W9-AFP-953

QUIET TRIUMPHS

QUIET TRIUMPHS

CELEBRITIES SHARE SURVIVAL STRATEGIES FOR GETTING THROUGH THE HARD TIMES

MARY ALICE WILLIAMS

HarperResource
A Division of HarperCollins *Publishers*

HarperCollins books may be purchased for educational, business, or sales promotional use. For information please write: Special Markets Department, HarperCollins Publishers, Inc., 10 East 53rd Street, New York, NY 10022.

FIRST EDITION

Designed by Joseph Rutt

Library of Congress Cataloging-in-Publication Data

Quiet Triumphs : celebrities share survival strategies for getting through the hard times / [edited by] Mary Alice Williams. — 1st ed.

p. cm.

ISBN 0-06-270245-9

1. Life change events—Psychological aspects. 2. Celebrities—United States Interviews. I. Williams, Mary Alice, 1949– .

BF637.L53Q54 1999 99-29561

920.073—dc21

[B]

99 00 01 02 03 ❖/RRD 10 9 8 7 6 5 4 3 2 1

To my mother,
Alice Mary Williams,
whose life has been a triumph.

CONTENTS

ACKNOWLEDGMENTS

No one accomplishes anything worth anything alone. Least of all me. It took guidance and research and a lot of blind faith on the part of many people in many rooms to get me through this Quiet Triumph.

Margaret Loesch and all the men and women of Odyssey, especially Jeff Weber, who fought to keep the program alive and thought to let me tackle this book. Jeff devoted the better part of two years to supporting all my efforts. His best trick was to encourage me and then leave me alone to write from my own heart, my ferocious research (provided by Chris Dibernardo), and voluminous transcriptions (provided by the inestimable Kimberley Clark Waddy).

Ellen Rodman brought me there, and Christopher DiBernardo, who became part of my mind and then part of my heart, kept me there.

Doug Wyles and Peter Goldsmith made the program work and kept me laughing.

John Rokosny and the crew did the scut work to make it look easy.

Carl Mark Raymond, the man with three first names, believed in this project long before I did. Linda Cunningham and Marion Maneker, with velvet glove and cattle prod, pushed me along.

I am ever grateful to Abby Adams for her clarity and Leslie Bennetts for her trust. When the subject matter, or my own doubts, clouded my computer screen, Father John O'Connor reminded me that the task was worthy and Joseph Martin and his very extended family reminded me that the road is worth it.

My husband Mark Haefeli walked with me every step of the way. And our three indomitable daughters, Alice, Sara, and Laura, sacrificed a lot of Mom time and assured me unbidden that while I am in heaven waiting for them to get there, God will provide a computer so that I can keep writing.

INTRODUCTION

> He who learns must suffer. And even in our sleep, pain that will not forget falls drop by drop upon the heart, and in our own despair, against our will, comes wisdom to us by the awful grace of God.
>
> —*Aeschylus*

I had a perfect sanctuary. Being a television news reporter is a cool job on its face. It is a difficult job practiced imperfectly. But it is a noble profession. The need to know is as important as the need to believe or to love. It is essential to democracy and to our collective ability to make healthy decisions. I am humbled to have been a part of that.

But I also used it. For me, it was not a career as much as it was a hiding place. I'd become so accustomed to chaos that if it didn't exist, I would have had to invent it. Television news thrives on chaos. I used television as a personal safety valve, to try to make sense of the chaos from the sanctuary of dispassionate distance. In my own life, I was never sure what was real, and television news forced me to reality test what was true. By having access to decision-makers and eyewitnesses, I could find what was really true about a given event on a given day, insofar as that's humanly possible.

I've interviewed and palled around with enough top-flight reporters to know that we are, as a breed, so busy studying other people's lives that our own lives go unnoticed. I was so focused on minding other people's business that I was wildly successful in neglecting my own.

Renegade journalist Hunter S. Thompson wrote, "The TV business is a cruel and shallow money trench, a long plastic hallway where thieves and pimps run free and good men die like dogs." It is enshrined in nearly every TV newsroom in the nation.

It is not an entirely godless profession. However, time constraints and competition can force us to edit out the dignity inherent in every person we cover if we're not careful. The fact that we get our biggest breaks covering the really bad stuff puts us in the position to risk losing our faith in people if we're not mindful of it.

But the real world was coming for me, like a cudgel that would finally convince me to look at my own humanity. I didn't get the Odyssey show, *Quiet Triumphs*; it got me. In case you've missed it, *QT* is a touching, joyful, practical (critics have called it gripping), sometimes funny, always moving acknowledgment that no matter who you are or what your station in life, people go through tough times. They just do. They experience personal challenges during which they feel isolated, afraid, and alone. Each survivor on the show has found strategies to get through it and prevail.

A year into production, the boss said, "You know, when you began this show you were just walking through it." No, I wasn't. When I came to Odyssey, I limped there. I am a Catholic. The newspapers like to refer to me as a "practicing" Catholic. Ever heard of a practicing Protestant? I am named for the one person who, more than any other in human history could intuit God's will in her own life. (My husband likes to remind people that I have a lot in common with the Virgin Mary. He says, "I'm married to a saint.") But I'd long since forgotten the way she accepted God's will in her life. While I kept practicing my religion I kept forgetting acceptance. My spirituality was limited to praying for minimal traffic and a decent parking place. And by the time I arrived at Odyssey, I had a poverty of spirit so severe that six months into it I would be brought face-to-face with the power of hell.

But you are exactly where you're supposed to be. On *Quiet Triumphs*, I was able to listen, really listen, to the spiritual journeys our generous guests shared on our show.

Anthropomorphized angels among us is a concept as hot in Hollywood as it's been since Jimmy Stewart was standing on that bridge in the Thirties having lost sight of the fact that it's a wonderful life. But I don't think they look like matinee idols. They come more humanly wrought with less lucrative contracts and no back-end percentages. They visit through the voices of people who've struggled.

I've learned from them that what is most personal is most universal. That magnificent epiphanies come from ordinary places. I have been given real freedom. I have been given amazing grace. I've been given the bravery to start my own personal journey back.

Coming out into the glaring sun and looking at what is true in your life is not easy, but it's not boring. Few people remember what is at the bottom of Pandora's box. It is hope. Just when I believed I had lost everything—my ability to laugh or trust or even pack school lunches—it was a final shard of hope that allowed me to reach out and get help. I made a lot of mistakes during the climb back from my self-imposed prison. One of, I hope, the good things that came from it is this book.

Every one of the people in these pages are celebrities. They have talent and intelligence and the drive to have accumulated impressive credentials and great wealth. And none of it has inoculated them against all that it means to be human. I've learned that when you face a crisis you can't work through or think through, sharing the wisdom, strength, and experience of those who've been there, is the best way out.

The men and women who have been open enough to talk with me about their real lives have only their own experience to share. They've lived it all. They've nursed parents into death and buried children. They've overcome career-busters from stuttering to stage fright. They've swallowed that acid steady-drip of fear that comes with the diagnosis of a terminal illness. They've watched loved ones murdered. They've lived with the guilt of suicide and the anger and confusion of divorce. They've seen Satan in the carpets of seedy hotel rooms searching for that last stray grain of crack cocaine. And they've seen God.

Not everyone spells out his or her difficulties or provides the details of what happened to them. They don't have to. Because it's not nearly as important as what happened in them and how they got through it. My goal is not to exploit the prurient, but to illustrate the process.

It's a process that you never entirely finish. At first that seems too onerous for words. When I began mine, utterly exhausted from awareness, I thought, "My God, will I really have to do this for the rest of my life?" But very soon I realized what a relief it is to be able to consciously travel with real joy in search of myself.

There are vastly different paths. One size does not fit all. That's as true in a personal journey as it is in ready-to-wear and pharmaceuticals. I'm reminded of the story of five sightless men confronted with an elephant. One felt the animal's leg and pronounced it was a tree. Another felt the tusk and proclaimed that it was a paving stone. The tail was a snake, and so forth. None of them could figure out the truth alone. But once they put their convictions together, they recognized the one True thing. They got it right.

Some people in these pages are a good way along the road. Some are still enmeshed in the struggle. The loneliest of them are only just beginning. There are stages, and each one is worth celebrating. These are snapshots of what they were feeling at the moment we were talking.

You may not like them all, as I do, but you may come to appreciate the experiences that have informed them, fired them, and drawn them to their beliefs.

Each of them is on a path in which they're finding strategies to get through their trial and triumph. In knowing them in a new way, you may come to know yourself as well. I have.

Neil Simon remarked after our chat, "You never asked me where I got my ideas!" I don't ask people about the wonderfulness of themselves, or their brilliant careers, or how they think the rest of us should live. We don't tackle geopolitics, or ideological conflict, or the plagues of the planet. I promise. I still believe the need to know is as important as the need to believe or to love. I have recently come to believe that motive is more interesting than behavior. What frames people's lives and their thoughts is more significant than what they do.

I began these conversations armed only with solid research on their outward lives and a vague notion of their inward struggles. But, in fact, I never know what will happen in the conversation. Neither does the person with whom I'm talking.

A word on alcoholism. These pages are riddled with its fallout. It was not intentional. There were only three people whose struggles with that disease I specifically wanted to explore, but the vast majority of the celebrities I interviewed brought it up. At first I thought there must be something about growing up around alcoholics that causes people to choose the spotlight, as if basking in the applause of total strangers somehow redeems them from the devastation it causes. The only other possibility is that alcoholism is just that pervasive. I now believe it is that pervasive. I think if I had interviewed only physicians, or only Wall Street traders, or only left-handed garage mechanics as a group, I would have found the disease had tarred them too. There is scarcely a family untouched by it.

Many of the people you'll come to know in these pages, I have known for years. They were heroes or mentors or friends. Some I'd never been privileged to meet face-to-face but only through the dark glass of a screen. Neil Simon said to me years ago, "We all know each other." I think what he meant was that those of us who've lived public lives share an understanding of what that means, what sacrifices we've made in terms of anonymity—privacy. We share various degrees of notoriety. But what we share most is the glorious human condition.

These are their stories. With few exceptions I have excised my part in the conversations to allow them to reach you unfiltered.

What has astonished me most is how quiet they are. (All except Rod Steiger. He was loud. So loud it was as though all the oxygen had been sucked from the room.) There is no self-pity in their speech, no particular drama in the words they chose. Each of them has spoken not with rancor or grim resolve, but with a calm acceptance of what is and a genuine gratitude for it. Each has come through a journey to arrive at a peace.

Every day, I learn more from them than could fill five books. I am learning that you can't change the painful past. You can't fix it or forget it or wish it away. But you can come to accept it and use it as an opportunity to change yourself in a way that gives you strength and serenity and happiness. I am learning that isolation will kill you. When I'm living all alone with my own thinking in my own head, I now know I'm in a bad neighborhood and I'm going to get mugged. I am learning that taking the risk of trusting and feeling and actually talking about it isn't as frightening as it sounds. That it's human to suffer losses, give them a name, grieve them, and go on. That you always have someplace to turn. The best power-tool is prayer, and for jump-starting your day, the words, "Thy will be done," are a darn sight better than Starbucks. Without the ability to call on someone a lot bigger than you are, blame, shame, guilt, and resentment only lock you in the victim role.

I am learning the freedom of grieving and forgiving. I am learning that humility is not humiliating and that there is no weakness in surrender and that there is precious little glory in being the captain of your ship and the master of your fate if you're adrift in your little boat all by yourself. Above all, I am learning that while you can't decide what happens to you, you can decide what happens in you.

If there is a through-story, a common thread that connects their stories, it is a reach for faith. Not tub-thumping religiosity, just a simple belief that they are not alone, that they are unconditionally loved, and that a power greater than all of us can do for us what we cannot do for ourselves.

I've learned that people can weather the worst of crises and get better. If they think smart and reach out and hope, for God's sake, people get better. And they can be genuinely happy. Joy is, after all, not the absence of sadness. It's the presence of God.

In India, weavers incorporate a mistake, a flaw, into every magnificent carpet they produce. The imperfection is a culture-wide reminder that nothing human is perfect. The fact that we have nobility, even heroism despite our humanity is worth illuminating. It's a triumph. A Quiet Triumph.

QUIET TRIUMPHS

CHAPTER 1

JACK KLUGMAN

With a face like a wharf punk and a voice that could make a respectable drain cleaner, he was as unlikely a heartthrob as ever came out of a picture tube. Yet he's been a part of American popular culture for about as long as television images have been flying through the air.

At a time when poverty wasn't a war but a way of life, Jack Klugman survived depression-era Philadelphia on the strength of his greatest attributes: the wits of a jackal and the tenderness of a teddy bear—an odd coupling for a man who, with his alter ego Tony Randall, would define odd couples.

Fear can be a great propellant, and it certainly was for Klugman. If it doesn't paralyze you, it can help you reach your dreams, or at the very least, it can help you get to the other side of calamity. For Klugman, fear is what propelled him into acting. And when throat cancer threatened his livelihood, his life, and his very identity, Klugman used his fear to open himself to the love of neighbors and strangers. It was these people who were the key to his survival.

Klugman is also a gambler from way back. Following his success as one of the finest character actors of all time, he has put together an impressive stable of racehorses—one in fact, Jaclyn Klugman, placed third at the Kentucky Derby in 1980. But Klugman has been rolling the dice for as long as he can remember. As a kid, he knew all the bad neighborhoods where the poverty was worse than his own. These were the places where even the most needy street vendors wouldn't go. So the enterprising young man would buy two pretzels for a penny in a good neighborhood and sell them at a penny a piece in a bad one. He always knew how to double his money.

Klugman says that poverty can teach lessons that privilege cannot. His two-for-one income helped support an impoverished family. His mother made and sold hats out of her kitchen for the grand ladies who'd force their limo drivers to suffer the squalor of South Philly just to get their hands on her chic chapeaux for a buck a piece. She'd stitch those hats day and night while raising six children. Klugman says though his father, a housepainter, died too soon, he might as well have been his mother's seventh child.

Every freckle-faced kid with a pocketful of dreams to be a star can tell you acting is a calling for either the patient or the certifiably mad. Only a fraction manage to get a first break. Jack Klugman got into the business through the back door, and made it not so much because he was good, but because he was a male—and scared out of his wits.

This is a true story. The gambling is what got me into it. I owed a loan shark, who was also a friend, some money. I couldn't pay him, so he turned the debt over to a couple of guys who were going to hurt me a little bit. I went to him and said, "Uncle Tommy, you know I always paid you!" And he said, "Jake, listen. I got a hundred thousand dollars out on the street. And you don't pay me and I don't do anything to you, I lose all that money. Now I don't want to hurt you, but if you can give me some money before they get to you . . . "

I had to get out of town. Since I had the GI bill, I remembered my brother knew a guy in the Army who had been to Carnegie Mellon University so I went there. There were twenty-seven young girls. Sada Thompson was one of them, and Nancy Marchand. Wonderful people. They were seventeen. I was twenty-three. And I had to audition. So they gave me *Our Town.* Well, if I did *Our Town* it would sound like Marlon Brando doing it from *The Godfather.* So right in the middle of it I started to hyperventilate. I had never spoken in front of two people before and here, there were twenty-seven kids and all I could do was hyperventilate. Afterward, I saw the teachers and they said, "You're not suited to be an actor. You're more suited, Mr. Klugman, to be a truck driver. Not that there's anything wrong with truck drivers, but you're really not ready for this. However, as you see, we don't have any men to do scenes. So, for this reason only, we'll take you. But in January, we'll have to let you go." "Okay," I said. I figured by that time I could raise some money, give it to the loan sharks, everything would be all right again.

The first scene I did with them I rehearsed for three weeks. To really understand how I felt at the time, you need to know another story about my childhood. I had a rich uncle, and when I would go to his house to eat, they very often served chicken. But I'd always say I wasn't hungry because I didn't actually know how to eat this chicken. We never had this much to eat at my home and I didn't even know how to pick up the pieces with my fingers. Since I didn't know what to do, I'd just say that I wasn't hungry.

But when I walked on that stage and acted in that scene, I knew I was more comfortable there than I had ever been in real life. I knew how to "eat the chicken" on stage. I'm really not comfortable in life, but onstage I'm at home. And that's why I knew this was for me. I always believed that I would have to work to subsidize my acting, but this profession has been good to me.

I do have a big ego, and if it's questioned then I'll fight back. In many areas I'm maybe even cowardly, but in acting, I'm a lion. There was a guy—a wonderful director—who used to give me a lot of work. One day I was doing a *Twilight Zone,* and he wanted me to do something. And I tried. I said, "It doesn't work." He said, "But I got a great camera angle." I said, "I don't care. It's just not true. It's not honest." "But Jack, you'll look good," he said. And I said, "Do you think I really care what you think? I have to crawl under your head, be what you want me to be. Next week I'm going to work with another director. Now you want me to crawl into his head and be what he wants me to be? Before you know it I'm a chameleon." The only person with me all the time is me and I have to please me.

⁓⁓⁓

Jack Klugman may sound an ego-stricken wretch, but in fact he is a remarkably humble man. Standing on a stage or before a TV camera is the ultimate team sport. No one can succeed alone, though the loneliest among them insist they have. Klugman genuinely believes that he contributes to a performance but not more so than the other players.

It was this kind of collegiality and mutual respect that forged the basis of his lifelong devotion to Tony Randall, who played opposite Klugman as the quintessential fussbudget Felix Unger in Neil Simon's The Odd Couple. *It was during the early-Seventies Broadway run of this play, as his character*

Oscar Madison was tracking up Felix's freshly waxed floors, that Klugman experienced for the first time the warning signs of a disease that threatened to silence him forever.

I was doing *The Odd Couple* and I was on stage. I had replaced Walter Matthau, and I was getting laryngitis. Back then I was a heavy smoker. I went to one doctor who thought it was an allergy and he gave me cortisone, but that didn't work. Another doctor told me to quit smoking, so I quit for three months, and it cleared up. But then I went back to smoking, and I continued for years. When I finally was diagnosed with cancer, I certainly knew what caused it.

I believe that you can't be a victim. When you're a victim you start to blame. Though I do think the tobacco companies knowingly are killing millions of people, I believe that blaming them does me no good. Instead, I believe you've got to get off your butt (forgive the pun), and say, "What can I do about this situation?"

In the beginning, I admit I did blame. I blamed Fate. "Why me?" Even though I knew that smoking was terrible, and I did it anyway, it still felt like God had gone out of His way to choose me. You'd think His schedule would be busy enough without going out of his way to choose me. I see this at the racetrack all the time. A guy loses a horserace by a nose and says, "They won't let me win!" And who are "they?" He says, "Fate." I believe his is just a negative way of becoming important. Fate didn't go out of her way just to see you lose a horserace. You're just not that important. So "me" isn't the issue here.

The first couple of years were difficult for me. I believed that I would never act again. I went to every doctor, every specialist, all over the world. They all said, "You can't get a sound anymore." They had taken out the vocal cord. I didn't know what to do so I prayed every day. Even though I never went onstage without a prayer, this was different. I'm not what you call a religious man. But I do believe, in this case I guess, I had no alternative. For there was no place else to go, nothing else I could do.

I did read plays out loud in the privacy of my own home, but I would never let anyone hear me. I really gave up in many ways.

It's not like acting is my best friend. It's all I can do. I can't put a bulb into a socket. I can't play games. I don't know how to fix a carburetor.

Klugman did the only thing that made sense. He dug far back to grab hold of his dearest dreams and started over. A year after the surgery, The American Cancer Society invited him—begged him—to make a speech. Being thrust in front of an audience without his most valuable instrument seemed too daunting. But he looked fear in the face and did it anyway. And that's when he learned that by giving other people hope, he found hope.

I had no voice at all. I said, "No, I can't do this." And they said, "Please. Two hundred and fifty cancer patients and their spouses are going to be there, and we'll be giving them each a little tree plant which is what we call a gift of life. It will mean a lot to them to hear your experience, so please, it's very important."

I said, "I'll try it." So I went to Atlanta, and it was hot. I had an amplification system, but I still couldn't hear myself. I was so angry. I hated those people for bringing me there. I felt so humiliated. They all knew me as a successful actor, and now I couldn't even talk. I didn't want sympathy, and I didn't want anybody to feel sorry for me. But I did the speech as best I could. Afterwards, all five hundred people came up to me and I had my picture taken with every one of them. Then I gave them the "gift of life," the tree plant. Not one person just said, "Hi." They all said, "We love you. We prayed for you. You're going to get better. We swear, we know you're going to get better." Five hundred people! Talk about crying. I couldn't believe it.

You can't do it alone. I had so many people that helped me. Oh, the people that wrote letters. It's unbelievable. You don't know where it's going to come from. All you have to do is hang in there. You've got to try. You've got to believe.

People would say, "You really can help people. Go to a hospital and get your picture taken with them." At the time I thought, How is that going to help them? But I learned that it does. And at the same time, they showed me love and concern and empathy. They needed my help, but I needed theirs as well.

Back in 1991, Jack Klugman was "finished." After a twenty-year bout with cancer during which his voice had been sacrificed, the doctors had given up hope that he'd ever speak again. Certainly the producers weren't taking any bets on Klugman's comeback either. And the critics, they had moved on to their next victims. But what the doctors, critics, and producers didn't consider was that love can always throw the equation. When Tony Randall needed to stage a benefit to raise money for his non-profit National Actors Theater, he called Jack. He wanted Jack to go back onstage, and though Jack would do anything for Tony, this was a big request. But Jack did do it, and the result was miraculous. Klugman was awarded with a seven-minute standing ovation.

Tony called me and said, "Listen, I understand I need to raise money for my National Actors Theater. If we could do *The Odd Couple* one night, I think we could raise a lot of money."

I said, "Are you crazy?" At that time, I could only whisper. I said, "I can't even talk to you on the phone. How am I going to get onstage?" At that particular time, my voice teacher Gary Catono was working with me, and we were trying to get a sound out of me. Just one sound. "There's a sound in there somewhere," he said. And I said, "You don't hear a sound. You hear money, is what you hear." He said, "No, I swear, it'll work." And then one day I just made a little sound—an "Uh." And Gary said, "There it is. Tell Tony you can do it in six months." So I called Tony, and I said, "Six months, I'll be able to do it."

And what a night it was! I went onstage even though I couldn't control my voice. It kept breaking. I went onstage after the audience had listened for eight minutes to four guys with normal voices. And then I said my first line. People started to shuffle. I thought, oh my God. And at that moment I hated Tony Randall so much. How was I going to get through this night? So I said the next line and I'm there sweating. About the fourth or fifth line Tony said, "What do you have to eat?" And I said, "I have green sandwiches and brown sandwiches." Tony said, "What's the green?" And I said, "It's either very new cheese or very old meat." And the audience started to laugh. I could just feel them, and I could hear them actually settling into their seats. We went on to play that fabulous performance.

That opening night I had very little voice. My kids, who had seen me do *The Odd Couple* God knows how many times, told me, "That's the best performance you ever gave of *The Odd Couple.* Your concentration was keener and deeper than it's ever been." It's like, if you lose one arm the other one gets twice as strong. You lose this, you make up for it.

Tony was there all the time just giving me confidence, saying, "You're doing this." And that's what happened. Every time I'd say, "Tony, this is crazy," he would say, "No, you can do it." Oh, I love that guy.

If you're the luckiest actor in the world, you get to work with Tony Randall. Every night it's a joy. It's a challenge. You don't fear going down, because he'll pick you up, and vice versa. I have a line in the play which just describes us well: "I know what he's thinking and he knows what I'm thinking." One person, that's what we are. You can't separate us. You can't like his performance and not mine, and vice versa. We come together as a package.

Well, after the first curtain call, we thought it was over. Tony and I were talking, and I was hugging him. And the stage manager said, "Don't you hear them?" I said, "What?" He said, "They're still standing!" Now these are not theater people. These are guys who paid twenty-five thousand dollars for a table for ten people. These are not just fellow actors. The curtain went up, and there they were, standing, every single one applauding. I started to cry. I cried. And Tony cried. And they cried. And Miss Helen Hayes and Sylvia Sidney were in the audience. They were together. Sylvia asked Helen Hayes, "Have you ever seen so much love go from an audience to actors and back?" And Helen Hayes said, "Never in my life have I seen anything like this." Well, that was one of those nights, and I'll never forget it. I can't ever top that. It's an epitaph.

CHAPTER 2

TONY RANDALL

Tony Randall's fond memories of that night are tinged with bitterness. Tony Randall is not a bitter man, it's just that his feelings are so intensely felt—especially when it comes to Jack Klugman. The night in question was the benefit performance to raise funding for Tony's dream, the National Actors Theater. It was the "Jack and Tony Show," and they brought in a million dollars performing their best trick, The Odd Couple. *When he recalled Jack Klugman's comeback from throat cancer, Tony Randall was weeping openly.*

> The ravages of that terrible disease were apparent in his voice. It will remain with him the rest of his life. It's a rasping sound, but you get used to it. The *New York Times* critic wrote that he should be ashamed to go on stage with a voice like that. People can be so cruel and sadistic. Instead of saying what a hero he is to overcome this, to be so indomitable and to win. It hurts that they treat him this way!

When you talk to Tony Randall, you get used to the wild emotional pendulum. One moment he's conveying pathos, the next a wry sardonic humor, the next a glee that would rival all of Santa's elves put together. He is brilliant, acerbic, and driven. Sometimes he seems brusque but only until you realize that it is because his mind is spinning with ideas.

There is today barely a hint of his Tulsa, Oklahoma, roots in Tony Randall. He has had a celebrated acting career on Broadway and in

Hollywood. He had a marriage of fifty-four years and a passion for books, opera, witty banter, and the real-life stuff that stars rarely get to peek at. When he reached his seventies, instead of looking at a life well spent, he began it all over again with a new wife and children. Through it all, he's shown us that it's never a good time to give up waiting for your miracle.

Tony Randall's first miracle was Florence. She married him, supported him, put up with him and adored him for more than half a century. He won't talk about her lingering death from cancer. It is too private, too dignified to share. If there were potholes or heartbreaks that are part of any marriage, he holds them secure in his heart. And he puts a button on the happiness they did share as real partners, just the two of them.

In the early days of our marriage, Florence was the breadwinner. She gave me pocket money. I wasn't working. Young actors were always out of work. That's the story of our business, but it never humiliated me. Because we were a team. That's the lucky thing about it. It was always "us." We certainly wanted children. It just didn't happen. At one time we tried to adopt, but that didn't happen either, and that was rather heartbreaking. We resigned ourselves to it and finally stopped thinking about having children. And we were happy. If ever there was a happy marriage, that was it. I was certainly happy with my work. Maybe that's one of the reasons our marriage was so great!

From time to time I would go on the TV game show *Password,* but I would always practice at home with Florence before the show. Invariably, she got everything wrong. Whatever I would say to her, she would somehow botch it up. It was so maddening and funny at the same time! If I wanted her to say *pins,* she would say *needle.* Or she'd say *hypodermic!* When I'd finally say I was after *pin,* she'd say, "Well, what does that have to do with hypodermic!" It was both frustrating and hilarious. I realized this scenario could make a great *Odd Couple* show. The next morning, I went into Gary Marshall's office and I said "the guys" (my term for Felix and Oscar) should go on *Password.* He immediately called one of the writers and asked him to write an outline for a show. This episode happened practically overnight, and I'm particularly proud of it. That was totally my baby.

It is testament to how Tony Randall's wife Florence inspired him, and how his best friend Jack Klugman implemented his passion. TV experts voted the "Password" show from The Odd Couple *to be the fifth greatest TV episode of all time, sitcom or drama!*

I thought I'd never marry again. When Florence died I really thought that was it for life. But life is full of surprises. In fact, I always thought Florence was immortal. When I was young, I thought my mother was immortal. But she had a serious heart condition, and she used to say to me, "You're not always going to have me." I just didn't believe it. Now I believe it!

There is one thing that you must have—and this is purely a matter of luck. You must have good health. Early this year I had pneumonia, and I was in the hospital for two weeks. And that's the only time in my entire life I've been ill. I think I work too hard to have time to be sick. I'm lucky I've never had the terrible problems that some other people have.

For some years after Florence's death, Tony Randall became the every girl's favorite bachelor, including me. When I have to be away, my husband arranges his schedule to stay home with the children, and I make personal appearances at dinners and galas stag. I have never been comfortable walking into a room full of strangers. So one hot July night at a costume ball in Saratoga Springs, Tony Randall sidled up to me and said, "Got a date?" I said, "Yes, you." I have never been more grateful for the company of such a charming, funny man. Women who were available sought his attention too. But Tony Randall remained a confirmed bachelor until he met Heather, who would become his second wife. Her opening line was, "National Actors Theater. Fifth floor." And Tony Randall felt nineteen again.

She was twenty-two when she joined the theater as one of the interns on *The Crucible.* I saw her at the first rehearsal, but I didn't pay much attention to her. I did notice, however, that she was the hardest working intern. That attracted me! Then after

Florence died, I renoticed her. So, I'm married again now to a wonderful, fun woman. At twenty-six, she's getting a little old for me, but at least she's given me Julia Laurette!

At seventy-seven years old, Tony Randall became a father. This was the blessed event heard round the world—news I greeted with a belly laugh. Tony and I were neighbors in the same old apartment building in New York City. Flush with hopeless infatuation for my firstborn baby, a Gerber prizewinner if ever there was one, I was out strolling her and ran into Tony and the great opera diva Beverly Sills. There's a reason Beverly's nickname is Bubbles. She did all the right things. Fell head over heels for my gorgeous little dreamboat. Tony Randall positively recoiled. I figured he'd assessed her as far too sticky for his taste. The image of Felix Unger being invaded by a baby, with her attendant explosion of multi-colored plastic, was just too perfect. Turns out he's not a neatnick after all.

Since our conversation, he has become a father again. I'm glad I got him early, fully smitten with Julia Laurette in the first blush of fatherhood.

It's the most wonderful thing that's ever happened to me. It does, of course, change the focus of your life. It changes the way you look at yourself. You forget yourself and start thinking of her future only.

And there's his other baby, The National Actors Theater, which is now firmly entrenched on Broadway. Everyone said it couldn't be done. Why would the United States need a national repertory troupe just because every other civilized nation has one? Why should Americans fund one just because every other nation funds theirs? Tony Randall's crusade to launch NAT made Don Quixote's look like a cakewalk. But he did it. The theater not only presents world-class drama but provides thespians-in-training the opportunity to work in all aspects of theater from dramaturgy to set design.

My second balcony is for students. For them, every performance costs ten dollars. All our shows have free student matinees, and for the special matinees we'll have about 1100 kids from schools all over the country. Those kids are so responsive. They're what audiences ought to be. But every student matinee costs us thirty-five thousand dollars, which is the price we have to pay. That's why the leading figure in any nonprofit organization, from the symphony orchestra to museums and colleges, spends all his other time fundraising. And that's what I do most of the time as well.

Note to the Reader: I have steadfastly tried, in the course of writing this book, to excise my own involvement in these conversations so that you can get these stories unfiltered. In Tony's case, I have purposely reinserted myself into the conversation so that you can get a glimpse of the depth of his passionate defense of his ideas, however curmudgeonly they might seem.

Maybe baby Julia has fired him up with the grave responsibilities of parenting a child in this world. But I don't think so. I think I would have gotten this lecture anyway. All I asked was, "Why is it so important to present the classics and why was he willing to lose a ton of money on every single matinee performance?" I had no idea I'd be walking into a buzz saw. See how his intensity escalates in this interchange:

TONY: We are introducing students to Ibsen, and Shaw, and Chekov. This heritage is so important. Our educational system is awful, and the truth is that the arts are good for you. You are not a complete human being if you don't know Beethoven and Mozart. They are the peak of the Western civilization! We are all beneficiaries of this. If you haven't been introduced to the classics, you have been robbed in your education. You are deprived.

MARY ALICE: I'm very worried about Julia! This kid is going to be exposed to everything, isn't she!

TONY: It's going to be jammed down her throat!

MARY ALICE: But what if she prefers rap? Hip-hop? That's your payback, Papa. You know that? You're going to cram Beethoven and Tchaikovsky down her throat.

TONY: I can pass over Tchaikovsky.

MARY ALICE: Well, Mozart or Bach. (Babies love Bach.) But when she turns seven or eight, she might surprise you with rap, or bubblegum rock!

TONY: Not in my house!

MARY ALICE: You have to let her.

TONY: No! It's degrading stuff!

MARY ALICE: But she does have to individuate from you. She has to say: Here dad look . . . I have my whole culture too! You have yours and I have mine!

TONY: Nonsense! She has nothing. She has what she learns, that's what she has!

MARY ALICE: What if her best friend listens to the Spice Girls!

TONY: I have no idea what you're talking about!

MARY ALICE: I'm certain you don't but you will!

TONY: What responsibility do I have as a parent if I say: *Your best friend is right and I know nothing?*

MARY ALICE: No. But I'm bringing this up, Tony, because my children too have been exposed to all sorts of classical music, books, classics, and the theater. Yet there comes a time when you find them standing on the kitchen table, using the ends of toilet paper rolls as microphones, singing along with the Spice Girls or LeAnn Rimes. I didn't introduce this music to them, but as their mother, I better make a point over the next forty-eight hours to learn about these groups. When I've done this, I've learned something every time—like the Spice Girls are singing about the power of girls, and that's a positive affirmation. Okay, LeAnn Rimes is singing classic country, Patsy Cline music. So I talk to them about Patsy Cline, and about country music and its roots. In other words, with kids sometimes you have to just go with the flow. If they're interested in something, maybe it's our responsibility to learn about it as well.

TONY: I suppose so. You may have some sort of specious point, but I'm too old to change.

MARY ALICE: Go home and have this discussion with Heather. Let me know what she says about the Spice Girls!

TONY: I know what she'll tell me. In fact, Heather liked [the

Broadway rock musical] *Rent.*

MARY ALICE: Oh, so can one assume that you did not like *Rent?*

TONY: It was unbearable. I think it's evil stuff. It had a terrible, loud sound amplification and I couldn't understand one word. It didn't seem to hurt Heather's ears, but it certainly hurt mine. So I sat through the whole show with my fingers in my ears. That's the one generational difference between us!

* * *

Tony Randall draws on lessons in his life that are cross-generational. The value of work and the investment of love.

* * *

I'm one of those people who works. If there's a secret I know, the secret of it all is, there is no secret. I think it is a fact that everyone in the world who's made anything of himself is a workaholic. We are. All of us. I went one period when I was a fairly young fellow, about 365 days without a day off. The job is all we know and all we want to know. We're voracious about it. We never get enough. And we frequently neglect everything else in life. I'm not that kind. I'm not neglecting everything else in life.

Love! I think love has informed my entire life. I've always loved acting. I've always loved the theater as others love their religion. And I loved my wife, every minute I knew her. And now I love my new wife and baby. I think love is the only answer. I have been very fortunate. I was adored by my mother and my sister. I was that kind of boy, adored by women when he was a little boy! I think boys who are adored by their mothers have feelings of invincibility.

But imagine all of this happening to me at my age. That in itself is remarkable. The most remarkable things in my life have happened after I turned seventy. I've never heard anyone else with a story like that.

Woody Allen said if you want to give God a good laugh, tell him your future plans.

* * *

I'll add to Tony's list of work and love: passion. Passion, for anything, can get kicked out of us along the road. I've learned from talking with Tony that the trick is to dust off every so often what you feel passionate for and then open yourself to loving. Loving what you do and who you are and what you share with people you love.

CHAPTER 3

HUGH DOWNS

One would expect a person to swagger just a bit after he's logged more hours on television than any human being, dead or alive. He'd have a right to. But Hugh Downs never learned to swagger. He reported on history and made history, hosted The Today Show *and* The Tonight Show, *sailed the South Seas, and relocated the South Pole (this bears some explaining: the South Pole is marked by an actual bamboo pole stuck in ice pack, which drifts. So the pole occasionally has to be moved to reflect the true Polar South. In 1982, Downs was the one who got to move the pole). That's true. He's even made it into the* Guinness Book of World Records. *If TV has a voice of authority and wisdom, that voice absolutely belongs to him. But no one calls him Mr. Downs, at least once they get to know him. Approaching his eighties now, he is genuinely warm and modest and congenial, and his indomitable curiosity keeps everyone around him thinking young. He is the standard bearer for the notion that competence rather than a calendar really is a measure of anybody's ability.*

It's a little known fact that Hugh was actually on television before he'd ever seen television. Come to think of it, that may have given him a leg up. He got to mold the entire idiom. Thank Heaven it was he. There are a few annoyances inherent in the technical aspects of television anyone who hasn't tried it might not be aware of. Like the sound of your own voice. It's sounds different on the outside than on the inside. Then there's the feedback. The words you say are fed back into your ear a fraction of a second after you've uttered them. If you focus on the echo of your words coming back at you, it can make you nuts.

Hugh got used to that but never to that newfangled teleprompter. To this day, he never reads a teleprompter. He hates them.

Hugh launched his career in the depths of the Depression, and his inauspicious start was what you'd expect from any greenhorn.

My first job began during the depths of the Depression. The local radio station was looking for an announcer. So I auditioned. At the time, it was clear that I didn't know the first thing about announcing. However, the station manager took me aside and told me that I had the job. It was surreal. It wasn't until years later that I understood why he hired me. The station hadn't had the money to hire a professional. But regardless of the reason, I was hired by the station and began my career as an on-air announcer.

When I began broadcasting, I had to overcome the worst case of mike fright. It was pure agony. Every time I had to do an announcement or a commercial on the air, my palms would sweat and my pulse would race. My blood became icy and my knees turned to jelly. It was awful because I had to make sure that it would never show up in my voice. I went through months of such agony before I got over it. There were many times that I wanted to quit. And I probably would have if it had been a different time. However, it was the Depression, and there were not a lot of opportunities out there for me. In retrospect, I am glad that I stuck with it. I wanted to be a broadcaster and I knew I could do it. The fact that I got over my fright completely taught me a great lesson about the resilience of the human spirit.

In 1945, right after the war ended, an experimental television station, WBKB, in Chicago's Loop, invited me to do a broadcast. It was an amazing opportunity for me. At the time, I had never seen television, and they assured me that I was going to reach a big audience. (At the time there were 400 TV sets in all of greater Chicago, mostly in bars.) They asked me to do a newscast on their television station. So I did it. After the broadcast was over, I said to the producer, "I've never seen a television program." And he said, "Well, we're going to do another program in forty-five minutes and there's a television set out in the lobby if you want to watch that." So I went out to the lobby and watched my first television program. It was hard to imagine my face on that screen; it was something that would take me a long time to get used to.

At one point in my career, I came very close to interviewing

Albert Einstein. At that time, I was working for NBC on what they called *The Wisdom Series.* In 1953, I interviewed Frank Lloyd Wright, and that was fascinating. I was slated to interview Einstein, but we had to postpone it because Einstein was sick. Unfortunately, Einstein never recovered. He never got well, and I never got the chance to meet him. That is one of the greatest tragedies of my life.

There are things that I probably wouldn't even try, in the way of record setting—mountain-climbing feats or something like that. But if I feel I can do something, I find that you can do it unless your judgment's very bad about what your abilities are.

Resilience could be Hugh's middle name. Sure he's suffered the slings of aging. Both knees went. But since he's always turned setbacks into opportunities, he agreed to televise his surgery, allowing masses of total strangers to peer into his sinews.

But he's got the eyes of an astronaut. He's never worn corrective lenses and is still flying airplanes, if only to keep his pilot's license current.

Staying current is the fountain of youth. Hugh believes learning takes the limits off longevity.

I am not a young man. I am a man who has experienced a great deal in my life. I am not upset that I am growing older. In fact, I've always said there's nothing wrong with getting older or being older. We all hope that we will live long and prosperous lives. Therefore, I don't understand why so many old people are the victims of ageism. They're in a group that, with luck, everyone will join. When I think about ageism, the only thing I can think of is our society's obsession with youth. We are living in a time characterized by a "Pepsi generation" mentality. While it is better than it was ten years ago, ageism is still the prevalent issue we have to deal with today.

Harvey Wheeler, a scholar at the Center for the Study of Democratic Institutions, said he honestly believes that when the enormous population of baby boomers become the elderly, they will be such a strong force that our culture will change. It will be a culture based on older people. Harvey Wheeler thinks there'll be so much cachet and prestige to being older that cosmetics companies will begin to bring out lines of cosmetics to help young people look older. That's an interesting thought. And then we might, like several Asian cultures, come to revere age and make use of the wisdom that the elderly contain. I love the idea and hope to see it happen real soon.

Walter Pitkin wrote a book years ago called *Life Begins at 40.* When it came out, I was around eleven years old. At that time, I honestly believed that life ended at forty—forty was old. I thought my parents and my grandparents were all in the same old ballpark. But then as I grew older, I realized that I had completely missed the boat as to what aging is all about. When you are young, you think old people go around thinking, "I'm old." However, they don't. Everybody thinks he's thirty-five. To this day, whenever I look at myself in the mirror, I always expect to see a thirty-five-year-old man staring back at me. Then I realize that I'm looking at a plainly middle-aged person. And it never fails to take me by surprise. Therefore, I believe it is most important to focus on how you feel inside, because how you feel is important in determining how you live life.

However, it is a fact that no matter how young you feel inside, you can't stop the aging process. As people grow older, they are faced with different kinds of medical problems. As I have said before, I am not a young man. I am a man who has lived a long life and has experienced a great deal. Therefore, it is inevitable that I too would experience some sort of problem that affects the elderly. In my case, I was lucky—my one problem was that my knees went bad.

I am kind of ashamed that I don't have a Heisman Trophy to show for having ruined my knees. If I had, it would have been a better story. But my knees went bad because of a series of dumb accidents.

Before my knees went bad, my philosophy had been that there's no such thing as a permanent injury. You get injured and then you get well. But let me be the first one to tell you, that philosophy is not true. Once I had really ruined one knee, the other one began to suffer because I was favoring the one that was hurt. Then the cartilage went and the bone began to erode, and with that erosion came traumatic arthritis. Since a lot of people have bad knees, I was persuaded to go public with my surgery to show people suffering from the same knee problems as I was that they were not alone.

At first, I was resistant to going public with my knee surgery. I thought it was of a more private nature. I tried to get Barbara Walters to cover for me by just saying that I was away. However, after much persuasion, I realized that by coming forward I would provide a great service to the viewer. So I did. Since my surgery, I've received hundreds of letters from people who want to know the name of my surgeon. They too want to have knee surgery. I am really glad that I did it and that I shared it with others.

Being old is not bad, unless you've run afoul of real bad luck with a disease that you can't control or, worst of all, if you suffer the shipwreck of the mind in one of the brain diseases like Alzheimer's. Being hurt is bad. And that's what you try to avoid. And you have to have some luck. I have been lucky.

Aging can be a tough process. However, it can also be an amazing one. I did a PBS series on aging where I interviewed Dr. Walter Alvarez. Dr. Alvarez made many of his medical breakthroughs after he turned sixty-five. If he had been forcibly retired at sixty-five, our society would be at a great medical loss. His story is such an inspiration to me. And it is more common than one would think.

In my segment on centenarians, I learned a great deal about the elderly. I interviewed around six people, but my favorite subject was Mary Elliott, then a 102-year-old woman who was a part of the University of Georgia experiment on people who lived to be over 100. In our interviews, she told me great stories. She told me about the time that the University of Georgia folks went to her house, to examine her as part of the project, and she offered them refreshments. She said they wouldn't eat a thing. One of the people from the University told her that he couldn't eat anything because he was allergic to milk. Another told her that he couldn't have eggs because of the cholesterol. Mary just sat there looking extremely puzzled. Finally, she told them that she could eat whatever she wanted and that they should not be so hard on themselves. I loved that story. Mary Elliott died at 105 years old. She was a great lady who taught me a lot about aging and youthful spirits.

Whenever I think about Mary Elliott, I think about her spirit. She was a woman who loved to learn and loved to live life. She was not your typical preconception of the elderly. She was a woman who was with it, strong and sharp. She was a great inspiration to us all. Whenever I ask doctors about her sharpness, they all tell me the same thing. Apparently the brain is somewhat like a muscle. If you go to bed for six weeks, you'll find you can't walk. Your muscles atrophy and you lose skills. If Mary Elliott had shut down her brain, retired, and just sat on her back porch with a fishing pole and didn't do anything, doctors believe that she would have deteriorated much faster than she did. Yet, since she challenged her brain, her IQ kept up, and she was able to continue to learn. Therefore, I believe that the challenge comes from the desire to keep active. If you can keep active, there's no reason to stop learning even when you turn 100.

My advice to all on the aging process is not to retreat from whatever challenges cross your path. A lot of older people use the excuse of being older for saying, "Well, I don't want to bite that off, maybe I can't chew it." But I say, "Go ahead and face the challenge. Take the chance. Take the risk. If you fail, learn from your failure. Failure's not as bad as not trying." Because by trying, you will learn that no matter what the outcome, life is something that is special and worth trying out.

I apply that same sort of logic to my marriage with my wife. We have gone through some hard times together. When we first got married it would have been easy to say, "Well, I'll try this but I can always bail out, there's always divorce." However, we didn't. We took the challenge of staying together and decided to really make our marriage work. Even though we went through a stormy first and second year (I'm talking about clothes tearing and dish throwing and stuff like that) we never thought about splitting up. We made our marriage work and I am happier than ever that it did.

Friends of the Downs like to refer to Hugh's wife as the "Sainted" Mrs. Downs. Because she is *a saint. And because she's managed to remain in a solid, growing marriage to a television journalist for well over fifty years. That may be a world record. When I was newly married, Hugh told me to always consider marriage a third entity. It's not the sum of two people. On those days when everything goes to hell in a handbasket, that third party can hand you a one-way ticket back to serenity. That advice has been a tally light in my life more often than Hugh will ever know.*

Gratitude is all in your attitude. They say that old age is the midnight snack of life. When Hugh finally gets finished with lunch, I'll confirm that with him.

CHAPTER 4

BARBARA BARRIE

If you believe there are no "second acts" in life, then I give you Barbara Barrie. One of those gorgeous ingenues who's still gorgeous in her seventies, Barrie has a figure that still stops traffic. She has thirty-five years worth of credits and acclaims under her twenty-two-inch belt. Fans know her as the loyal, loving mom in the Oscar-winning film Breaking Away, *or as the long-suffering wife on the long-running television favorite* Barney Miller, *or as a funny feisty grandma on the hit sitcom* Suddenly Susan. *But Barbara Barrie is much more than an actress; she is a survivor. In fact, her greatest challenge in life came off-screen. Facing down a disease that has all too often done its deadly work in silence, Barrie's greatest legacy may not be the portrayals of women she's infused into our culture through theater, film, and television. Rather, it may be tucked in the pages of a book she wrote about her own private battle with a disease that's usually not mentioned in polite company. As a subject, colorectal cancer is unappealing. The fact that she's portrayed it with such candor and grace and enormous good sense only demonstrates what a remarkable woman she is, not to mention all the public support she has brought to the countless others who are currently coping with this disease.*

Barbara woke up to this grim reality in 1994. She was working in Charleston, South Carolina.

I couldn't see on the set. We were doing [the TV miniseries] *Scarlett.* I came out of my trailer to do a scene and I literally couldn't see. Everything was fuzzy. And I thought, "I'm really sick here." But I somehow did the scene, and finally got back to my hotel. I had an idea that it might be my colon because I had been ignoring symptoms for a year. I called somebody in the yellow pages and he was very unhelpful, so I ended up taking myself to the hospital in Charleston, where I got terrific care. It was decided by the next morning that I had cancer. They saw it. They did a sigmoidoscopy (which is really taking a little picture), and there it was, a little volcano—a very big tumor.

In fact I had had symptoms for thirty years. I had always been told that I was actually okay when I was given tests. In the last year, I had severe bleeding and severe weight loss but I thought, They've always told me I'm okay, I'm not going to worry about this. Besides, I was having a very good time in my life and I didn't want to stop it. In retrospect, this was a big mistake because the minute you have bowel changes, or loss of weight, or bleeding from the rectum, you should get yourself to a doctor quickly and say, "Help." And once you're over sixty, the minute you get symptoms like that, you should run to the doctor and get examined. But I didn't do this. Instead, I just ignored it. I couldn't have done *Scarlett,* or the movie in Canada, or continue to renovate my little house that my husband and I were working on. I realize now how insane my behavior actually was.

When I was a girl nobody said the word cancer. In fact, my grandmother died of this when I was seven. My great-grandfather did not die of it, but he did have some bowel dysfunction that eventually turned into cancer. My uncle died when I was twenty-three. I went to the funeral in Chicago, and nobody told me what he died of and nobody mentioned it at the time. Cancer was the forbidden word. I had an idea that cancer was the problem, but I didn't know how rampant this disease was in my family.

When I heard the word cancer, I thought, Uh-huh. Yeah. That's it. It was like the other shoe dropped. Deep down I kind of knew. But I also knew that I wanted to finish my work. I had worked on that miniseries over a period of three-and-a-half months and I had only one scene left. It was a hard scene but I had to do it. Though, I wasn't in any pain at the time, I was totally depleted. I couldn't see very well, but I finished it!

Ever the trooper, Barbara Barrie finished the film. She told no one; not her fellow actors, who must have known something was up; not me (though we had had a long conversation at the time); and she didn't even tell her own children.

I didn't want to burden anybody. I didn't want to tell them. I guess it's because I'm an overprotective Jewish mother. They were furious when they found out. To tell you the truth, I really didn't think I was that sick. I thought, I'll have this operation and I'll be fine. For some strange reason, I never doubted my survival. I just didn't think my adult children needed to come home for the operation. I thought I'd be out of the hospital in eight days. (It turned out to be fourteen days.) I wasn't being devious. I just was not worried. And also, I didn't want to burden them, though I now realize how wrong I was about this. At the time I felt that if you give them the really horrible news that their mother might possibly die, then it might do some terrible harm. I was wrong. But my husband Jay said at the time, "If you don't tell them, they'll never forgive you." So I did, though it took me days to come to that decision. In the end, my sister-in-law also called them and said, "You better get home." When I saw them walk into the apartment the day before the operation, I was dumbfounded . . . in fact, I could almost cry right now thinking about it. Isn't that funny? I have never cried over this. I thought, here are my kids. These are really good kids. They are so interesting, these children—these grownups. And I thought, we're a really great family!

They made all sorts of funny jokes about it. When I told my children that I was going to be wearing what looks like a baggy for the rest of my life, my son said, "Have you seen it?" I said, "No, I don't know what it looks like." And he said, "Will you have to declare it as carry-on luggage when you go on the airplane?" We all laughed. And then he said, "Will it be a Vuitton bag?"

They all took me to the hospital the next day.

The doctor that I originally chose to do the operation is one of the very best colorectal surgeons in America. However, he was going on vacation, and I panicked. I decided that I didn't want him operating on me and then leaving right away. So, I went to another surgeon at a different hospital, who turned out to be someone who should never have performed this operation since he really wasn't skilled enough to do it. He was listed, by the way, in *New York* magazine as one of the hundred best doctors in the tri-state area. However, he really didn't know what he was doing, and in the end he performed two very bad operations.

By the time Barbara was diagnosed, she had a level-three tumor. That's as bad as it gets. The cancer had already begun to invade her lymph nodes. Her surgeon was faced with performing a colostomy, having to extract a good chunk of her rectum. It's a procedure that when performed often enough, over a long period of time can be considered routine. But Barbara's wasn't routine. It was painful and grotesque. The surgical site, called a stoma, became perforated, and her colon had prolapsed and broken through the wall of her abdomen.

Barbara Barrie became a victim of the healthcare system. Modern medicine is backed up by great science, but in the end it is an art, not a science—particularly when it comes to surgery. Through a combination of miscues, bad timing, and karma, she was in for a very rough ride.

In fact, my colon was actually hanging out. I kept saying to him, "Why is it doing this?" "Oh, that's the way it looks. It'll shrink," he said. But it didn't. In fact, it got bigger and longer. It's called prolapsing. It got longer and longer and longer. I was told by the first surgeon (who I did not use), that it should look like a little rosebud. This was certainly no rosebud. So my surgeon stitched it up. But it too was no good. The stitches got infected and it was a mess. At this point, I was in terrible pain. I couldn't control my body, and I finally realized that I had to get help. I went back to the first doctor who in turn performed a miracle operation, and finally I began to heal.

Now I know you must always find out how many of these operations the surgeon has performed, and how many were successful. I didn't ask those questions unfortunately. My current oncologist tells me that patients who take an active part in their own recovery get better much faster and in greater percentages than people who are passive patients. You have to work with the doctor. If you and your doctor are not working together, then you have to do something else. But if it's a good doctor, as my current oncologist is, then it's a partnership.

I wrote the book *Second Act* because I believe that colostomy is the last forbidden word in medical jargon. People just don't want to know about it. This is something that is so frightening to them that they don't want to hear about it. They don't want to know about anybody who wears a pouch that catches feces. The fact is this whole business is totally controllable. It's called irrigation. I decided that my life was so great after this operation—and that I feel so wonderful and so vital—I wanted people to know not to be afraid. And they need to know that you shouldn't ignore the symptoms of bowel dysfunction if you have them. Your body and your life can get better.

I had a cousin who elected to have an ileostomy because she was so sick of being in pain all the time. Her life began when her ileostomy was completed. She travels all over the world now.

Even if young people get this disease, there is no reason why they cannot have children. In fact, some babies are born with this condition, and they actually have a colostomy "built in" before they leave the hospital. The point is that taking care of your colostomy is about as bothersome as brushing your teeth in the morning. After that you can run, jump, play tennis, or make love! And that's something that people just don't know about. I wear one-piece bathing suits and leotards and I go to the gym and you just can't see it. It's part of my body. The difference is amazing.

It hasn't changed my family life at all. I guess my kids appreciate me a little more, although we've always had a great relationship. My husband is easygoing and it doesn't bother him. When we make love, I say, "Oh, this thing is crackling." He says, "Yeah, yeah, well, no big deal." It's nothing.

I've never really been angry about this. Though it took me a whole year to get rid of the first doctor and even though I never really healed from the first operation, I wasn't angry. I was perplexed. I knew something was wrong and I'd ask myself, Why can't this be fixed? Why am I in pain all the time? Why is this not working? Later, though, I thought about suing. I didn't. I believe that nobody means to hurt you. The first doctor who did my first colostomy did do a good job in one facet: He did get all my cancer. When he said, "I got it all," I reminded him that this is what is said on television shows all the time and then the husband dies four months later. But he said, "No, no, I really did get it all." And he did, so how could I be angry with him now?

I'm told that at the two-year mark after the first operation, if your cancer hasn't metastasized, you're in really good shape. When I got to the three-year mark, my oncologist told me, "This should be a day of celebration." It was an especially important milestone since I had begun with cancer in my lymph nodes. Now I consider myself a patient who's been cured, but I also have a chronic condition. I never know when it might come back, yet, I can't really think about that. I just have to live my life. Now, I consider myself to be a patient who's been cured, but I also have a chronic condition. That doesn't mean that you don't ask for help along the way.

Terri Haus, a hospital staffer, is a good example of this. She helped me in my many moments of bewilderment and showed me how to do things. Sometimes she would just talk to me. I believe it is essential to people like me who have to learn to care for a "new body" (a body that needs to be irrigated in this case) to have someone who knows what to do and can also listen. To me, Terri was both a practical help and also a great spiritual help. If it hadn't been for her, I'm not sure I would have survived. I certainly would not have known what to do. She taught me how to use the apparatus, how to irrigate, how to put the pouch on, where to get it, how to live with it. But she did all this with such spirit and such humor and such a joy of life that she helped me find my joy of life again. She was truly an angel.

Before this happened, I never thought about God much, but I did belong to Overeaters Anonymous for a few years. In OA they talk a lot about a Higher Power. I do believe in a Higher Power. A Higher Power certainly took care of me during all of this because I never doubted for a minute that I would not survive. I'm not saying I became religious, but I am saying I was very optimistic. My higher Power helped me to stay this way. The Jews think that what you do in this life every day is your heaven and your hell. And so, while I'm here, I try to be the best person I can be. Sometimes I slip, but I always try.

I feel as if I'm at the top of my life now and I feel that this is one of my legacies. I love my children, and they're the best thing that ever happened to me, but beyond them, my second legacy is to tell people about colon cancer—rectal cancer. It is nothing to be afraid of and you must take care of yourself. Like me, your life can be wonderful afterwards, and it's definitely worth the fight.

Barbara's book, Second Act, *is a feat of derring-do if ever there was one. For a glamour queen to share every detail of her trial down to the most unglamorous aspects is a rule-breaking breakthrough, not to mention an act of humility and courage. Through all the indignities she suffered on her way to getting well, Barbara never slipped into the blame/shame cycle we humans are so good at. She didn't blame bad doctoring; she didn't blame her familial genes; she didn't take it out on her husband; she didn't even blame God (who probably wouldn't have minded a bit). Instead, Barbara was ready to accept grace from the most unexpected places. How she handled her illness is a lesson for us all. She was open enough to let her Higher Power and others help her both spiritually and practically. And they did. That's how it works.*

CHAPTER 5

BETTY ROLLIN

There are more than 135 million women in America. Grown-ups with attitude, humor, wisdom, and intelligence, who can achieve anything they set their minds to. If ever we decided to organize a political movement, there'd be no stopping us. I'm convinced of that because women have already done it once. And it was a barn-burner.

Breast cancer is not the greatest threat to women's lives in America. Its mortality rates fall well below that of heart disease. But you wouldn't know that from the noise that's been made about it. And a welcome noise it is! Twenty-five years ago, a convention of breast cancer survivors could have filled up the train station in Fenimore, Wisconsin. Today, a convention of survivors would have to rent the entire state of Utah.

It was a campaign launched from the White House—by the women in the White House. In 1975, First Lady Betty Ford had the generosity and good sense to have her husband the president hold a press conference to announce that she was facing a mastectomy. It made banner headlines. Up until that moment, the word wasn't in the spoken lexicon. It was a word always whispered and usually mispronounced. And the media disgorged mountains of data that, collected for the first time on a national basis, demonstrated the pervasiveness of the disease and the rather woeful state of medical knowledge about it.

In a stunning one-two punch, days later the vice president of the United States, Nelson Rockefeller, called an emergency news conference. He swaggered to the microphone with his trademark Rocky smirk and said to the assembled White House press corps, "Ladies and gentlemen, you're not going to believe this." His wife Happy, the Second Lady of the United States, was at that moment having a mastectomy as well.

One of the young reporters on the story was NBC correspondent Betty Rollin. She didn't know then that the lump in her left breast, the lump doctors had called a cyst and dismissed, was malignant.

There I was, reporting on breast cancer, and I too had a lump. I thought to myself that I should have my lump looked at. My internist was the world's nicest guy. But nice guys don't always make great doctors. He told me, a woman with a hard lump in her breast, to go away and come back in a year.

He dismissed my condition. What a mistake that was.

He didn't suggest a mammogram. Mammography existed at the time, but he didn't say I should have one. He assured me that everything was fine. But I couldn't ignore the subject of breast cancer. I was reporting on it. Still, I couldn't help but feel a little bit pushy when I returned to his office later that year. Finally, I got what I wanted; I had a mammogram. To his horror and mine, my lump turned out to look cancerous. Wow. Who expected that? There was no history of breast cancer in my family, there was no reason I should have had this disease. I was undone.

It wasn't First Lady Betty Ford, but working stiff Betty Rollin, who earned the dubious title of Miss Breast Cancer 1975. First she cried. And then she laughed. And then she broke all the old taboos and wrote about it. First, You Cry *was a breakthrough book. And nobody would publish it. Who wants to read about somebody losing a breast? As it turned out, practically everyone did.* First, You Cry *became a national best-seller. She could not have imagined at the time that doing something to make herself feel better helped a powerful number of other women feel better too.*

My surgeon told me just before my surgery that I might have cancer. I was such a coward. I immediately fainted. In a way I think that my book should have been called *First, You Faint,* because my initial reaction was not to cry; it was to faint. My knees turned to jelly and I fell to the floor. I guess the doctor picked me up. And the next thing I knew, I was lying horizontally on a sofa. That was just hearing that it *might* be cancer.

When you hear you have cancer or that you might have cancer, it's shocking and so frightening. In my opinion, it is that initial shock, the first stage, that is the absolute worst. Once they take your breast off or do a lumpectomy, you have something else to do: you cope; you deal with it. There is no time to be afraid.

Today, the terror is diminished by the fact that women have been educated to take charge of their medical care. We are taught that we can participate in our medical decisions. We are told that we have time to research our options and our medical specialists before surgery. But such was not the case back then. Being powerless, over anything never mind a threat to your very life, is a very scary thing. And Betty was powerless.

1975 was a very different time. It was a time when nobody even said the word cancer. Nobody said the word mastectomy. So the concept that I was going to make the decision myself did not exist. All I knew was that this surgeon said that I probably had something malignant and that I should get it out and, if necessary (if he thought it necessary), the breast would be removed. It certainly didn't occur to me to wait. In fact, I wanted to do it as soon as possible, which is what I ended up doing. A few days later, my breast was removed. Nowadays the patient is much more involved in the decision-making process. Not that, in my case, I would have decided differently. A modified radical mastectomy seemed like a reasonable way to go then. And for me, it does now.

Having a mastectomy is very rough at first, and not only because it's cancer. It is also the realization that you're suddenly missing a sexual part. You don't need me to tell you that breasts are important. Breasts are part of your sexual equipment. And if you lose one or two, it's not pleasant. You will come to terms with your loss later, but when it first happens to you and you're a young woman, it's tough.

Everybody's really nice to you if you have cancer. It's not a time when people are going to be mean. I have to say I didn't mind the pity. I've often said that I think pity is underrated. There's a certain kind of pity at the right moment that's actually very pleasant. Sympathy, pity, kindness, love, and affection are all very nice.

The point is, there are stages. And I think the best advice you can give someone is allow yourself to feel whatever you're feeling because you are in the midst of a process.

There's a time at the beginning of all of this when you feel perfectly lousy. You may not even want to get out of bed. The first day I went home, I was in my old surroundings with what I felt to be a hideous new body. Somehow, being home was much more depressing to me than being in the hospital. I guess it is because it was appropriate to be sick in a hospital.

I really wanted to get right back up. When you're struck and you fall down, very few people want to remain on the ground. It's a natural impulse to want to go on, and most people are able to do just that. However, if sometimes you just want to lie there, that's okay too. You shouldn't feel guilty; you don't have to be such a great sport right away. You should cry as much as you want to and then get up when you feel like getting up.

When something like this happens to you, you should be nice to yourself. You should also be a little self-indulgent. I think it's good to say, "If you're going to feel lousy, let yourself feel lousy because then you'll feel different soon."

Nowadays we tell everybody about everything. While sharing your experiences with others can be helpful, sometimes you wish people would stop telling you everything. However, sometimes sharing is the only way to get through an experience. I am a writer; after my experience, I just sat down and started to write. For me, that worked. I don't believe that everyone should write a book or share their experiences right away as I did. However, I think eventually you should probably share because you'll feel better. And at the very least, you'll find out that you're not alone, which is a major comfort.

In the late Seventies, Mary Tyler Moore made a movie about breast cancer from *First, You Cry*. It was a very brave movie for her to make because at that time, people still weren't talking about the disease. However, she brought it forward and presented a message that couldn't be ignored: You can have this disease and live through it. I think that is a wonderful and true message.

Throughout my book and throughout the movie *First, You Cry,* I used humor to get through my situation. For me, humor was a great way of battling the disease. And it is a wonderful way of fighting. I believe that when people laugh, they put themselves far ahead of the game.

Being ahead of the game is essential, because cancer patients, no matter how long their disease is in remission, are chronic patients. There is always the threat that the beast will come back to bite you when you're least expecting it. In 1984, nine years after Betty Rollin's first mastectomy, the cancer reemerged in her healthy breast.

It was different the second time. I felt less terror because I was more experienced. But I was extremely angry. I felt like screaming, "Hey, I did this already! I mean, leave me alone, you know? Enough already!" All I could think was, Here goes the other breast. I was miserable.

For a while, after my second mastectomy, I didn't talk about it because I felt like a failure. With the release of *First, You Cry,* I had given so many women hope. Yet, what did they have to hope for? I had gotten cancer again. However, after several years had passed, I noticed I was still breathing! And I decided to talk about it. Then I realized a lot of women get it twice—and live. So that was a comfort to me and, I hope, to those I was able to reach.

The idea that cancer can improve your life sounds like a bad joke. But with gratitude and the right attitude it can.

You would not believe it but cancer survivors are a merry group. I think we are merry because we know that we could have croaked! And if you really grasp that fact, you are immediately cheered when you realize that you haven't.

After my second battle with breast cancer, I became more focused and a lot more grateful. I now noticed that I was alive, and before I had cancer, I didn't pay any attention to that. So in a weird way, I think that my bouts with cancer gave me a better life. I think many cancer survivors feel that a scary disease improves your life. It's not even a matter of stopping to smell the flowers. Maybe some people like to smell flowers—I don't mind flowers but it's not my favorite thing to do—but it makes you pay attention to what you care about and who you care about. Essentially, it keeps you on track. And that's a very good thing.

Every week I hear about somebody who gets this disease and doesn't make it. And for what reason? Just luck. That's it. Why did I live and she didn't? It just doesn't make any sense. If you're one of the ones who is lucky enough to live, you feel humble and grateful.

Every woman is at risk for this disease. Sometimes women think, Oh well, nobody in the family's had it. Let me tell you firsthand, if you're female, you're at risk. Therefore it is your duty to yourself to keep getting checked and keep having mammograms. If cancer is caught early enough, you will likely get the opportunity to live. I feel lucky because I consider each year that passes a small victory.

CHAPTER 6

MICHAEL YORK

What is breathtaking about Michael York is not that he's a gorgeous California-blond with an Oxford honors-student accent (he is), but that in an industry pock-marked with narcissistic superstars whose self-importance ranks in their minds right up there with motherhood and the flag, he is the essence of humility. He doesn't talk much about himself. But I couldn't get him to stop talking about his wife!

There is still a bit of the buckled swash of a musketeer in his appearance but maybe that's just his famous profile, which he procured at the age of three by breaking his nose. He says he was trying to fly.

Many great actors portray characters who are larger than life. But they've got writers. They embark on exotic adventures, lose their hearts in great romance, confront and conquer tragedy and trial, and undertake quests of spiritual and emotional discovery. A very select few of those actors take these elements with them, through the stage door, and into the real world. York is one of them.

But the moment that really informed his life came not in Shakespearean garb at the Old Globe, but in Wales, in despair. What do you do when you're twenty-five, the heartthrob of Western civilization, and your girl dumps you? He returned to London contemplating what possible spin he could put on his predicament in order to carry off a dignified interview for an American magazine.

I lived in London at what used to be the Old Imperial German Embassy, a great Gothic pile of a place. It was very dark, with huge vaulted ceilings and big rooms. I waited there for my appointment with this journalist from an American magazine. I was under the impression that it was an Irishman named Pat, Pat McKelley. But when I opened the door, I found this dazzling blonde.

I invited her in and made her tea. We chatted and, after time, I said, "Well, if there's anything you'd like to ask me . . ." She told me later, she thought, "Oh, no. Just another conceited actor. I can't bear it. How can I get out of here?" I thought, since she was coming from New York, that this was a new type of interview where you humiliate your interviewee to get them to babble on.

When it came time to take the pictures the light was gray. It was London, after all. She asked if we could meet the next day. After that, we just had this instant connection. That was it.

I was doing a film in India, *The Guru,* directed by James Ivory and produced by Ismail Merchant. When they were still in their Indian phase of shooting, Pat was with me, and it was glorious. I asked her to marry me in India, because in India they have wonderful weddings that go on for three days. We were very happy.

Then suddenly she fell ill—seriously ill. In fact, she was dying. And we happened to be right out in the desert, in this little town called Bickinee. It's one of these things that happen in life. You don't anticipate it, but it takes on enormous subsequent importance. I can only describe it as a miracle. The Maharajah of Bickinee had just donated the operating facilities to a hospital, and there happened to be a surgeon who had been trained in New York who was about to get the train back to Delhi. They found him at the railway station, brought him back, and he performed this operation to take out all this gangrenous intestine in her. Before going under, she fought like a demon to live. I knew that she was exceptional, that there was something about her. And she did survive against all the odds. It was a very dangerous operation, after which the Indian doctor said: She's in God's hands now. Which is rather wonderful, and actually quite reassuring.

The reason she'd fallen ill was not because of India, but because she'd been given drugs by a London doctor to prevent her getting sick, and these drugs contained sulfa, to which she was allergic. So once she was back in England again, and very weak, one doctor said she could only exist on codeine. Massive doses of codeine, for the rest of her life.

It's had huge cosmic payoffs. What should have been something very negative, a life sentence to drug addiction, has in fact turned into something incredibly positive, because in the course of getting well again, she found alternative therapies, and in the mid–Sixties, this was unusual.

Someone introduced us to homeopathy, and all kinds of natural homeopathic therapies, which of course now, is very mainstream. Everyone knows about it. But then it was sort of unusual. So, she systematically explored them all, and I would have the great pleasure of watching her turn from strength to strength. And now she's the strongest person I know, both spiritually and physically too, which is wonderful. For the last couple of years, she has been researching a book on alternative therapies. She feels very strongly that it's time that the orthodox and the alternative join hands. They shouldn't be mutually exclusive; they have so much to offer each other. She has been interviewing doctors all over the world who feel the same way, and this is all going to be another book.

So those very difficult and strange and stressful days in India in fact produced the most powerfully positive result. And I think this happens to people. What you suspect is life changing and negative is often life changing and positive. Maybe the payoff doesn't come immediately, you have to wait for it further down the line.

Patience is a key factor in the success of our marriage. We've also shared everything. The good and the bad. We've made an unspoken vow that we would spend our lives together. And because she was a freelance photographer and a writer, it was much easier for her to travel with me. She would come with me, and laterally, I would go with her when she'd exhibit. I think it's important to share things. As I said, it's the good with the bad.

I don't mean to harp on about my wife, but she's done another book, which I thought was really interesting, in which she photographed and interviewed seventy-five people over the age of seventy-five who hadn't retired. It was a book of great inspiration from wonderfully dynamic people. One of the factors that linked them all together was that at some point in their lives, they'd been through an incredibly stressful, negative period, that changed their lives. In fact, it usually was the one factor that turned their lives around and pointed them in a very positive direction. This was a very, very common factor.

The pattern of life is just like a wave. Even the calmest ocean has waves. It's up and down. That's where energy comes from. You just have to let go of the familiar—to dare. You have to do what your children are doing. They attempt to fly. They are not afraid to explore the unusual or the unfamiliar. I don't mean you should turn into a daredevil or put your life or your happiness at risk. But I suppose in a way I've been lucky to be conditioned like this, because every job is a new departure. I feel that I am sailing into the unknown all the time. I can usually say that whatever one does, it's never a totally negative experience. Even if the work itself is judged to be bad, usually one has a wonderful life-enhancing experience. You go somewhere. Or you meet somebody who becomes a friend. So in the end, rarely is anything ever totally negative. I'd rather regret the things I've done than the things I haven't done.

One of the things he didn't do was the film Love Story. *Michael York was originally cast as the male lead, and all his instincts told him to go for it. But his advisors suggested he decline. York turned it down. He says he'll never choose his advisors over his instincts again.*

I think it's very useful to be associated with a smash hit. I think people like to be successful rather than the other. But that's not regret. I think something very positive came out of it. I do believe that you have instincts, and you must obey them, whether you call it the higher self, as a lot of new age books do, or that other knowledge. I believe it is in there, and maybe if I had done the film, I would have ruined it. It would have been the wrong combination.

In *Hamlet,* Hamlet says, "There's a divinity that shapes our ends, Rough-hew them how we will." Often I think it's the other way around. The divinity rough-hews our ends. We finish the ragged pieces into something lasting and valuable. I would like to feel that there is a thread of destiny that goes through everything. Yet you can change it too. You don't have to accept a negative lot. If it's all preordained, then what's the point? You have the power too.

I always look ahead. I'm thankful for the past, but I love the present, and I think the future is even more exciting.

The human body regenerates. We don't live with the same old body year in, year out. It's always a new constantly changing thing. So everything's new and fresh.

Nice view from a guy who earned his bread on the strength of his youth and vigor and earns it now on the strength of his maturity.

Woody Allen once said ninety percent of life is showing up. I think ninety percent of it is attitude. We all tend to think that our own stresses were created just for us. That's an illusion that makes us victims. It's also dead wrong. The most serious stresses are pretty universal. If you truly believe you are exactly where you are supposed to be, however uncomfortable it is, then you're on the road to learning something important. You're learning to turn negative illusions into positive truths. Those are the ones you can put in the bank. Then, like Pat and Michael York, you wind up with a stockpile of dividends you get to draw on.

CHAPTER 7

PAUL SORVINO

If you saw him bawling like a baby when his daughter, Mira Sorvino, accepted an Academy Award and gave her dad the credit, you might not imagine that Paul Sorvino has a positively volcanic presence, as though there's always something in his imposing stature that's about to erupt. When he fixes his gaze on you and holds it there, you cannot look away. At least, I can't. His intensity is too great.

Paul is a man who has very clear ideas of who he is and what he's here for no matter what other suggestions may come his way. As an actor, and, yes, a director, he's animated a gallery of memorable characters in seventy film and television roles, playing everything from a hardened criminal to Henry Kissinger. Just when the hit TV series Law and Order *was on a roll, Paul quit to pursue an opera career. He's performed with the Seattle Opera and appeared in a Gala at the Metropolitan Opera in New York.*

His life was shaped by a terrorizing father and a brutalized mother, from whom he was wrenchingly separated in what felt to him like a kidnapping. The fact that he didn't repeat the abusive cycle on his own children is a near miracle. But then, being alive, being able to breathe, much less sing, is a miracle.

Paul is one of the millions of people who suffer from asthma. People not afflicted may think it just means you can't run track. It is far more serious than that. It is not curable, and if left untreated, it can be fatal. Paul Sorvino learned to treat his asthma in a drug-free way—his own way. And he is fanatical on the subject. He wrote the best-selling book How to become a Former Asthmatic *and formed a foundation to get the word out, particularly in deep urban areas like the South Bronx, where minority children are most at risk for contracting the illness. And every ounce of his passion, not to mention his dis-*

posable income, gets poured into it because he knows his method has worked in his own life. More important than that, it saved the life of his four-year-old son.

I had asthma from the time I was ten until I was twenty-five. It became pretty serious. At that time they were giving me steroids, which they still prescribe for asthmatics. But they gave it to me in some serious doses, and it made me very introverted. I am naturally the very opposite, which is gregarious, and emollient, and voluble. It made me paranoid and strange. To make matters worse, it didn't work. I still had asthma. Steroids didn't really take it away.

I was going to quit this Broadway show I was in because of it. And the two actors in the show, one whom I was understudying, Robert Burr and the late Herb Atilman, said, "You have asthma? You're leaving the show?" I said, "I can't sing." I'm a tenor and I couldn't sing high notes. They said asthma can be cured! I said, "Are you out of your mind?"

They showed me these exercises in the lobby. They put me through a series of breathing exercises which are based on yoga. I was at that time on a bronchial dilator, four pills a day, and on those steroid pills. After I'd done these exercises for about an hour that day I needed half the medication. The next morning I was out of the asthma attack completely. I didn't have another for two months.

Over the years I began to teach these exercises to anybody who had asthma. In twenty minutes very often I can show somebody this technique and they do it and they're free of the spasm. I'm not allowed to use the word cure, but if you don't have symptoms anymore you put a name on it.

I've stopped the spasm in twenty minutes in people who have had it for twenty years—people coming out of hospitals. Let me explain what it is. Asthma is a blocked off function of breathing. It's very simple. You have a trachea coming from under your larynx, or voicebox. That becomes a *Y.* The two branches are called the bronchi, and they branch out and become the lungs, leading to the little air sacs, called the alveoli. There is a muscle sheath around these two hose-shaped branches which in people like me, and others who are so disposed, constricts. The muscle sheath closes. So instead of having a healthy opening that air can pass through, you have a tiny opening or no opening at all. This can come from edema from allergies. It can come from excessive secretion of mucus. It can come from the spasm, or any combination of these.

The medications serve to relax the muscle sheath. To a degree they work, but they don't work forever. After a while, they make you sicker, and sicker, and sicker. So by the time you've had steroids for several years, you look very different. Your musculature is very different. You're very debilitated after a number of years on cortisone.

What I do, and what I teach people to do is this: Standing erect, you take a deep sharp breath in through the nose, and let the air expand your belly to its fullest. Then you blow out very hard through tightly pursed lips. If you just did that, four times a day, for five minutes each time, you would probably relieve most of the symptoms of your asthma. I'm here to tell you I haven't had asthma in thirty-four years.

Asthma is not what people think it is. First of all, it needs a redefinition. It's not a disease. If it were a disease, I couldn't have been cured in one hour. If it were a disease, I couldn't have saved my son's life with these exercises.

That was the most horrifying day and night of my life. My wife called me to tell me that our son Michael was having an asthma attack. I couldn't accept it because I'd had asthma, and I didn't want to believe that my son could have it. I jumped into the car and rushed home and found him in the back yard, sitting almost slumped over, his face all swollen. He was very allergic and still is.

He said, "I can't breathe." He was four years old. So we called the doctor and he told us to come right over. On the way, I had him in my lap and his eyes were rolled back in his head, and I thought he was going to die. We rushed him in, and the doctor gave him a shot of adrenaline immediately. With asthmatics, that makes you breathe right away. With him, it didn't do anything. The doctor listened while I was trying not to panic. I was in tears, but I was trying not to make Michael frightened, though he was almost unconscious anyway. And the doctor said, "I think his left lung has collapsed. Watch him for a few minutes, I'll be right back. If we can't stop it here, we'll have to go to the emergency room." He came back in a few minutes and Michael was barely breathing. I said, "We have to do something!" The doctor gave him another shot of adrenaline, and that started to bring Michael around. I've never heard of two shots of adrenaline for that.

I took Michael immediately to a specialist, and he filled him up with more injections. The child was on four medications. He was breathing but he was careening off the furniture because the steroids usually act like some kind of high. It gives you a very excited kind of behavior. He was really jumping, running, crazed.

That night I slept in his room, and I said, "Look, Michael, if you can't breathe you have to wake me up. Okay?" At two in the morning he woke me up saying, "I can't breathe Daddy." I tried to show him the exercises, but he was a little boy. He couldn't or wouldn't do them. I was going crazy thinking, My boy is going to die! If he can't breathe with four medications in him, the most powerful they knew, he'll never survive. And his face was swollen, so I knew everything in his trachea was all swollen.

I prayed, "God, help me. What am I going to do?" And somehow I got the inspiration to make it a game. Anything that would make him blow out hard against tightly pursed lips. I said, "Mike, we've got to blow. The little bird can't fly, Mike. We have to help the little bird fly. Come on Mike." He was a heroic little boy, and I knew this. He was always a helper. And I said, "The little bird can't fly. Come on Mike. We have to blow. Come on Mike, let's help the little bird fly. Oh Mike, let's blow out the birthday candles!" I worked with him for nearly an hour. And within an hour he was breathing, freely. I took him back to the specialist two days later, who said, "This is the same boy you brought in who was out of it? This is a different boy." Mike was very skinny and not a strong little boy. Cute little boy—handsome as you can make them. And now, he's twenty years old, six-foot-two, big, beautiful, handsome, healthy.

I cannot read about other children dying. I become depressed. I put so much of my time and some of my money into the Paul Sorvino Foundation. People would write to me, and I would return phone calls as far away as Maui. And I would be on the phone an hour, trying to teach them breathing exercises. I used to rack up $2,000 phone bills. I never charged anybody for that. But I must get this done. I've got to get it done! I can't go to my grave understanding that I had this great secret which saved me and my son, and thousands of others. Through the book and the videotape that's available now, I estimate we've saved 200,000 people, at least. And we have so many to go. There are 30 million asthmatics, maybe as many as 100 million asthmatics worldwide. There's so much work to do. It is hereditary. I wish I could put everything else aside and just do that, but of course, I can't.

There has been a lot of resistance from the medical community because you must know that eighty percent of an allergist's patient base are asthmatics. Yet certain allergists used to give my book out. I do understand certain of the resistance that I have encountered in trying to promulgate these techniques. One doctor on NBC asked me, "What would you say to those who say it's voodoo?" Why would I lie? I stand to gain nothing! It's a nonprofit organization into which I put all kinds of time and money and from which I take nothing. I said, "I'm telling you this because it works. Because it saved me and it saved my son and so many others, hundreds of thousands of people."

Finally, the American Medical Association honored me for my work with asthmatics at their annual convention in San Francisco. That was wonderful. They gave us a grant because we're trying to build a center, and conduct studies, and publish very shortly.

I was blessed with a phenomenal mother. Her name was Mary Maria Angela Maria Martea Rensey. All Italian men think their mothers are angels. I'm here to tell you that my children pray to her as if she were a saint. My mother was the most extraordinary of women. Were one to design a mother, accepting, loving, intelligent, beautiful person, that's the mother that you would design. She was all accepting. My mother's dead seven years now. My son just said last night, "Daddy, I miss grandma so much." They all say that. Everybody's life she touched, everybody who came within her sphere, she took in. Just took them in.

I had a talented but difficult and dangerous father. He used to beat the hell out of me! He was a very insecure, very talented, very intelligent man with no education whatsoever, who would periodically go through almost manic stages, where he would beat up my mother, and beat me up. He was a terrorizing individual. And so I grew up with this terrible fear. My parents split when I was ten. My mother took me to California. She tried to take my two older brothers, and they wouldn't go. They were afraid to go.

My father kidnapped me when I was twelve. I didn't see my mother for another five years. I couldn't even see her. We were forbidden communication. She wrote three or four letters a week—tearstained letters—but we were under such domination, we were not allowed to write back. I wouldn't even do it. I was afraid I would get caught! When I was seventeen, she stopped writing. She couldn't. He would beat the hell out of her. That's why she left him, because he'd beat her up. By then I was six feet tall. It was a little bit different. After a few months during which no letters came, I said to my father, "I think mother's dead!" He said, "No, she's not." I said, "How do you know?" He said, "I know where she is! She's in Bridgeport, living with her father, taking care of him." I said, "I want to see her!" That's the day I became a man. We saw her the next week. The whole family, including my father, drove up to see her. But can you imagine a father calling my mother names every day, forbidding communication. Oh, it destroyed me for those years!

My son Michael, whom I adore so much, like all my children, said, "Daddy, I know your daddy hit you a lot. How come you don't hit me?" I said, "Michael I knew it was wrong!" By my mother's example, by what she was as a human being, and by what she did trying to protect us, I knew right from wrong. Everything that I feel is valuable from a human point of view is from my mother. She was very spiritual in her own way.

I'm not sure where my spirituality lies. Something's there. Perhaps we're too small to think of ourselves as just ants or flies, that there's nothing beyond this. I would prefer to think there is. I would prefer to rest my case with the notion that some extraordinary, magical, brilliant phenomenal ultra hypergenius created all of this. The word in this language is God. So let's call it God. Something is there. But I don't think He's interfering with us. I think he may have moved on. But we'll catch up to him, the universe is expanding.

CHAPTER 8

PATRICIA NEAL

Because his soul was a pawn in the eternal war between God and Satan, the story goes, Job lost everything and kept asking why. Only when he accepted his lot, forgave his tormentors and put his life in God's hands did he receive all that he had lost and more. There are some people who seem to have the lot of Job.

The great actress Patricia Neal's life seems to have been Job incarnate. In her public life, she had great fortune. In private, she watched one child maimed and another buried. A series of massive strokes wiped out her abilities, and thirty years of domestic oppression erased her self-esteem. And all the while she searched for understanding, as a Baptist, a Methodist, an Anglican, a Catholic. Always searching for peace. She has found it, but her journey was punishing beyond measure.

Patsy Louise Neal was born in Kentucky and raised in the hills of Tennessee. Tennessee hillbillies, like biblical heroes, as Neal puts it, "don't conk that easy."

At twenty-one years old, Patricia Neal sprung from the publicity mill of the great studio system in Hollywood a full-blown star. In the film version of Ayn Rand's novel The Fountainhead, *she was paired with the indomitable Gary Cooper. It was a pairing both electric and catastrophic. Their torrid, years-long affair was the worst kept secret in Hollywood, replete with blow-ups and break-ups, recriminations and reconciliations that only furthered the pain for all involved. She became pregnant. He wouldn't leave his wife. She wouldn't have his child. In 1952, Patricia Neal had an illegal abortion. It ended their affair and framed her life, because he had been the love of her life.*

Their breakup led Neal to a state of near suicidal depression. On the rebound and desperate for babies to heal the gash guilt had torn in her heart, she met author Roald Dahl. Dashiell Hammett told her not to marry him because he felt Dahl possessed a capacity for Olympian cruelty. Neal didn't listen and she immediately married him anyway. Unfortunately, Hammett was right. Neal has written that Dahl froze her out, insulted everyone she cared about, refused to speak to her for days, and told her he loved her a grand total of three times.

I married Roald Dahl because I wanted children. I thought he would be a good daddy. After waiting two years, I became pregnant. I had a baby. I was so happy. Yet, even though I had a new baby, I couldn't ignore the horror our marriage had been before I became pregnant. It was just hell on earth.

They had three children in five years: Olivia, Tessa, and Theo. Yet the choices she had made seemed to boomerang. She viewed it as life-crushing retribution. In the short span of the next five years, Patricia Neal began to lose all that she held dear.

It began in 1960. The family's nanny was strolling Neal's third-born child, Theo, in his carriage. All of a sudden, a taxi came out of nowhere and hit the stroller.

When I heard the siren go by, I was at the A&P. I thought to myself, What is it now? I looked and saw that it was a taxicab. I looked again and saw that it was a police car. I thought, Thank God, not knowing my son was in it. When I got to the corner, our housekeeper was there. She was looking for me. She told me what had happened. I dropped my groceries. It was just horrendous. I ran to my husband, Roald Dahl, who was working in Clifford Odets' apartment. He lay down his pencils, and we went to the hospital. We were told that Theo would die. Roald went into Theo's hospital room where he saw the nurse giving Theo a lot of medicine. He thought it seemed like too much medicine, but the nurse assured him everything would be all right. Roald left the room and stood by my side. All of a sudden, we saw the doctor running into Theo's room. The nurse had given our baby three or four times too much medicine.

The accident caused Theo to suffer massive head injuries, and his recovery would be a lifelong struggle. He had lost his sight. The family fled the perils of Manhattan for the relative security of Dahl's native England. It was 1962. At that time, epidemics were widespread in the city of London. But they hardly ever reached the little hamlets in the hills. As a result, inoculations were rarely given to children living in the countryside, and when the German measles (later called rubella) struck, it was a killer. Patricia Neal buried her first-born there. Olivia was only seven.

Roald went to pieces. He really did. I think it's the most tragic thing that ever happened to him. He never got over it. He couldn't believe that he had a daughter and that she had died. He had a sister who had died at the same age. She had appendicitis. His father, heartbroken over his daughter's death, caught pneumonia and died about two months after his daughter. With the death of our daughter, Olivia, it was like Roald was living his childhood losses all over again.

We were so brave when Theo got in his accident. But this was different. Roald just went to pieces when our Olivia died.

The real torture was when she died. I remember I was up all night. Roald came in and he was just crushed. I remember the sun coming up. It was a fabulous sun. I remember saying, "My daughter Olivia is no longer here." It just breaks your heart. I got ill. It was like God was making the same mistake twice. But you've got to get through it. You can't give up because of tragedy; you must be strong and move on.

In fact, Patricia Neal did move on. Soon after Olivia died, a new child was born—a daughter named Ophelia. Yet the living can never replace the dead. Neal has written that she felt Olivia's death was retribution for her aborted child, as was the guilt over it that she has carried ever since. However, Neal continued to grasp for strength through it all. In 1963, she won an Academy Award for her role in Hud. *She had a fifth child whom she named Neal. Yet, her tragedy was far from over. On February 17, 1965, the thirty-nine-year-old Patricia Neal, in her first trimester of pregnancy, was bathing her daughter*

Tessa when she felt her body betray her. She suffered three strokes in rapid succession. The right side of her body was paralyzed. Her vision was impaired. She couldn't speak. Her final thoughts before she fell into a coma were, I have children to care for. I cannot die.

Horrendous is not an accurate description of hell. Patricia Neal credits Roald Dahl with being the single most important agent in her recovery. He did devote himself to her with religious fervor. But the way he did it must have added to her pain. Dahl was a brutal taskmaster. Neal's 1988 autobiography, As I Am, *described her battle to regain basic motor skills, and was also filled with palpable vitriol for the way Dahl treated her. His method lacked compassion or warmth or even common decency. Today she tells snapshots of the same story, but her words are softened and infuse him with higher motives.*

Roald wanted me to live. I didn't want to. But in the end, I agreed to try. He went to see me every day when I was unconscious in the hospital. One or two times, he'd shout at me. He'd do anything to make me regain consciousness. Then I finally opened an eye. It was really a horrendous thing to go through. When I first came to, I couldn't say a word. My speech was all wrong and I saw everything in double. I had to walk with braces on. I was paralyzed. But he was tricky. He would shout at me, screaming, "I'm going to make you get out of this!"

When Neal needed water, only a sip of water, Dahl would refuse her such pleasures until she could pronounce the word water properly. This may sound like an acceptable tough-love tactic today, but back then, tough-love tactics hadn't been adopted or even invented. It didn't feel like love to her. When she sunk into depression and was unwilling to go on trying, Dahl offered to show her where he kept the razor blades.

That's right. Oh, he was being funny, you know. He just didn't want me to feel sorry for myself. He was tough. Oh, I could have killed him at times. But he really wanted me to get well, and he wouldn't settle for anything less. He said that I was the mother of his children and he wanted me to live.

Yet his intentions made things difficult because he liked running everything. I remember Tessa was so distressed by my disability that she began to back away from me. Everything was "Daddy." Daddy this and Daddy that. When I would try to get her to talk to me, she'd only say, "Daddy." I would lose my temper. Roald would then say to Tessa, "Talk to Mama now. Talk to Mama." And she would only say, "Daddy." It was just horrendous. They would go for a walk and would go up the hill and I couldn't do any of this. I was so bitter. We had some terrible times. It was a really difficult period of our lives.

Six months after she'd been slammed with that series of strokes, Patricia Neal experienced a miracle. The child that she had been carrying wanted to be born. Miraculously undamaged by the physical blows her mother's body had taken, Lucy Dahl was born with no complications. Neal's doctors were astonished.

*Dahl had driven Neal to a recovery that was almost uncontainable. Three years after her strokes, the great Patricia Neal was back in a film—*The Subject Was Roses, *for which she received another Academy Award nomination in 1968. She received a thunderous ovation at that Academy Awards ceremony when she walked onto the stage as a presenter. Things seemed to be looking up for Neal. Yet at home, life was becoming extremely difficult.*

I guess I have a lot of guts. That's about the only thing I can think of. Roald and I lived together for thirty years. Some of those years were very happy. But toward the end a lot went wrong.

We are physical, emotional, mental, and spiritual beings. When one of those aspects takes hits, you can recover. But when all of them are under attack, it can feel like a runaway train.

There is no greater outrage to a woman's self-image and emotional stability than infidelity. Dahl flaunted his indiscretions in their home. Yet, Neal, like many wives, found solace in her denial that these affairs even existed.

I really am an idiot like that, because all these girls would come in my house and I'd say, "Aren't they lovely?" I adored them all. Yet, in retrospect, it seems that my husband knew them a whole lot better than I did.

In 1972, Patricia became fast friends with a fashion coordinator named Felicity Crossland. She considered Felicity to be her best friend. It turned out to be a double cross. Her newfound best friend was having an affair with her husband, and even the children knew all about it. Neal's daughter Ophelia informed her mother of her father's actions. It was like history was repeating itself. But instead of playing the role of Gary Cooper's mistress, Neal was now the woman scorned.

For all his might as an author and authoritarian husband, Dahl was, in the end, a cliché. Just another philanderer. He married Felicity four years after Patricia Neal divorced him. But it took years longer for her anger to wane.

The door to forgiveness can swing two ways. Neal had experienced a wonderful act of forgiveness years before. During Neal's affair with Gary Cooper, his twelve-year-old daughter Maria had been devastated by her father's open infidelity. Neal thought Maria would never forgive her for what she had done.

When I became ill, Maria wrote me a fantastic letter. At that time, I could barely write, but I wrote a card saying, "Thank you, thank you." And then, in time, I ran into Maria in France. It was fantastic. I love her. She's a very good woman.

Resentment is a killer, and it gets heavier the longer you carry it. It is easier to forgive when you yourself are forgiven. Maria Cooper had forgiven Patricia Neal. Now it was Neal's turn to let the hatred go. It was time to begin healing her heart and her soul.

At the end of Roald's life, I was able to forgive him. It was my son's thirtieth birthday, and I wanted very much to celebrate with the family. I wrote Roald a letter which said that I was willing to forget about my pain and anger. Roald was so thrilled. That was the last year of his life. It was thrilling to see him so happy that I had at last forgiven him.

I guess I was just so tired of this hate I was going through. For God's sake, you know, who wants this? It seems so silly to hate. I hated Roald. But now, when I think back on him and the way he cared for me, I think he did a wondrous job. It was a terribly difficult thing that he did for me. A lot of other people also did do many things for me. I'm very grateful to them all. You never know who's going to be there for you when you need them the most. Roald was there for me and he really was a fantastic man. I see his wife Felicity now. She's good to me and I like her.

We're not all perfect. I don't think there's anybody in this world who's perfect. I'm like everybody. I have good points and I have bad points. We're all human. I'm sorry about some of the things I've done, but I like myself.

In terms of what has happened in my life, I don't quite understand it. I don't know why some people are picked on and some people aren't. But you just can't be a sissy. You can't give up. There were times when I was so indignant, so furious about all this. Somehow, I don't know when it happened, I came to believe that we do live in a fabulous world. Sometimes, when I think about all the amazing countries and the oceans we have on Earth, I become so happy to know that I'm here. I really adore life now. I even adore the fact that you never know what's going to happen in life from one minute to the next. Now, I'm just going to continue to do the best in this life. I don't conk that easy.

CHAPTER 9

ROBERT GUILLAUME

There is a part of Robert Guillaume in every character he's played on television. He has the literate intelligence and compassion of the "Boss" on the smart TV sendup Sportsnight, *the discernment of* Benson, *the butler turned lieutenant governor, and the wisdom of the old mystic Rafiki the baboon from* The Lion King. *He is also very funny. And his birthname is not Guillaume. In the interest of attaining a more sophisticated image, he adopted the French translation of* a perfectly good name—*Williams.*

Bobby Williams was born into the Great Depression and grew up poor in St. Louis, Missouri. His father was gone before he ever knew him. His mother was an alcoholic. He, along with his sisters and brothers, were turned over to their grandmother when Bobby was still a toddler. She supported them all by doing the laundry for the priests at the Catholic rectory nearby. And he was angry.

Kids from broken families bear scars. When the solvent in which the family disintegrated is alcohol, kids exhibit specific behaviors. And acting out is one of them. Guillaume describes himself as a choirboy who hung out in pool halls and had a bit of a problem with authority. He has confessed that as a kid he got into a pattern of destruction, theft and other rotten behavior. He has said it was like swimming against the tide of the ghetto to avoid it. His loud mouth and explosive temper got him suspended from grammar school and expelled from parochial school. At the age of seventeen, Bobby Williams joined the army. When his Southern captain said, "This army isn't big enough for both of us" (he actually said that), Bobby quit.

He washed dishes and cooked candy and took a job as a trolley driver so he could sing to his passengers along the tracks and work his way through college.

It was then that he molded the mouth that had gotten him in so much hot water into the instrument of his salvation. It may have seemed impossible for him to become the upwardly mobile champion implicit in the American dream, but he could play one on television. On stage, Guillaume was nominated for a Tony Award for his portrayal of floating crap game owner Nathan Detroit in the 1976 all-black revival of Guys and Dolls. *Guillaume's TV character Benson went from butler to lieutenant governor, and when the series ended in 1986, he was even running for governor. Guillaume scored another triumph on Broadway when he was cast as the first black actor to play the title role in* The Phantom of the Opera, *where he breathed his own monsters into the role of the madman.*

At this best of times, in a wash of great critical acclaim and personal victory, Robert Guillaume lost his son. Jacques was thirty-three years old. Robert blamed the ghetto, saying its long arm had reached Jacques and programmed him for this kind of life and death. But he also blamed himself.

~~~~~~~~~~~~~~~~~~~~~~~~

My son died. He died of AIDS that Christmas. Jacques was a wonderful, wonderful young man. I always feel that he never really thought enough of himself. He was extremely talented. He was a much better singer than I ever was, much more natural, and had gifts that I always wished I possessed. I had no doubt that he would have made his mark. I really don't know how he came to this particular end, but I remember feeling helpless. There was nothing I could do about it.

And one of my lingering regrets is that I think Jacques thought I looked down upon him. Jacques was a homosexual. He thought I was ashamed of his sexuality. I was not. Jacques thought that his sexuality was a factor in our relationship. It was not. I loved my son and I think he loved me. I just wish that he felt that I loved him as much as I did.

Jacques was a gifted man. And I'm still so sorry that he didn't quite understand how gifted he was, and that we needed him, that we wanted him to be alive, because he was carrying a banner for us. He was carrying a torch for us, he was leading the way, which is what I thought I had always done for my family.

Jacques' death occasioned me to say, "The long arm of the ghetto had programmed me for this kind of life and death." Growing up in the ghetto had programmed me to act in a cer-
~~~~~~~~~~~~~~~~~~~~~~~~

tain way without my knowledge. My life was subliminal. Things were happening to me and suggestions were being made to me that I really wasn't all that aware of at the time.

I was never aware growing up, that any negative impressions about myself were just nesting in me. But I now realize various suggestions had seeped into me that I was ugly. I felt this when I was very young, around eight or nine. I began to feel, gee whiz, black skin, and big lips, and a big nose—my goodness, how am I ever going to do anything with that? I know other guys who grew up looking exactly like me who didn't feel that. I thought I could overcome almost anything other than the fact that I was not an attractive person. It produced a lingering anger in me.

So in my dealings with people, I would get into trouble. I would get into arguments. I would not be as charming as I had the ability to be, because I was always on guard and defensive about one thing or another. Yet even though I would get angry, I never thought that I was doing anything wrong. In retrospect, I think that most of my life I had been shooting myself in the foot! I'd been trying to pretend to be one thing or another and not quite pulling it off.

I have confided before that my mother was an alcoholic. My sister told me that that was kind of harsh, so I've had to rethink it. It was a while before I really could forget my characterization of her, but then one day I had the realization that, actually, she was only nineteen years old when I was born and had had two or three kids before I was born. I saw that there were events and circumstances that may have accounted for her behavior, so I am inclined to give her a little better reading than that she was simply an alcoholic. That she was an alcoholic and had gotten involved with whiskey was a fact, but the reasons behind it lead me to remember her much more gently.

But she never made me feel that I was special. I remember that all I ever wanted someone to do was touch me! I wanted someone to touch me.

My grandmother to me was sort of a miracle worker because whenever she disciplined me, I never once thought that it was out of anything other than just love. She wanted me to get the best out of my own life. She managed to discipline me without taking away my spirit and self-esteem. She had an intimate bond with me. I guess the basis of it was love. My grandmother was intimately involved in everything I was doing. Good or bad, she was there. I remember being so disappointed in myself that I was never able to repay my grandmother for all of the things that she did for me. Had it not been for her, I would have been nobody.

But in spite of my grandmother's love, I still carried such anger. Maybe it was the long arm of the ghetto—the idea that even if you get out of whatever situation you were in, there are attitudes in your personality that still lead you back to the lifestyle that you are more familiar with. I don't know. What I do know is that understanding my behavior has been a continuous and unfolding process which has given me the strength to grow.

I do think of my own complicity in Jacques' death. I had left him, his brother, and their mother to follow a dream of mine—a career in show business. But even though I left, I never felt comfortable about that. I felt guilty for having followed my own dreams rather selfishly and not being with their mother and them. It still haunts me.

I think that Jacques, for all of his dangerous liaisons and dangerous connections, was still an innocent in a way that I've never been. However, I think that we are all innocents in a certain way. We all walk in a certain atmosphere of redemption.

I believe that whatever is in me was put there by the God that I pay homage to. When I was younger, it was Catholicism and the church. But I feel like I am a child of God. And I feel that I walk in a certain light because of that. If I were to put that in the vernacular I'd say I have always felt lucky. I have always felt that things will work out for me, and I could go into anything and come out relatively unscathed. Yes there is a God for me.

I think that I will see all of my relatives in the past again. That's my fervent hope. I think that they understand something that I'm going through now.

No amount of success can banish long-simmering anger. And no esteem in which a person is held by others is enough to build it in oneself. That's an inside job. And if you tackle it, you can find a separate peace.

CHAPTER 10

RICHIE HAVENS

Richie Havens' voice always rasped of too many cigarettes and other drugs. His music was a scratch-track for that time between hootenanny and hard rock when the chords were loud and abrasive and the lyrics were play-as-you-go. Even in the Sixties, when it was brand new, it smacked of too many needle passes on the turntable at 33 RPMs.

Richie Havens' background was as wild as the American West and as weird as the beatnik era at its best. His grandfather, a member of the Blackfoot tribe of Montana, moved to New York with Buffalo Bill's Wild West Show. Havens' mother came from the West Indies. And nothing so informs his identity as the fact that he is the real McCoy, a native-born, full-blood American.

Richie grew up poor, the oldest of nine children in the war-time Forties. In the Fifties, he hit the beatnik circuit in New York's Greenwich Village, where he performed his poetry and drew portraits and never thought of picking up a guitar. But his Dad was an ear piano player and Richie inherited the talent. Eventually his self-taught quirky guitar style gave him a first-class ticket to the college concert tour and the top of the charts. But his defining moment, the one you likely remember best, was Woodstock and his unforgettable performance of his song, "Freedom."

Strangely enough, the song didn't exist before I went onstage at Woodstock. In fact, I wrote it onstage. I guess the song came to me when I was being transported by helicopter to the stage. As I flew over the crowd, I realized that we had finally made it. We were no longer underground where they'd put us; we were now above-ground. People of all ages were there, singing, dancing, and laughing. That was part of what made the word freedom make sense to me. When I flew over the crowds, I realized that this was the freedom we were talking about.

But there are more important freedoms, harder won. Making a life that is productive and creative and worthy and, most of all, your own is a kind of freedom. Sustaining a loss and learning from it that there is a lot you get to keep is freedom too. He's said, "Most of the time we're struggling against ourselves because we've never been properly educated about how to deal with common, normal things." The struggle, all by itself, is also a freedom.

My grandmother raised the first five of us (I have four brothers and sisters who were born after I left home) because my mother worked nights. My grandmother was a very special person, and I was very close to her. When I was thirteen years old, she died. Her death was very hard for me. I felt as if I was lost without her. Yet I knew that I had to continue on. Therefore, in order to feel better, I began to reminisce about my grandmother; and by reminiscing, I was able to keep her memory alive.

I was born in 1941. During that time, many people were hungry and went door to door asking for food. As a child I remember my grandmother would answer her door and invite any person in search of help into her home. She'd say, "I have some food, but you go into the bathroom and you wash up. You get washed and then you come and sit at my table and then we can eat." She would feed these people off the street. She was such a special person.

She happened to be born on Christmas Day, which made her a very religious person. She was Methodist. She used to have her five children kneel around her bed on Sunday mornings before they went to church. I remember being the baby on the bed, surrounded by people kneeling all around me. When I was about eighteen, I asked my mother how long these Sunday morning sessions would take. My mother told me that it would take my grandmother a half hour to bless everybody in the world. She would say, "Bless the hospital, the people in hospital, bless the people who don't have." I believe that this memory makes up the better part of me. Through her Sunday rituals, and the way in which she would invite people in need into her home, my grandmother taught me an extremely important lesson: She taught me that every person on this planet is equal, and because we are all equal it is up to us to help others. This ideology, while simple, gave me the strength and guidance to work through the hard times in my life.

At one time in my life, I had four daughters. Eight years ago, my first daughter passed away. When she was born, she had to stay in the hospital because she had pneumonia. And during her life, while her pneumonia plagued her in different ways, we never thought that it was life-threatening. But we couldn't have been more wrong. When she was twenty-four, she started to have very devastating headaches. She went to the doctor and no one really knew what was going on. The doctors were not able to figure out where the headaches were coming from. It was an extremely frustrating and nerve-racking time. Because the headaches would not go away, my daughter was admitted into the hospital. She was only there for three days. She died three days after admittance. My daughter died in the hospital.

It is very difficult for parents to explain the depths to which one plunges when one's child dies. It's one of the most difficult things one will ever have to deal with—so difficult in fact, that many parents are never able to recover from their loss.

My daughter's name is Nancy. She was a wonderful woman with two children of her own. When she died I was devastated. However, I soon realized that I had to pull myself together for the sake of her children. I had to be concerned about the mental and emotional health of Nancy's children.

I admire my grandchildren a great deal. They are the most wonderful kids. They are strong, compassionate and wise. My grandsons will forever miss their mother, and that's something that will be a part of them for the rest of their lives. Therefore, it is up to us to help one another. By staying connected to one another and by using her memory to make ourselves better, we are able to keep the best parts of us alive.

When my daughter died, it would have been easy for me to

blame God. However, my grandmother taught me that death is not an end to life. Rather, it's another beginning. Death just takes us to a different place in a different time. Therefore, with my grandmother's lessons, I am able to achieve a sense of comfort in my loss. My daughter's new life is just a new beginning.

I am an American. I was born here. I believe in freedom. I have a sense of spirituality that I want to share with others, and I am going to do it by communicating, lending myself, and sharing my ideas with others.

Richie Havens puts his convictions where his mouth is, all in the name of giving people freedom. He has been active in promoting education and literacy. He has worked to raise funds for AIDS research. He is a founding member of "Save the Whales" and actually helped invent the harness now used to tow beached whales back to sea. He also founded "The Natural Guard," a group that teaches children about the environment. Mention any of these causes to him and you're in for a few hours of nonstop lecturing. Hearing Richie speak, you might think he's a bit laconic. He is not. He is intense about everything he spares his breath on, because his message is about Freedom. It always was. And he's never taken freedom for granted.

CHAPTER 11

BEN VEREEN

The curtain went up on the darkest of tableaux. All I could see, in a blacklight glow, were his teeth, glinting like a neon pinpoint marking an off-road trail. Ben Vereen was a born off-roader—a combustible talent that ignited the Broadway stage in a breakthrough production called Pippin. *I saw it seven times. As the Leading Player, he was larger than life, all mindgames and magic, all spirit and body. He moved with the fluidity of a panther and the energy of a solid rocket booster. I didn't know at the time that he'd trained at the pulpit. I also couldn't have guessed that twenty years later he would take me through the debris of Bed-Stuy, Brooklyn, through the beat-up remnants of street riots, to the row house where he grew up with people who never spared the rod. And right there, taunting him from across the East River, just past the docks, was the skylined fortress of the Big Time, Manhattan. It was so close you could practically kick it. Yet so far that no common ghetto kid could ever imagine reaching it. Ben Vereen not only reached it, he damn near toppled it with all of his Tonys and Grammys and Emmys.*

Just before Christmas of 1987, he lost a real treasure, and thereafter went hell-bent toward losing himself. His fall was like a plummet from an orbiting star, complete with flameout on reentry. But it took five years to land. His body was crushed, his abilities erased, and all that was left to him was spirit. That's when he learned that spirit is enough.

It was December1987. Ben's daughter Naja was sixteen years old. He had taken her with him to perform in Los Angeles, and then put her on a plane heading home to her mother. Naja's life ended in one of those mindless collisions on the New Jersey Turnpike. Eleven years later, he still weeps at the memory of the first words he heard.

"You better sit down." I sat down and I got the word, and I tried right away calling to see if Nancy was all right. Because I thought I had lost them both. I couldn't get through to the hospital. I found out later that she was okay. When I got to the airport I was in such bad shape. I had to fly 3,000 miles. So they sedated me, and I stayed sedated.

You've got to understand, I'm a child of the Sixties and so drugs were not a new thing. But when you use drugs, you are an addict. Period! I believe that there are no recreational drugs. When my daughter died, I threw myself into using. When my mood picked up, I took more drugs. It's a selfish thing, because I was not considering the feelings of the people around me. I was not thinking about my family; I was only thinking about myself.

After the accident, we as a family would go to the movies and watch happy films. I remember there was a film out that year, *Planes, Trains, and Automobiles* with John Candy and Steve Martin. I'd watch videos that were supposed to make me laugh, although they didn't make me laugh.

It was as if I didn't have any laughter in me. I was scared. While I wanted to keep positive notes such as laughter inside me, I found that I couldn't. It seemed to me like somebody had snatched my air out of me. I felt like I was walking around waiting to exhale. It was awful. I needed an escape, so I plunged right into my addiction. I found myself falling deeper and deeper. I remember so-called friends who were trying to make me feel better saying, "Yo, take this man. Yo, take this man. Yo, here's a bottle of scotch. There's more booze at the wake." In retrospect, I know that they were trying to anesthetize my feelings, because they had been taught by societal rules that feeling pain is bad. I for one don't believe that anymore.

Drugs rob you of all of your feelings—they pacify your good and bad feelings and leave you in a state of numbness. It's a bad place to be in because sooner or later you are going to have to deal with your feelings. The sooner you do it, the better. It is a tough process to go through, though. Even if you are strong enough to put down the drugs, not using them is even harder. It's as if the drugs are beckoning you, going, "Yo, I've been waiting for ya!" And there's no way to get out of dealing with them.

The last straw for me was when I was in the bathroom and my daughter Milika came in. I was such a wreck. I tried to run. When I realized that I was running from my own daughter, I decided to run in a more positive direction. I ran straight into rehab.

I believe that spirituality is the key to survival. If you can find a way to both hold on to spirituality and make it a priority in your life, then you will be "walking in the light." Now, after going through rehab and coming to terms with my daughter's death, I no longer have my back to the light. I, too, am walking in the light.

Then I came to a place, where I realized, that feelings are never going to go away. Now I don't want to ever lose that pain. I tried to and it didn't work. I'm okay with it now because I keep that child inside, and I bless the time that I spent with her. I'm thankful, because it was a special time in my life, I can go on now because by feeling this pain, I am being healed.

I know that every time I breathe in air, I am breathing in a piece of Naja. She is there, comforting me. I can always reach her. Sometimes, however, I think it is important to let her go. I do and she goes and does her thing. But I always know that she's in the universe. She is in every sunrise and every sunset, in every raindrop and every snowflake. When I feel that I can't go on, it is she who makes me. I can hear her say, "Dad, come on you can do this." And when I had the accident, it was she who was right there with me.

Vereen's own accident in 1992 was ghastly. Though Vereen was on his way to spiritual recovery from addiction and emotional recovery from the death of his daughter, his body was damaged beyond repair. Details are murky, in both Ben's mind and in police reports. Was he driving at night when his car veered off the road? Or was he jogging, not driving? Was he hit as he crawled alongside the roadway? Whatever the specifics, we know that eventually Vereen became airborne. A car driven by a business associate had thrown him eighty yards into the air and slammed him down on the ground with a force no body could have endured.

I don't remember anything about the accident. I don't even remember getting into my car. People have had to tell me what happened. I know I woke up in the hospital, and my wife Nancy, my children Koran, Kebara, and Milika were there, and I thought to myself, "What are you guys doing here?" I tried to speak, but I couldn't! I looked down, and I said, "This isn't my bedroom!" And then I realized that I was in the hospital! I tried to move, but I couldn't! Finally, I thought, "Uh oh. I'm in trouble."

When the doctors came in, my daughter Kebara tried to communicate with them for me. She read my lips so that they could understand what it was that I was saying. The doctors told me that it would be at least three years before I would walk again. When I asked if I would ever sing again, they said, "We'll remove the trachea and put in a plug. You'll be able to talk again but we can't say that you'll ever sing again!"

I had to believe in divine providence. I had been telling people that they had the power within themselves to do anything, and all they had to do was wake up the giant within themselves. Yet, while I was professing my ideas to these people, there I was, unable to do anything.

"Father, I can't do anything!" I said. "I've been going around the country telling people about Your greatness! It's me, it's me oh Lord, standing in the need of prayer. Standing here! Lying here, unable to move my body, not able to even get off the bed, not able to feed myself! Father it's me! Help me! They're telling me I will not walk again for three years! And I'll never know how to dance again, or sing again. Father it's me! I'm here! It's me!"

I never questioned, "Why are You doing this to me," because when I talk about the Father, I talk about the universal Father. When I talk about spirituality, I'm talking about universal spirituality. I'm not talking about a clique or a club. So many organizations try to teach people the right way to guide them up the mountain. I believe that there are many trails to the top of the mountain, but there's only one mountain top. I want to be on the mountain top! I want to talk directly to universal Father, Mother, God, Buddha, Allah, Yahweh, Elohim, or whatever you want to call that higher consciousness. I want to talk to Them.

Through my hard work, and by turning it over to God, to Elohim, to whatever you want to call that higher power, I was able to walk on Broadway ten months later.

And what a night it was! Ben Vereen walked out onto that Broadway stage and sat down in the wheelchair placed center stage. As he sat down in that chair, he was once again illuminated by a familiar spotlight, and he was charged with energy. He went right into his song and dance, dancing right there in that wheelchair and bringing the house down. Ben Vereen, despite the tragedies, was and is the quintessential show-off.

Yes I am! That's why I am here! I have a friend whose name is Mary Verdes Fletcher, and she has spina bifida. She's had it all of her life, but she's always wanted to dance. When I was doing *Jelly's Last Jam,* she sent me a poster of her dancing in a wheelchair. Now I work with her, and we're looking to build a school. When we bring the ablebodied and the people with physical disabilities together to do concerts and dance, it's like, "Yeah!" I want my friends in the wheelchairs to know that there are no limitations to what they can do.

Sometimes I sit down and think about Stephen Hawkins, the man who wrote a couple of books about the universe. And I say, "Father, Mother of God, if you can send your vision through a man who has Lou Gehrig's disease, then who am I to complain? I am able to walk! Able to talk! Able to have my limbs! Who am I to complain? Who am I? Thank you! Thank you, every morning, thank you. My bills might not be paid. I may not get that job, but thank you!" Because when one door closes, another one opens. We just may not see it.

If Vereen's words ring with an evangelistic spirit, it's because he was molded for the pulpit. His aunts spotted his gift for preaching early on and imbued him, body and soul, with the Word. Vereen, of course, wanted to become a Broadway star. But a part of him also wanted to be a preacher, and still does. He's been trying to integrate the two tracks for a long time.

It has been a struggle to bring them together. I finally decided that in order to bring peace to my consciousness, I would have to combine the pulpit and the stage in order to deliver my message. It's all about the message and how the message is delivered to the people. My shows are pretty much about the good times and the good feelings of life. It's about you feeling good about you. That's my message, that's my sermon, and that's my ministry.

My spirit is lifted when the people are turned on. I believe that when I am turned on, they are spiritually lifted. Even though we seek salvation by going to churches, to synagogues, and to mosques, salvation is only delivered on an individual basis. We must first seek the kingdom of heaven within us. A great teacher by the name of Jesus taught us many years ago how to seek first the kingdom of heaven.

Why did I choose show business? It was a calling. It's what I do. It's what I love doing. I love entertaining people. It's magic. I get such a kick out of it. There's nothing like being on the boards. And whether I'm acting or I'm singing or I'm dancing boards all across the world and touching people, I can go the other route and be able to preach to people and give them sermons. I go out and I talk to people about overcoming adversity. I talk to them about spirituality. And I enjoy that. But there's nothing like the boards.

CHAPTER 12

MACKENZIE PHILLIPS

She was Everykid. A spunky, sassy little sister who somersaulted across the screen in American Graffiti *looking normal as apple pie. It was 1973 and Mackenzie Phillips was only twelve years old. And nothing about her life was normal.*

America had just rolled out of the Sixties, and much of young America was launched on a sex, drugs, rock-and-roll adventure. No boundaries. No kidding. One of its principal proponents in what turned out to be a "self-will run riot revolution" was Mackenzie Phillips' dad, rock icon John Phillips, leader of the Mamas and the Papas. Mackenzie was his firstborn child in what would become a crazy quilt of an extended family with three different mothers, a dizzying array of step-siblings and family friends who hung on for cash and hash. Her mother was Baltimore socialite Suzie Adams. Mackenzie's life might have looked golden, hanging out with the best bands of the era, jetting across the continent weekly, becoming a teen idol before she finished high school. But her California dream was a mind-altering nightmare.

My mother was my father's first wife. She was from this socialite Eastern seaboard family. She and my father, a half-breed Cherokee and very strange, divorced when I was eighteen months old. My father would come and pick me up in a Lear jet (this was when the Mamas and Papas were huge). I'd walk into his house, and the Beatles and the Stones were there. I remember Donovan sliding down the banister, and helping him make hash brownies. I was probably ten years old. And my father's attitude was "whatever turns you on." I'd visit my dad on the weekends with all this partying going on, and then I'd go home to my mother during the week to go to school. My mother's attitude was the opposite. "Know which fork to use, and sit like a lady, and cross your feet at the ankles." So I was getting all these different kinds of messages. It was very, very confusing and so I developed two different ways of dealing with life—one for my mom and one for my dad.

I wasn't forced into show business by my family, but I don't think I had a choice internally. It was something that I had to do. It was just there in front of me. I put together a rock-and-roll band at school in the fifth grade and we performed on an amateur night at the Troubadour, which is a legendary place in Hollywood. I was twelve years old singing lead in this band when Fred Russe, who was casting *American Graffiti* at the time, was in the audience. He liked my act and so my first job was in *American Graffiti,* and it just sort of went from there. But I had always been a performer as a child. I'd stand in the living room yelling, "Ma! Hey, everybody! Sit there, I'm going to put on a show!"

To anyone who hasn't tried it, being a star must look awfully good. Television and the big screen may put you in a position where everyone can love you, but it also leaves you in a position where everyone can judge you.

Mackenzie Phillips earned a place in the catalog of household names as a result of her role as daughter Julie in the television sitcom One Day at a Time. *She was already using drugs, and her condition only degenerated into a downward spiral that threatened to destroy both her life and her career. As she headed toward the bottom, increasingly emaciated and unreliable, she was fired. Then rehired. Then fired again.*

For a lot of years I just liked being high. It was cool. It made me feel good. But retrospectively, I look back and see that I wasn't equipped to handle anything. So I used drugs and alcohol so that I could be physically present but I really didn't have to be emotionally present. Anything that could change my mood or alter my mindset or make me not feel was good. When my difficulties became so public, I closed in on myself and hid.

By then everything surrounding the Phillips family had gone bust. In 1980, the Phillips were forced into their first taste of recovery. For them, sobriety became a family affair. John Phillips, one of his wives, one of his band members, and his firstborn child all went into rehab. And the family members who didn't check in got an apartment nearby. Only John knew there was a hidden agenda.

My father was arrested for trafficking narcotics in 1980 and was facing federal prison. I was living in Los Angeles at the time, though now I wouldn't call it living. I had been fired from *One Day at a Time* and I was holed up in my apartment. My father called me after his arrest and said, "I'm in a rehab, and I'm trying to get clean. I'd really like for you to get clean, too." What I didn't know at the time was that he really just needed me to help him stay out of jail by doing some publicity with him. So we went on every talk show that existed. We were even on the cover of *People* magazine. As a consequence of that, my father did not go to prison. He only served thirty days. But through this I did get my first taste of recovery. Unfortunately, the place that I went with my father espoused a strange way of getting and staying sober. They said that if alcohol wasn't your primary drug of choice, you could continue to drink. So I stopped doing cocaine and all the other mood- and mind-altering substances, but I continued to drink. Eventually, through drinking, I earned my "seat" in Alcoholics Anonymous.

I have now read a lot about Moderates Anonymous and it makes me very uncomfortable. Any time that I hear, or any other alcoholic or drug addict hears, that we can still drink like ladies and gentlemen, it is frightening. I don't want to go out and have that drink and only then find out that I can't handle it. I just don't want to do it. I have friends who got clean and sober and stayed that way without any outside help from any type of program, and that's fine for them. But I need the extra help.

In 1992 I was sitting in my house and I was out of drugs. I couldn't drink myself drunk, and the doctors that I was scamming prescriptions from found out about each other and wouldn't write any new prescriptions for me anymore. Finally, the moment came. I don't know where it came from, but I picked up the phone and I called a counselor that I knew from a rehab. I said, "I need help." I was in detox by sundown, and I have been sober six-and-a-half years now. I believe that that was a divine moment. I believe that this desire to stop did not come from me. The days when I still want to rage now, I ask my higher power to take that feeling away. The days when I want to control and manipulate (like when my son is walking too slow, or maybe he's not getting in the car fast enough), I say "God, just please guide me through this. Give me the strength to not react." That prayer helps me through the day all the time.

The interesting thing about it is that my recovery is not about fighting the urge to drink or use. I believe that once we get sober and stay sober for any period of time, we're left not necessarily with a drinking problem, but with a residual thinking problem. I don't wake up in the morning and think, "Oh, my God, how am I going to get through the day without drinking or using?" It's not an issue for me anymore. But I still have the "isms," the stuff before I got sober, where I wake up thinking, "Oh, my God, I hate myself so much." And some days I wake up steeped in self-loathing. But something gives me the strength to not pull the covers over my head and call and cancel doing whatever is in front of me. Something gives me the strength to say, "That's okay. It's going to pass." Something is showing me that there is another way to live every day, and that I don't have to be in the dark anymore.

I think many people might disagree with me, but I believe there is a genetic predisposition to alcoholism and drug addiction. All you have to do is talk to people who have this problem and you'll find that somewhere in the family, somebody else has it. Clearly my father had a severe drug and alcohol problem. Anyone who's read his book or read anything about him knows this. And he has a lot of kids. I can say that all of us have had battles with it, and most of us are sober. I firmly believe that alcoholism is a family disease.

I also believe that for comfortable, easygoing, longterm sobriety, everyone needs to come together as a family and say, "We are going to get through this and we will help you. We will not isolate you, we will not ostracize you, nor label you. We will recognize it as a disease and we will help you by working on ourselves as well." And it's quite a decision since most family members don't want to get into it that deeply. It may take the alcoholic getting well and staying well for a period of time for the nonalcoholic spouse or family member to realize that they might have some issues to deal with, too! But certainly, at first, there's a, "Wait a minute! This isn't my problem! I'm not the one who has the problem here! You're the one that needs to go and get well and deal with this, and I'll just continue doing what I've been doing all along!" But that's controlling the situation, and I feel that that's part of the sickness of the spouse or family member of the alcoholic. That control, that "I've got to be the one to keep this together. She isn't going to be able to do this without my absolutely incredible help!" It's that person who ends up manipulating everything—when the meals are eaten, when the kids are going to be around the parent. And that's a sickness in itself. It's a control issue. It's a dependency issue. I don't mean to say that everybody needs the twelve steps or that everybody needs to get well. But certainly there has to be some sort of realization at some point by the family member or the spouse of the alcoholic that this is a family problem. The "getting well" is a family accomplishment, but so was the "getting sick."

There are programs for families and spouses of alcoholics and addicts. At the time, my husband started going to one of those programs—two years before I was able to get and remain sober for any length of time. It was such a huge help to me when he started saying, "This isn't my problem. The fact that you can't deal with what's in front of you isn't my problem, and I'm not going to get involved." Before this, he would say, "Okay, let me fix this for you. I'll make the phone call and tell them you can't make it. I'll do this. I'll cancel that. I'll make sure Shane, our son, gets picked up from school." He came to the point after going to this particular program for a while of being able to say, "Honey, this is your problem." And then I'd have to deal with my own wreckage. Eventually, the clarity came to me.

I now don't have anyone that I need to forgive except myself. I'm working on it. I have a friend who said to me the other day,

"You seem tortured sometimes." And I said, "Well, it took me many years to get sick, and I can't expect to recover and get to the point where I want to be in just six years." It's a daily reprieve based on a spiritual contact.

As an alcoholic, I have been prey to what I would call the god of self-sufficiency for so many years. "I can do this alone, I don't need anyone. Anyone who is spiritual or has a religious background is weak." For me, religion or spirituality was a crutch. That's because I wanted to be in control of the show. I didn't want to say, "Okay, universe, God, whomever, take this. Guide me. Help me. I trust and I believe." That's a hard thing for someone who's worked so many years to control and manipulate the unmanageable aspects of one's life.

I also know that there's sometimes a misconception about people who are involved in twelve-step programs—that we're holy rollers or Jesus freaks or born-again Christians. Maybe some are, but I am not. I don't go to church or temple, but I do have a strong belief in a power outside of and greater than myself. I woke up this morning, and before I lifted my head from the pillow, I said, "Good morning, God. It's me, I'm still here. Just help me get through the day. Just guide me and give me the strength." And then, I always add, "And thy will, not mine, be done." I don't believe that God ever had anything against me in the first place. In fact, he sat up there and probably said, "Oh, you poor little babe."

But I do believe that there's a purpose for me on this planet. I came so close to dying so many times, and miraculously I survived, so I must be here for a reason. What I say now is that if I can come through what I've been through and finally realize that I didn't have to live that way anymore, then anyone can. My life is better than it's ever been. I am a mother to my son, a friend to my friends, and a worker among workers.

I don't have it all figured out, and if I ever do, I'll probably be in trouble. And there's a part of me that is still broken after almost six-and-a-half years of sobriety. But it's not the destination, it's the journey, and hopefully I'll never reach that destination. I'll just keep traveling on this path and finding new things about sobriety and myself every day.

There is a notion that taking drugs is a choice—that you really can "just say no." But for a child who was spoonfed drugs before she was old enough to understand the consequences (let alone make conscious decisions) becoming an addict can't be called a choice. Nobody chooses to become an alcoholic or addict. Before Mackenzie knew it, her craving for drugs wasn't a matter of willpower, it was cellular—biochemical—and most likely genetic, since it's estimated that children of alcoholics and addicts have a four-times greater chance of becoming addicts themselves.

When Mackenzie finally did receive some help with her addiction, she was given some seriously questionable advice. While most people in the drug treatment field believe a twelve-step program is the only reliable treatment for addictions, there are still a few stalwart souls who feel differently. However, to my knowlege, there is no research to support the theory that alcoholics can learn to be moderate drinkers. In the end, Mackenzie was fortunate. Though her whole family was sick, and they got sick together, they also went into recovery together and got well together.

Anybody who lives with the hell of somebody else's addiction can certainly feel justified in saying, "He's the one who caused the problems! All I'm doing is trying to hold the family together! I'm not the sick one." But there is solid anecdotal evidence that when the family agrees to become part of the recovery process, the alcoholic or addict has a far greater chance of making it.

Mackenzie speaks of her "spiritual contact." Many people throughout history have found relief, humility, even simplicity and immense power in the notion that we are not alone, and not solely in charge of everything on the planet. It is miraculous to realize that we are not only worthy of unconditional love, but we actually can receive it from a power who created us as beautiful people. I have come to believe that spirituality is key to recovery from addiction, and very often that higher power is all that stands between an addict and the next drink or drug.

CHAPTER 13

FRANCES STERNHAGEN

Few actors can claim the breadth of career that defines the work of Frances Sternhagen. She has brought to a breathtaking variety of roles a fierce intelligence and compassion. She has outlasted an entire generation of ingenues to become one of the crown jewels of the American stage, bringing to life the miraculous language of theater. This is not chump change. The highest compliment an actor can receive isn't a Tony Award. It's a handle: working actor. The fact that she did it while raising six children is amazing. The fact that she did it while living with an alcoholic husband for forty years, without losing her self-esteem, her ability to work, or her grasp on reality is darn near miraculous. Frances Sternhagen has embodied women in conflict and women at peace. Perhaps she played the roles so brilliantly because she's lived them.

Before we were married, I had been told by his roommate what a wonderful guy he was. So I was looking forward to meeting him. We went to a party, and Tom had been drinking. I just thought, this is supposed to be the wonderful guy I've been hearing so much about? He's kind of like a moron. I mean, his eyes were sort of glazed over and he was saying things that were kind of ridiculous.

But the next time I met him, he was sober, and it was like night and day. He was a changed person. Very bright, very witty, very compassionate, fun. But I didn't know anything about alcoholism until we'd been married about six or seven years. It just wasn't talked about the way it is now. Alcoholism has been with us for generations. But at that time I really didn't know there was anything I could do about this. But finally, I read or heard about something called AA and I looked it up. For the first time, I learned about Al-Anon, a support group for the family and friends of alcoholics. So I went to my first meeting, and of course everything I said was, "Yes, but . . . " meaning, "Yes, but he's not so bad. Yes, but my problem is different." And they said, "You're saying a lot of 'Yes, buts.' Do you have a problem with alcohol? Is alcohol affecting your life in any way?" And, yeah, I guess I do. Alcohol does affect my life. Right then you start to learn to change your behavior as best you can and start putting the focus back on you and not in the futile hope that you can change somebody else so that they'll get into recovery.

As the home situation got worse for Frances, she took what was one of the hardest steps she could take. She picked up the phone and called for help. It probably saved her life. But she went one step further. She got very tough.

I went to the family court. It was very hard. It took so much courage to just go there. But oddly the family court is actually not a tough place. It's a place that wants to keep the family together. Of course, at the time, it felt ghastly to me. I couldn't believe I was going to family court! And when I went, this particular family court was quite unattractive and cold looking. The walls were kind of that awful beige or glossy green. And I felt rather like a traitor being there and having brought my husband there. Then I met someone who really understood and was compassionate. He said to my husband, "It looks like you really have got a problem. You have a choice now. You can change and do something about it or you can leave the family and go out on your own. Which would you rather do?" And of course Tom said, "I'll do something." I was sitting there thinking, "Oh, shoot!" I was thinking, this is going to be a real challenge. He's going to leave and I'm going to have to do everything on my own. I wonder if I'm up to it. But then he said, "I'll stay home."

Tom never really accepted AA. He went through four rehabs. Each time I had gotten to the point where I thought I couldn't take it anymore. I would do all the right things. Finally, he would go to the rehab. The disease of alcoholism is insidious. He would be sober and go to AA for five months. And then he would become what they call a "dry drunk." This behavior includes not going to AA meetings. Slowly beginning to say they were stupid, that it was a waste of time. Then the irritability sets in. I, as the codependent or the "coalcoholic," would begin to hope that he would start drinking again. Strangely, every time that he finally did start drinking again, after six or eight months of being sober, he would go through two months of being very pleasant while he was sneaking his drinks. But it was a pattern. The whole cycle would all start over again. He would get to the point where he would be drunk at certain times each day, and at night he would fall. We would go to a party of some kind and he would be embarrassing to the children. They knew what he was doing and what was sure to come. And they would be afraid of it. After I started going to Al-Anon, I was finally able to talk to the children about it.

When I was a child, my father had been sick with Parkinson's disease (before they knew what it was) and his behavior was difficult. Of course, I watched my mother's behavior, and this was a pattern that I was also to follow. She was always trying to help make things better for him. There was no such thing when I was growing up as taking care of yourself first so that you can be strong or be understanding of somebody else. She'd always say, "What can I do for you? How can I make things better for you?" My mother, like a lot of young women in her time (and in ours for that matter), liked to be the rescuer. I don't know why that was. It's not unlike domestic abuse. If you are a victim of this, or maybe if your mother was a victim, you're very likely to become one yourself. This is just like child or spouse abuse. If you watched it as a youngster, you will perhaps become a child abuser or a spouse batterer yourself. Now there are avenues of help for this that people just didn't have in the past.

But after I began to understand the pattern of behavior in alcoholic homes, that's when I suddenly thought that there was something wrong here. I had to stop whatever was happening. We know now how we can damage our children. You get to a point where you know you've got to do something. The disease of addiction drives people, because of their own shame and their own being locked into something that they can't seem to get out of, to some kind of abuse of whoever is closest to them. And that's when the spouse, whether it's male or female (and there are plenty of women alcoholics as we know) says, "Wait a minute. I am being treated in a way that no human being really should be putting up with. I am beginning to be ashamed of my behavior. Somehow I am allowing this. I've got to stand up for myself. I've got to say no."

People think that I work all the time or that I have worked all the time. I've had quite a lot of times when I didn't work. And there were many times when I turned down jobs that I simply couldn't do because of the kids. After Helen Hayes performed in Washington, D.C. (where my mother lived), my mother went backstage because she knew I had worked with Miss Hayes at one point. Helen said, "Oh, Franny could have been such a star if she hadn't had all those children." And my mother just said, "Yeah, well, thank you." She came back and told me and I just said, "Well, I did." What do you do about that, throw them back? No. But there were many times when I just had to say no. At the time it was hard, but it was okay. I simply knew what was the most important thing. I think the kids knew. It was hard, especially when the older ones got more of the brunt of my husband's drinking behavior, as older children tend to do. But all my children eventually went through their own therapy programs or attended the children of alcoholics meetings. And I know that there were times when they responded to those programs with, "My mother wasn't there for me. My mother didn't do what she should have done." Now I think they understand. Some of them have their own children now and they understand how hard it was for me.

It got harder. In spite of all the education the Sternhagen kids had in the disease of alcoholism, in spite of all the open family discussions, despite the gift of the twelve steps of Alcoholics Anonymous upon which all the family programs are based, the genetic bullet for addiction worked its inexorable course. One hopes knowledge will give children power to make wise choices about taking that first drink or that first drug. But heredity is a powerful aspect of destiny, and the permissiveness of the Sixties and Seventies didn't help. Her oldest child did become an alcoholic and drug addict. Another one quickly followed. But the Sternhagens were able to find the Hyde School in Maine, which involves the whole family in the treatment of kids. It's a formula that can work.

For Frances there was still work. The American theatrical community is, in and of itself, a family. Actors all seem to know each other, and they all know each other's problems and family situations. For Sternhagen, her coworkers provided a daily dose of salvation.

There were times when I was so glad to go to work because I could just get away from my problem at home and really infuse the work that I had to do with whatever was going on at home. I'm the kind of actor who does not change a performance. The other actors don't know from one night to the next that I'm doing anything different, except sometimes I will hear somebody say, "Wow, you were really doing something different tonight." And it wasn't that I moved anyplace different or had a different intention. It was just full of an emotion that I somehow had to get rid of.

In 1991, Frances Sternhagen was shooting the television miniseries The Golden Years. *It was a strange theme. In the storyline, she and her husband are in their seventies when the husband runs into some weird science and starts getting younger while she stays rooted in time. It was a proverbial blue moon, and Tom, her real-life husband, came to the set.*

Tom never liked to come to wherever I was working. I believe it was hard for him to come and see me in a place that was successful, when his career was on the slide. This particular time, I asked him to visit me on the set when I had four or five days off.

And I was quite surprised that he agreed. He also agreed not to drink when he was with me. We had a wonderful four or five days during this particular show. Two weeks later he died suddenly. This was a difficult time for me, not only because Tom died, but also because I had to relive our separation in the television show as my "husband" in the story got younger. I felt very vulnerable as if I were going to lose him. And of course there were a couple scenes where he did have to go someplace else. But those moments when he had to leave, and I didn't know if I would ever see him again in the show, the rest of the company was very aware of what I was bringing to the role. I really had to control myself from breaking down on many occasions. But the support of friends carried me. After Tom died, the company flew me home in a private plane. Tom had loved flying, and I recall as I went up in the plane, I said, "Tom, you would have loved this."

Frances chose to stay married to Tom, despite the problems caused by his disease. Many people do make that choice for many different reasons. They remain married out of a conviction that families are not so easily disposable, or they have a durable belief in redemption or the healing power of love or the wisdom of raw courage. "Dumping the bastard" might seem the easy way out, but sometimes one finds that no matter how far away you run from your problems, they have a way of traveling with you.

There are no census figures or government statistics, no actuarial tables or websites stuffed with data that indicate how many people are living with active alcoholics. But it's safe to say it's in the millions. They didn't cause the disease of alcoholism, they can't cure it and they certainly can't control it. But most of them try like hell to change the addicted person without realizing they're contributing to their problem. The families and friends of alcoholics or drug addicts live in isolation because they're too ashamed to divulge what on earth is going on in their homes or their friends' homes. They live in fear of breaking rigid rules they didn't even know existed, rules which the alcoholic changes at the drop of a Kleenex. They live in a constant state of martyrdom, which only locks them into the victim role.

Why do women marry alcoholics? The most obvious reason is that they're seeking a guy just like Dad, and Dad was an alcoholic. Dad may have been a teetotaller but his father was an alcoholic and he has inherited the behaviors and thinking of an alcoholic. Alcoholic behaviors look normal to those who have a history of it somewhere in the family attic. It's believed that most people who suffer from codependence with alcoholics may have never even known the ancestor who predisposed them to it. But even if alcohol isn't hiding anywhere in the genealogy, caretaking might be, and they've learned to be people-pleasers who would buy peace at any price.

As for children, one of the odd realities of most alcoholic families is that the children, particularly if the drinker is fundamentally a good guy, don't blame him for whatever crisis or problem with which his alcoholism has infected the family. They tend to blame the sober parent because she didn't stop him.

Words can cut deep in alcoholic relationships, whether they come from the mouths of babes or from the addicted spouse. I've heard women say, "Well, he never actually hit me." Physical abuse, according to psychologists, is easier to get over than emotional abuse. He belts you, you bruise, the bruise goes away. It's the emotional devastation that maims you. The browbeating from someone raging away at the universe can leave permanent scars. The raging may happen well after lullabies and bedtime, but the children do know what's going on and they're learning from it. They're learning they're not safe and they're learning how grown women are treated. This is behavior that will very likely be repeated if it isn't halted in some way. And even if this family model does not repeat itself, coming to grips with the reality of one's sordid past can be a shock.

CHAPTER 14

LARRY GATLIN

For us Northerners, country music was hoedown stuff. It was a cut below hootenannies and about as déclassé a level as a Seventies hipster could sink. But the song of the South, notably Ted Turner, then referred to as "The Mouth of the South" was calling my name. In the pre-dawn of CNN, I had the golden fortune to spend a good deal of time in the heart of the confederacy. I was forced to swallow voluminous amounts of down-home food, Styrofoam coffee and country-western road songs. Maybe I was a victim of the Stockholm syndrome (that psychological peculiarity whereby hostages come to adopt the credo of their captors), or maybe it was a close encounter with Larry Gatlin and the Gatlin Brothers. But whatever it was, I can say I came to love country music.

"All the Gold in California" is in Larry Gatlin's pipes. He has a tenor that is positively ethereal. Ethereal is what he insists he eats every morning with bananas and milk. And a chat with him is out of control before the first question.

By the time he was seven years old, Gatlin had already begun his career, having gotten his big break singing on the radio and raking in more dough than a paper route—ten cents a week. When he was ten, Gatlin and his brothers entered a local talent show in west Texas and won. They beat out some wannabe named Roy Orbison. As the loser, Orbison won a Chinese dinner over in Midland and as the winner Larry got a nasty horse named Dan. In retrospect, Larry says Orbison got the better deal.

Beginning with his win at ten years old, Gatlin's life pattern became one of winning. He succeeded in virtually everything he put his mind to. In his career, he worked for the greats, including Dottie West, Streisand, and even Elvis.

By 1980, Larry Gatlin had built himself a stone mountain of fans, a truckload of number-one hits, a Grammy award, and he was on his way to the big screen and Broadway.

However, even though Gatlin seemed to be at the top of his game, the buzz surrounding Gatlin as a man was bad news. He was becoming known as an unpredictable boss given to violent outbursts, an unreliable husband and father given to taking extended timeouts from the family, and a grandiose, arrogant son of—uh—Texas down to his boots. It seems that all the great songs about joy and sorrow and love and dreams, songs he wrote and performed with his brothers, acted as a brilliant coverup for his not-so-perfect personal life. In fact, he was singing solo. By the mid-Eighties, Gatlin's coverup was over. He had misused all the God-given talents he had used to amass fame, glamour, and riches. His life just wasn't working anymore. He'd gone and thrown his life, his career, and his success away.

I really didn't mean to! I didn't do it on purpose. Let's face it, I was twenty-five, cute, and richer than I ever thought I would be. I had a lot of free time on my hands. My peer group was basically doing the Studio 54 thing in New York, snorting cocaine off the tables and doing it in the bathrooms. It was a nutty time. When someone handed me drugs in order to "pick me up" I just took them and didn't think twice. I knew that a "pick me up" was not a valid justification for using, but I began using anyway. My old Pentecostal granny had a saying: "Nothing good ever comes out of a whiskey bottle." I think she's right! Obviously, there are people who will differ with that opinion. But in terms of me, nothing good came out of my whiskey bottles, my vodka bottles, or my vials of cocaine.

Larry Gatlin spiraled for more than a decade into a hellhole of addiction. There is a misapprehension at large in the land that drunks and junkies are simply moral reprobates with wills too weak to walk away from their drugs of choice. People removed from addiction often say, why don't they just quit? They should just find a way to just say no. Experts in the recovery field tell me that it doesn't work that way. Sure, picking up that first drink, doing that first line, is a personal choice. But few of those who choose to use have any notion of the potential consequences. They have no idea that they are playing Russian roulette. According to statistics, ten percent of them will become addicts; they will ultimately have no choice but to continue using. The drug produces a cellular craving in their brain, and addicts can't recover without help. Experts have also told me that of all the addictions they work with, the single toughest to beat, is the killer combination of alcohol and cocaine. Addiction to alcohol and cocaine has a relapse rate of a whopping ninety percent. However it is important to note that in the end, alcoholism and drug addictions don't come in bottles, they come in people.

Well, that's true. The modus operandi comes in a bottle, but my choices were taken away by abuse and the addictive nature of the beast. For those of us who have tendencies toward obsessive-compulsive behavior, we face an inherent problem; we don't know when to quit. You know, it is like when you want to go to Bici and eat every piece of bread in the basket. I used to go into the 7-Eleven to get a six pack of beer, and I'd find that some idiot had taken one beer from the pack. My immediate response would be, "What sort of idiot would take one beer? Are they crazy, what are they going to do with one beer? Nobody drinks one beer. Let's get a case!" So at times our own cravings or whatever you want to call them, get the better of us. It is like that age-old fight between good and evil that is the crux of every great poem, of every great novel, of every great song, and of every great piece of art.

I became mean. I knew better than to act that way but I was so mad at me. I asked my friend Jack Bolin why it was that on one occasion I would act totally selfless, loving, spontaneous, and good, and then two minutes later, I would turn and do something that is demonic? And he said, "Larry, there are two of you. There is the one that God made, that is perfect and pure, loving and kind, and there's the one that Larry Gatlin made, the scared little boy, who has every neurosis, every fear, every desire, and every hurt. In my opinion it is that scared little boy which causes all the damage." I had become the Larry Gatlin that Larry Gatlin made. Even though I had become a star, I also became very lonely and very bitter at the same time.

I have a New Year's resolution; I no longer believe that I have to connect all the dots. In fact, I'm just grateful I have a lot of dots because a lot of people don't have any dots. You know, they have one or two dots. They get up and they go to work and then they come back. Back then, I thought every one of the dots were my responsibility, and if you were in the way of one of my dots, I would verbally attack you. I was that cocky. I wasn't spiritual. I wasn't allowing God to move through me. I was trying to do God's work without the help from God.

It has taken me a while but I think I have learned my lesson. I've been doing these auditions, seeing kids come in everyday and sing for me, and I have realized that playing God is not nearly as much fun as I thought it would be. I feel as if through their little five-minute audition, I have their lives in my hands. Are they going to get a part in this new play? I want all of them to do well, and some of them do and some of them don't. When I used to play God back then, I would never root for the kids. I was playing the role from a position of "every man for themselves." I was in a very lonely place. Over those ten years, I alienated myself from the spirit of Larry Gatlin, the godling.

He also alienated himself from Janice, his wife of many years, who stood by him through all his broken promises and all her busted dreams.

Toward the end of the bad times, she would ask me if I was doing drugs. I would respond, "No, I drink a little too much sometimes honey. But that's it." Finally, one night in Hawaii at a golf tournament, in front of Ben Crenshaw and his wife, and Tom Kite and his wife Kristy, and a bunch of other good friends, I literally passed out at the table before the entree came. It was not good. I promised Janice that day that I'd quit drinking. But secretly, I made my own revised promise to myself. I promised that day, that I'd never drink again in front of her. It was one of those little half-measures that all of us drunks try to say to make ourselves feel better. But it wasn't that easy.

One night, after a three-day using binge, I think I hit rock bottom. I was literally on the floor of a Holiday Inn in Dallas, Texas, picking lint out of the carpet and trying to put it in a free-base cocaine pipe. All of a sudden, I'd run out of drugs, I'd run out of money and I'd run out of friends. I was in that room alone, and I was scared. I crawled into the bathroom and saw this face in the mirror that I did not recognize. I didn't see a pitchfork, a red suit, a tail, and horns, but what I did see was demonic. I literally thought that I was going to die. I prayed to God to help me, and thank God, when I hollered, he, or she, or they, or it, was there for me. Somehow, God gave me the strength to get to the airport and to get home. My dear old friend and road manager Ron Carpenter called me the next day. He said, "Larry let's have lunch." And Ronny Carpenter didn't talk to me in that "Larry let's have lunch, it's time for the evening news" tone of voice! I knew he was going to tell me that he couldn't manage me anymore. It was a huge blow. I had lost yet another friend. I really needed to get help. I called my old friend Darryl Royale, who for many years was the head coach at University of Texas, and I asked him for help. I credit Darryl and his wife Edith with saving my life. Darryl didn't buy into my empty promises. He knew I wouldn't and couldn't quit on my own. He knew I had a disease.

In 1959, twenty years after Bill Wilson founded the twelve-step program called Alcoholics Anonymous, the American Medical Association determined that alcoholism was a chronic, progressive disease which if not treated would ultimately become fatal. Gatlin finally did enter a rehabilitation hospital. But he needed help to get there.

Darryl went with me. It wasn't a matter of him dragging me kicking and screaming to the hospital. It finally dawned on me that I needed help. Hey, I'm an intelligent guy. I mean, I'm not exactly the brightest flame in the candle shop, but I'm not the dumbest guy out there either! I knew that my behavior was no longer working. I knew that I was going to lose my family, my life, everything that I had worked for, and everything I thought God wanted me to do. Plus, I promised Darryl Royale, one of my heroes, that I would work to get myself better.

God put a series of people in my path during that experience that helped me become the wonderful guy I am today. Doctor

Purse at the care unit was especially good. During my stay, he taught me how to use prayer rather than medication to improve my conscience. I remember, I was shampooing my hair in the shower one night and I said, "Oh, God! Thank you for showing me the light!" Then it dawned on me: You idiot! If God had shown me all of the light, I would be blind, and I would still be blind, as if I was in the darkness. God shows us only a little bit of the light. We can't get all of that light at once. It is just like learning to do something new; we learn to tie our shoes slowly, we learn to do math, one plus one. It's not a quantum leap! It's not. It is a slow process. I believe that the absolute key to life is staying in tune with your spiritual self, the spiritual self that we all have. The quality of our life, and the spiritual quality of our life, is based on the realization that we all have it inside of us, but we need to learn how to awaken it. Dr. Purse said, "We are not bad people trying to get good. We are sick people trying to get better." We don't like to get hurt and we don't like to get our feelings stomped on! We don't like to have to make excuses for our behavior. We don't like our husbands or wives running around on us. We don't like all that stuff. We're human. It hurts! It's supposed to hurt! That's why we have relationships that are good and loving. When we hurt, that's how we know they've gone awry. But if you have a problem with the forgiveness of someone, I just suggest that you take a look in the mirror and say, "Who have I hurt?" and go ask them.

Gatlin refers to himself as a grateful, forgiven child of God. Forgiveness is a word that is so big it's hard for many people to wrap their minds around it, especially when they feel victimized and ashamed. It's politically correct to find someone to blame and cling to that resentment for dear life as a way of punishing the other guy. That way, no one has to look inward. It's what our entire criminal justice system is based on—blame, guilt, judgment, punishment. However, the problem with this type of resentment is that it only punishes the person who's polishing the grudge into a great golden insoluble lump. It's nice to know that there's an order to forgiveness. You ask God to forgive you. You come to believe that God has forgiven you. Then you get to forgive yourself. It is a simple process, but it is not easy.

Forgiveness is a daily and ongoing process. I am a type A compulsive. My motto is, I want all of it now. So as a result of my wanting it all too soon, I inevitably fall short. I was the quarterback; I'm the lead singer; I was the pitcher; I was the captain of the team. I thought if people followed me they would be all right—boy, was I wrong. I know that those people who follow me all fall down. So as a result of such behavior and actions, I have to forgive myself on a daily basis.

There is no question in my mind that I am a miracle! It is impossible to be crawling around on the floor, putting lint in a freebase pipe, with your heart going 200 miles an hour one minute and then be able to come back, and at almost fifty years old, feel better than you did at twenty-five. I can't believe it. I now run thirty miles a week and I hit a golf ball farther than I did when I was twenty-five. As a result, I have to believe in miracles. I believe in the miracles of the spoken word, the miracles of writing music, the miracles of being at God's place at God's time to do his bidding. My friend Jack Bolin once said, "Larry, if you will just get in tune with the spirit of the universe, the universe will stand up and applaud for you, and you'll get a parking place in front of every building you need to go in! And when it starts raining and there's not supposed to be a cab, one will show up!" I see it everyday! I see miracles everyday!

Larry Gatlin today has his very own theater (that's THEE-A-ter), and he still has that nasty old horse named Dan. He will tell you he's got a bald spot and a potbelly, but that part's not true. And he's got more to give than he ever has. Each person who goes to his performances gets a gift at the end. It's a song he wrote just before he got sober, after a particularly appalling display induced by an ingestion of too much of a really bad drug. To appreciate it, you have to hear the touchingly close four-part harmony, unaided by any instrumentation. It's all a cappella and from the heart. Its lyrics are: "May all our alleluias whether spoken or heard be mindful of your grace, Dear Lord, and not just lovely words. May all our tenderest blessings to the ending of our days be filled to overflowing with your never-ending praise."

Maybe God was rapping on his door saying, "Hey Larry. Call me. You need me now."

CHAPTER 15

SUZANNE SOMERS

Okay. I admit it. I couldn't stand her. I'd pegged her as a ditzy blonde—the kind that gives all of us true blondes a bad name. I'd been fighting her image all my life. She weaved through the movie American Graffiti *as an unattainable love object, and I loathed her. It was the first time I realized women could be objectified. Even years after the women's movement was in full flower, there she was on the nation's number one show,* Three's Company, *as Chrissy, the classic blonde bimbo with a heart of gold. The rest of America was laughing with her. But I thought they were laughing at her. I'm not laughing now.*

Suzanne Somers is a very smart lady—more introspective than any celeb I know, and a very open one. Because she's told her story many times now (to help clarify her own reality as much as to reach others who share her experience), she is at peace with it. It's compelling, and worth the retelling. Suzanne was hardwired for failure. She was born to a violent alcoholic father; she failed in school; she became a teenage mother and lived through a real nightmare when a car hit her son when he was only three. In spite of it all, she reached the height of fame and brought millions of dollars to her network. Then suddenly she was very publicly fired for requesting a raise.

She's a grandmother now, the matriarch of a blended family. She's also a five-time author and a zealot for telling her own truth. For Suzanne, the truth really did set her free.

I thought I was going to write a book about getting fired for asking for a raise. Then, as I began to write this book I realized that so much substance came out of losing the job, that this loss forced me to grow and think and evolve and diversify. But more importantly, it also brought the realization that I was defining myself as my accomplishments. Since *Three's Company* was such a mammoth success and there was such a huge response to my character, I equated that response to me as if I were this person. I was my accomplishment. So when I lost it, I had to think, if fame is that fragile, why do I place such importance on it? The search for that answer became the beginning of my next personal journey.

Suzanne Somers will always be associated with the word "bombshell." But the bombshell was not who she was but what she said and where she said it: the Barbara Walters interview. She just blurted out that she had been abused by her father, a violent alcoholic. It was a galvanizing moment for Suzanne (and for the viewers as well) as she saw, maybe for the first time, every horrifying incident in her childhood, and they stuck out in bas relief. She saw the alcoholism and abuse for what it was. She said that even the people who are not alcoholics in a family are also infected by the disease. Everyone gets sick. The interview was a first for national television, and it was a stunner. She had broken a canon law of alcoholic families—the code of silence. She told a dirty little secret shared not just by her kin but I daresay by thousands of families who were gathered around their TV sets at that moment. Her book that followed, Keeping Secrets, *became a national bestseller. And the process of writing it became the beginning of her journey to get well.*

Well, it took a long time to get so damaged, and when you finally decide that you want to repair the damage within you, you have to have a lot of patience. Part of this repair is forgiving all that had happened to you. Forgiveness is a process, and the process for me anyway is going back—as far back as I can remember—and reliving it. That's the agitating part, and it can be very painful. All those feelings that I had always pushed aside, I now had to force myself to remember by writing. Once I remembered, I began to understand. I'm older now, and I have a bit of wisdom to apply to what happened to me. My father didn't mean to treat me that way, he had a terrible disease. Once I understood it, then I was able to forgive him, but it took quite a process to get to that point. Once you can forgive, then you find resolution, and resolution brings peace. But that could take you your whole life. Simple it's not.

But Suzanne Somers does make forgiveness sound simple. The abuse she sustained as a child sure sounds unforgivable, but her story is a reminder that forgiveness isn't for the person who has sinned against you. He is out there in the world living his life and getting a good sleep at night. You're the one who isn't. As long as you're focusing on what he did, you can't learn to value your own experience. As long as you're letting him live rent-free in your brain, you're living as though his life is far more important than yours. You're not paying any attention whatsoever to your own feelings. So you're not getting on with this living business. When you're focusing on someone else, you're neglecting yourself. When you're focusing on someone else, you're trying to control someone else. Not only does that thing lack humility, but it can drive you to develop some pretty self-destructive habits. Abuse can be very tricky. It usually happens so incrementally, so subtly, over a long period of time, that you don't consider it abuse and it never occurs to you that all those nasty things being said to you are just not true. Your self-esteem is officially shot and you have lost your good judgment.

Recovering from the kind of outrage Suzanne Somers suffered takes focusing on yourself. If you really concentrate on yourself, on what you really feel and what you really think is best, you start to have options. The fact is you can't change much that's outside of you. You can't change the other guy. You can't change the past. But you can change you. In other words, recovery is an inside job.

I focused on the impact on me of my Dad's alcoholic drinking in my book *Keeping Secrets*. It was really shocking to me when I realized I had probably spent more nights sleeping in the closet than in my own bed just because of my Dad's behavior. Then I thought, How many other little girls are sleeping in the closet because of the fear of what might happen? How normal was it for my mother to round us up in the middle of the night saying, "We're going to the closet?" There was no "what's the closet?"

We knew what that meant. I'd grab my pillow, my teddy bear, and we'd all huddle in the closet with a lock on the inside. That lock was inside for the nights when we thought that we might get killed because he was so out of control. That is damaging, but you don't realize it because you accept it as normal. So I had to go back and take my life apart bit by bit until I wasn't angry with my father anymore. I don't want to blame him, because to blame him just keeps me a victim. And that means that the disease is still winning.

I remember appearing on a talk show and the host said, "Can we talk about something other than children of alcoholics, because that's been done?" And I said, "That makes me so sad. There are more than 76 million Americans in this country that are still affected by alcoholism and we still don't understand it." I have adult friends who have messed up lives. I know what their childhood was like. And they still, for all their brilliance, are not connecting the fact that they can't put their finger on happiness today because of what happened to them as a child. They keep saying, "Oh, it didn't bother me. My father was always drunk, and my mother was bringing guys home all the time, but that didn't affect me at all. And I think, how can that not affect you? How could you not hate women? How could you possibly even feel safe as an adult? Or how can you be a good father when that is the example that you had as a child? All of us learn by watching the first example in our lives about relationship skills, and if the relationship skills you're watching are so messed up, like the ones I saw, how can you possibly create a perfect relationship for yourself?

When she met the man she would marry, Suzanne followed another "rule" in alcoholic families, which is a direct outgrowth of keeping secrets. She lied. This is very common among children of alcoholics. When you grow up as she did looking at horrific behavior full in the face and then later hear those same grown-ups say that these things just didn't happen—Daddy didn't mean that—you understandably lose any grasp of what is or was real. Consequently you do the only thing you can under these circumstances: You create your own reality. And often, you don't even know you're lying.

I met Alan, and I was in love with him the moment I saw him. It's one of those lucky things. I walked into an ABC studio in San Francisco, hired out for a day as a prize model, the girl opening the refrigerator door on a show. He was the host, and he said hello, and it was one of those chemical things. I called my mother that night, and I said, "I met the man I'm going to marry." I can't deny that there were some serious complications, like he was still married. This did present a moral dilemma for me. But I had never reacted so viscerally to a person like I did with Alan.

At that time, since I didn't feel good enough to be who I was, I created a personality that I thought would be good enough for him. That's the shame of it all. I felt such actual shame about my real family that I couldn't bear to tell him the truth about my family background. So when I met Alan, I couldn't believe that he asked me out to dinner that very first night, and I certainly never thought it would go anywhere, so I just made up myself that night. I told him my father was dead, and once I had him dead, I made him what I would have liked my father to be—he was a doctor! And then I embellished even more and told him he was a brain surgeon and that he had left my mother an inheritance. Of course this was totally untrue since my Dad really had nothing. I told him that my mother was traveling around the world, and I created this picture that I thought would enchant him. This went on for over two years, because quite frankly I always thought it was going to be our last date. But it did go on, and two years into our relationship, on Christmas, I was in the kitchen making a soufflé, and he was in the living room. He walks in to the kitchen with a strange look on his face and he's holding a Christmas card. I panicked. He said: "What's this?" And I said, "Well, you know, ever since my father died my mother's been a little crazy and uh, she just can't deal with the fact that umm, my father's gone so she always signs the Christmas cards: Love, Mom and Dad." He looked at me and stared, and then said, "You're all messed up, aren't you?" I started to continue the lie, but he kept staring at me. Finally I said to him, "Yeah, everything I've told you is a lie. Everything.

Everything." I expected him to put down the card and walk out of my life forever, but he said to me, "You know, it never did ring true. Why don't we just start at the beginning, but this time with the truth?" And the truth made us stronger.

My own father was a psychiatrist. From time to time throughout my life, I've heard people say that psychiatry is bogus. Only weak people go there. Only the friendless. Only the hopeless. On that last point, they may be right. In some cases, it is only through a sense of utter hopelessness that people reach out for help. When people from alcoholic families go to a therapist for help, they must tell the family secrets to get well. Psychiatry is a safe place to begin spilling the beans. Suzanne Somers had been in therapy before, but this time it was different. Her doctor gave her a very practical exercise anyone can do at home. It's a helpful reality check. Make a list. What's good about you? What don't you like about yourself? The results in black and white can be pretty stunning.

What I liked about myself was always blank. There was nothing I liked about myself. I couldn't see anything good about myself because I was programmed as a child not to see anything good. Alcoholics are so filled with self-loathing, and without a family support system they know they will die. So they have to keep you attached to them at all costs. And so all the self-loathing my father had was visited upon his children. The mantra I heard from the time I was a child was that I was stupid and hopeless and worthless and nothing. And my IQ was a big zero. I believed this. I thought I was stupid. And that was reinforced by going to school and getting horrible grades—not because I was stupid but because I'd been up all night. I couldn't think. I couldn't learn. I couldn't focus. The circle closed tighter because then I became the object of ridicule by the other kids. By the time I became an adult, I didn't even understand what was wrong with me, but I knew something was terribly wrong.

People say to me, "Gee you're lucky. Everybody in your family drinks. Your sister, your brothers, your father, your uncles, your aunts your whole family. But you're the one who's okay. You don't drink!" But I think to myself, Yes I don't drink, but I'm still not okay!

In the beginning, I did not go to therapy for myself. I went because my son had been run over by a car when he was three years old, and he woke up every night with these night sweats and screaming and nightmares and I didn't know what to do for him. I wasn't making any money, and I had no child support. I was a single mother. I took him to the community mental health center. They charged me according to my ability to pay. In my case, they charged me a dollar a visit. After a year the therapist told me that my son didn't need to come anymore. "He's not having the nightmares anymore, and he's not afraid to cross the street, so you don't need to bring him anymore. He's well adjusted, and you've been a good mother." This did make me feel good since I was a teenage mother. But then the other shoe dropped. The therapist said, "But I'd like you to come into therapy." And I said, "Why?" "Because you have the lowest self-esteem of anyone I've ever met!" And I said, "Ever?" She said, "You walk in here and you apologize for who you are, what you are, how you look, what you say, where you come from, and where you're going." She said, "You're a walking apology!"

From that time on, I was in one-on-one therapy. I call this therapist the angel in my life. Sometimes you find yourself in the right place at the right time. This woman was the first person who made me understand that what happens to us as children will follow us through into our adult life unless we correct it for good.

My first marriage was as a teenager, and I married a very controlling man. From my perspective today, I chose, on a subliminal level, someone who was as controlling as my father was. We divorced, and then I met Alan. We had to go through his divorce, which was especially agonizing since his children had to experience instability for the first time. We had other issues, such as dealing with my child from my teenage marriage. And Alan had guilt about living with my son while he was leaving his own son. Out of loyalty to his own son, he began to ignore mine, so that his own son wouldn't feel threatened. This of course hurt my child, and the mother lioness came out in me. I found myself pitted against Alan. Despite the inevitable stumbling blocks, we did eventually marry.

Since Alan is strong, we started to fight because he wanted me to do everything his way. Having had such an out of control childhood, I wanted to control everything about my adult life. I wanted life on my own terms. But that didn't gel with the marriage because marriage has to be a give and take. So the arguments began, and we fought and we fought and we fought and we fought for ten years! We fought over everything. Now I realize I was fighting for a level playing field.

Sometimes Alan is the enemy, but I'm deeply in love with him. It's all so complicated. I really loathed his behavior toward my child. I am the only parent of this child, and no one is going to hurt him. At the same time, his children certainly don't want or need a new mother. I try hard to be nice and kind, but this only makes them more upset. Since there are no rules, we can only do what we think is right.

We are the first generation to use divorce to solve our relationship problems. As far as Alan was concerned, I couldn't leave. I sometimes felt it was a weakness. I just couldn't leave him. I was madly in love with him, yet at the same time, I hated him! It was very masochistic. I probably felt that I didn't deserve happiness yet—and yet is the operative word here. My self-esteem had improved because of the therapy, but still wasn't where it is today. However, at the bottom of my heart I never really wanted to get out of it.

The truth for me is what I'm about today. I sometimes get criticized for being so open, but I can't be anything but! The openness is what healed me and what my work is about. My "work" is about facing myself—all that I was, and all that I can be. But I must face it with total honesty. This change has been the most healing, and empowering, and freeing thing in my life. Even if I exaggerate just a little, to me this is a red flag. What's wrong? Am I depressed today? Am I having a little slip? Why did I think I needed to embellish the story? Was it so that people would think I am more than I am? I have to constantly check myself.

Regarding alcoholism, many people say to me, "How do I get my alcoholic husband sober?" And I always say, "You can't! No matter what you do. You can tie them to a chair in AA, but that won't work. The only thing you can change is yourself. And as you change and get well, then you have to make a decision. Do I stay, or do I leave? But by being an example, maybe the person with the disease of alcoholism will want what you have, which is peace! It's peace that we're all looking for. We all want to be peaceful. We all want to be demonless.

For the first time in my life, for the moment—because I don't know what tomorrow will bring—but right now, I don't have any demons. I am demonless. That's a huge accomplishment for me. There's nobody I'm harboring anger about. I've dealt with all those relationships in my life. I don't know about tomorrow, but today I wake up joyous and my goal is to keep doing the work to keep me feeling in the state I'm in now. Or perhaps it gets better. I don't know. I think it does!

CHAPTER 16

LINDA ELLERBEE

Linda Jane Ellerbee was a maniac. And I loved her. She was a brilliant writer before it was considered quaint to write an elegant sentence for television. She possessed two major attractions that softened up the hardest-get interview subjects (or three, depending on how you count). First, she had very imposing breasts. Second (or third), a mane of luxuriant brunette hair, enough for ten people—while I was cursed with towhead wisps that TV lighting shot through as though my hair were cellophane. She was worldly. She'd worked her way through a few husbands, a stint as a missionary in Bolivia (after which, she claims, the Methodists rewrote the rules that said something to the effect that no nineteen-year-old brunettes with bad attitudes need apply). God had not been in her lexicon unless the word was followed immediately by damn. She had two great kids, hard-smoking hard-drinking habits, and the mouth of a Texas trucker. She had attitude that could turn everything her way. As a cub reporter for the Associated Press, she wrote some smart-ass fake copy, punched the wrong button, and sent it national, getting herself fired big time, yet she ended up with a better job. She was very tough. More comfortable in a police precinct than the Waldorf. Even when I beat her on stories, which was seldom, her writing always made her stories better than mine. We were supposed to be rivals. Our New York flagship stations certainly were. But we were friends. Her brownstone in Greenwich Village, a monument to commune culture, was a watering hole where we would gather and sing—in harmony. We were good, too!

We both went on to the networks, living our lives in the upright and locked position. I followed all the rules, while she remained a maverick. In 1985, she invited me over for dinner, just the two of us, for girl talk. Dinner consisted of blenders full of margaritas. I was too much in awe of her to broach the subject of actual food. By 11:15 at night, confused and frightened, I left her nursing another jeroboam of whatever it is that goes into margaritas. I did not see her again for years.

At the darkest time in my life, when I had isolated from my friends and forgotten how to pray and even how to hope, Linda Ellerbee was on the phone. Transformed.

That change came when I got sober. I was dying inside. I just felt awful. My father was an alcoholic and therefore I thought, well I'll never be one. I've seen what it's like. But it's a disease that sneaks up on you. It is a disease that is a family disease. My father had it, and I have it, and it can get passed on to my children. It is also a family disease because when one family member has it, everybody in the family is affected. The family is forced to make one of two choices: They must learn how to accommodate their lives to this sick person, or they must leave the situation. There are no other choices.

One day I just realized that I had a disease. I realized that this disease caused me problems with my children and it caused me problems with myself. If I had a job at that moment, I knew that I would be fired. If I continued to keep on that way, I knew I would wind up dead. I had a couple of choices: I could die, or I could do something about it. So I decided to ask for help.

Both Ralph, my partner in life and in business, and my son Josh, who was living at home (my daughter was living in Vienna at the time), gave me the support and encouragement to ask for help. I remember holding Josh's hand when I called the Betty Ford Center. When I told all my friends and family that I was going to the Betty Ford Center, nobody asked me why. That said a lot to me. I was fooling no one.

When I first entered rehab, I fought (as many people do). I didn't want to hear about all this higher power stuff! I didn't want to hear about this God stuff! And finally I met a Catholic priest who made me want to listen. He said, "Linda, you haven't lost your faith, it's just buried under a pile of shit." And being a Methodist, I jumped back and said, "I didn't know Catholic priests talked this way! But I believe you're right!" With his help,

I was able to realize that I was not alone and that I had not been alone in a very long time. I was able to free myself, and since that time, I have been very comfortable with the word God and prayer.

You talk of triumph! I have not triumphed over alcoholism. I am a recovering alcoholic, not a recovered alcoholic. It is a struggle, and it will be a struggle all my life. I was struck by my friend's eulogy for another friend, who had been in recovery from alcoholism, and he said, "Here lies Joe, a recovered alcoholic." The day you die is the day you recover. Until then, it's just trying; it's just a struggle.

I don't like it when celebrities go in there and say, "I have been sober for eighteen years, or I have been sober for thirty days. It's too easy to slip. Many of us have slipped and fallen off and gotten back on. It's a constant struggle. For me, the two things I regard as my saving grace are my relationship with God and my AA group. God in many ways speaks to me through the people in the meetings. And I have to be in the meetings to hear it. I stopped going to the meetings for a while because I thought I had this all figured out. But I didn't. If I don't go to the meetings, I can slip; and I don't want to do that.

Anonymity is the spiritual foundation of Alcoholics Anonymous. If you're focused on personalities in the meetings, you tend to lose sight of the principles the meetings have to offer. Yet sometimes it is hard to understand how a celebrity can walk into a church basement full of strangers and maintain any semblance of anonymity.

First of all, there are no strangers in a twelve-step meeting at all. And secondly, there are no celebrities in a twelve-step meeting. Rather, there are only a bunch of drunks trying to help one another stay sober. I was in a meeting recently and a woman said, "One of the things I love about this is that this room is the only place in the world that I can go to anytime and always know that I am welcome." I feel the same way.

Alcoholics metabolize alcohol differently than nonalcoholics. It is likely that Linda inherited her alcoholism trait from her father. And it's likely she passed on to her children the behaviors she'd developed as a child to accommodate them. It was not her fault, that's just how it works.

My father was an alcoholic. How did I accommodate his behavior? Well, I was very careful about inviting friends over because I didn't know which daddy would be coming home for dinner. I also tried to ignore my father's behavior, as if by ignoring it, his problem would disappear. I now look at my attempts at trying to ignore my father's behavior as the old elephant in the middle of the room trick: Even if there was an elephant in the middle of our living room, we weren't going to talk about it. It's not healthy and it's not good. But that's what goes on in families.

Even though my father was the one with the problem, I was not angry with him. Rather, I was angry with my mother. I wasn't mad at my daddy because I understood even as a kid that alcohol is a sickness. But my mother was a "sane" woman, and she didn't have this disease, and I couldn't understand why she didn't fix it for me. Why she didn't protect me from it. And why she didn't fix it for daddy. So I was mad at her. It has taken me a long time to understand my anger towards my mother and to realize that my feelings towards my mother were very common in alcoholic households.

While Mama and I have had our battles, I do love her. I think I realized how much I loved her one New Year's Eve. I honestly believe that it was a night that changed our lives. My mother was living with me and my thirteen-year-old daughter. The three of us spent the night sitting up and talking. In our conversation that night, I learned that my mother had wanted a different life from the one she had. She had wanted to go into politics but, at the time, women weren't doing that. She'd wanted to work, but my father wouldn't let her. She talked about sex and said that my father wasn't very good at the foreplay part. Well, I almost fell off the chair! I had never had a conversation like that with my own mother.

That night, I also learned a lot about my daughter, Vanessa. Since Vanessa was more comfortable telling my mother about her dreams than me (her alcoholic mother), I did not know a lot about her wishes in life. Yet in that room, that New Year's Eve night, I became privy to information about my daughter that I wouldn't normally be privy to. It was a great night that made us know that somewhere along the way, we would be able to find one another. Today Vanessa is twenty-seven and we have found one another. However, we had to travel over a long hard road to get there.

When Vanessa was growing up, I was away from home a lot for work. I was part of that first group of women who came in to television and were told, "If you take time off from work for family-related activities, we'll know you're not serious!" Since I wanted to prove to people that I was serious, I didn't take time off. Now, when I look back, I know what a mistake that was. I should have told the networks, "Look, I want to be at that third-grade play today, and I'm going to be. So it is your job to find somebody else to go to Cleveland and cover that story. I'm sure that the network, Cleveland, you, and I will all survive." But I didn't do that. So my daughter felt that I wasn't there for her; and to top those feelings off, I was also an alcoholic.

Linda made amends to her children by focusing on herself and getting well. The twelve steps of AA, lived one day at a time, can be boiled down to six words. Trust God, clean house, help others. Do that and you can handle anything. Linda couldn't have known how handy those steps would be, because once she got sober, her challenges and changes had only begun.

I remember when the doctor said, "You have breast cancer. I know this is a pretty hard thing for you to hear, but I want you to just try to take care of it and live with it one day at a time." I looked at him and I laughed. I said, "Well, at least I am familiar with that concept!"

When I was first diagnosed with breast cancer, the surgeon that my family doctor sent me to became very impatient with me. I had a lot of questions. Everyday I would call him with more questions, until finally, one day he said, "There's this woman doctor named Susan Love who's written a book. Why don't you just get her book and read it? She's a feminist like yourself." I was incredibly ticked off. So I immediately called Dr. Susan Love and asked her if she would like to be my surgeon. It was the best move I could have made. It is important to remember that you have a right as a patient, and as a human being, to ask questions and to get answers. And to say, "Look at me, I'm alive!" Don't let anyone tell you differently.

When faced with a deadly illness, I have to admit that most of the clichés that you hear are true. I learned to stop and smell the flowers. I learned to stop putting off those things that are truly important. I learned to use the word "now" and to mean it.

I remember being in a Race for the Cure which took place in Helena, Montana, and there was this 104-year-old woman who was a 60-year survivor of breast cancer, and her granddaughter was pushing her in the wheelchair. And 60 feet before the end of the race, her little hand went up, and the granddaughter backed off. She got out of the wheelchair, and she walked around to the back. And this 104-year-old breast cancer survivor pushed her own chair across the finish line. That's the kind of noise women need to make on these kinds of triumphs.

I have not been quiet about my battle with breast cancer because I think that silence kills. For years, women were conditioned to be polite, and to suffer in silence. My mother had a friend with breast cancer. It was only spoken of in whispers. I want women who have breast cancer to be noisy so that more attention gets paid to this disease!

I was diagnosed when I was forty-seven years old. At first I prayed to God, "God, let me accept your will, whatever it is." But then at the end of that prayer, I would sneak in a little prayer that said, "I know what I said earlier and I meant it, it is just that it would be great if you would allow me to see fifty. Could I please see fifty?" Well, now that I'm fifty-two, my prayers are a bit different. However, they always start out the same. I pray, "God, please let me accept your will, but can I see the year 2000?" I really don't know what I'll say if I get to see the year 2000. But I do know one thing I'll say, and that is, "Thank you."

Of all the drugs that infest our society, from the schoolyards to the trading floors, the two most lethal are the only two that are legal: alcohol and nicotine. Alcoholism is a beast to recover from. It's estimated that only ten percent of alcoholics make it into AA rooms, and not all of those who wander in stay in. But those who've graded in degrees of difficulty the process of freeing oneself from addiction say alcohol is a poor fourth on the list. The second toughest to beat, second only to cocaine addiction, is smoking.

It is, it is! I swear to God! I was still smoking when I was diagnosed with breast cancer. I used to hate it when people would come up to me and say, "Don't you know that's bad for you?" I would want to reply, "Why, no, I just fell off this turnip truck here yesterday, and I didn't know it was bad for me." When I was diagnosed with breast cancer everybody said, "Well, now you'll quit smoking." And I said, "Well now, let me see. Let me see if I have this right. I'm going to have surgery, I'm going to lose both my breasts, all my hair, I may lose my life, I'm going to go through six months of chemotherapy, and you want me at the same time to give up a major addiction? I don't think so! I will quit smoking the day I quit chemotherapy." And I did. I used the patch.

I must say cancer is a great motivator. I quit smoking and I've almost never even missed it. Occasionally, I feel a temptation, but almost never. It was very hard to quit smoking. When I quit drinking I didn't have the DTs. They didn't have to tie me down in a bed and let me shake for five days. There were no withdrawal symptoms of that kind for me. But that's not true when you quit nicotine. I mean, I was a raging maniac! The patch was very helpful with that, and also everybody was very helpful in sort of keeping a distance for a while, and letting me be a little crazy! But I was very determined and I was able to say to myself, "Okay, you've done a couple of other tough things. You can do this because you really don't have a choice now. This has to go." I am a smoker who no longer smokes. I hate those nasty non-smokers. I'm never going to be one of them! The day I said good-bye to smoking, I was very sad.

Ellerbee is still a maverick who can't leave well enough alone. She's added to her toolbox of twelve steps a list of other ideals to live by.

The first one is, if you believe with all your heart that you are right, do it your own way, because only dead fish swim with the stream all the time. The second one is an old fashioned one: the best things in life aren't things. The third thing has to do with my politics. I believe that it's the duty of every citizen to keep her mouth open. The fourth is, if you don't want to get old, don't mellow. The fifth is probably the most important in this world: The best time to laugh is anytime you can. There are other rules. Always remember to set a place in your life for the unexpected guest, whether it's cancer or alcoholism or some other disease.

I remember my reaction when I was diagnosed with breast cancer. I was devastated. I went through the, "Oh, poor me, why me. . . . " But then I would see somebody much worse off than me. I would see somebody dying and I would think, "Well shut up fool! All you lost were your breasts, not your life." When you see people standing up and laughing who ought to be lying down and crying, it puts everything else in your life in perspective.

Everybody knows that we will all eventually die one day. However, that doesn't mean that we should give up on life. Rather, I believe that we should continue to do what we have always done. We should continue to plant trees that we may never see in their full-grown state. We should continue with our attempts to find cures for diseases for all people, even people we will never know. And we should continue to plan governments for the future even if the people of the future are not worth the democracy. In my opinion, these actions make up the best part of human beings. Even though we are mortal, we want our hopes and our dreams to survive ourselves. And to me this is a beautiful thing.

CHAPTER 17

POLLY BERGEN

Polly Bergen is one of those up-front women who is endowed with boundless enthusiasm for absolutely everything. And the clincher is, she fits it all in. She's on everybody's guest list and a ubiquitous presence in the Hollywood/New York access-way. And she's done it all. She's been a singer and recording artist when chanteuses ruled the airwaves. She's been an actress working without a net back in the days when all TV was live. She's lit up Broadway, and was part of the glorious musical machinery of the great MGM Studios. She took an unlikely product called Oil of Turtle and built a cosmetics empire, starting slowly selling by mail order and finishing big with a sale lock, stock, and wrinkle remover to Faberge. She's made a fortune in real estate and became the first woman elected a director of the Singer Company in its 124-year history. She has won an Emmy Award, run giant corporations, and written three best-sellers on beauty and fashion. She can eyeball your clothes and peg the label on the nose. And she never even finished high school.

I may have made her sound invincible, but she is really remarkably human. It wasn't all easy. She took a lot of risks, and twice suffered the consequences. She was born in 1930 in Tennessee. By the time she was nine, her parents were both working, and the cleaning, cooking, and caring for her baby sister was left to Polly. Her fifteenth birthday coincided with the virtual dawn of television, and she was among its earliest stars. She made her TV debut when she was fifteen, and she found the lure of performing irresistible. Already well on her way to a fifty-year-long five-pack-a-day nicotine habit, Polly left home and headed west to Las Vegas, a fifteen year old passing herself off as twenty-two.

Twenty-one was too obvious, so I thought if I made myself twenty-two, people would be more apt to believe it. The number one thing I did to make myself look older and sophisticated was to smoke. Smoking was a very sophisticated and glamorous thing to do in the old days. Long before anyone knew that smoking harmed you, smoking was used as a sexual innuendo in films. You were a very sophisticated woman if you had a cigarette and a cigarette holder. Both of my parents were very heavy smokers. I started smoking when I was about eleven or twelve.

Despite my age, I was never a light smoker. I was a medium smoker who eventually became a heavy smoker. I would smoke between two to three packs of unfiltered cigarettes a day. Sometime in the Sixties, the cigarette companies introduced a filter cigarette. They said that filters would get rid of all the bad stuff in cigarettes. So I switched to filters. They were much lighter than unfiltered cigarettes, and I began smoking more than I ever had before.

About five or six years ago, I attempted to stop smoking. I went to a doctor who believed that every day his patients should smoke less and less until they stopped for good. He wanted me to begin by cutting back one half of a pack. This brought me to two and one half packs a day. I thought I could do more, so I cut back to two packs a day. The next morning, I was very aware of my situation. Since I could only smoke two packs of cigarettes that day, I wasn't able to have a cigarette in my hand every single moment, like I had been accustomed to before. By 11:15 A.M., I had already smoked my two packs. That's when I realized that I had been smoking five packs of filtered cigarettes a day. It was a real problem.

Throughout my career, I considered myself to be a singer. Oh, how I loved to sing! It was the one thing that gave me great joy. However, my smoking was not helping my singing voice. I remember someone coming up to me and saying, "You know, you really have to give up smoking if you're going to continue to sing." I went home and really thought about it. And I remember making a joke. I said, "I can give up singing a chorus of 'Night and Day.' But I can't give up cigarettes." So in my thirties, I literally stopped singing.

I gave up what I loved the best and turned to acting full time. I think I'm fairly good at acting, but I'll never be as good an actress as I was a singer.

Smoking controlled my life. If I was flying cross-country, I would deliberately take a flight that made a stop so I could get off the plane and smoke a cigarette. At that particular time, you could still smoke in airports and then get back on another plane.

If I was going to see a play, I would pray that it would be an entertaining one because then maybe I would be able to manage to get through to intermission without taking a cigarette break.

I knew I shouldn't smoke, but I didn't want to stop smoking. There's a very big difference between those two. Knowing intellectually that you should not be a smoker and knowing in your gut that you can't smoke are two very different things. It is the worst addiction in the world.

The first time I stopped smoking was when I went into the hospital for a blood clot at the opening of my heart. I had come home one night and couldn't get my key in the door. I collapsed and was rushed to the hospital. It turned out that I had this blood clot, which I almost died from. Luckily, the doctors were able to dissolve the clot, and I came through the operation all right. I remember the doctor stressing the fact that I couldn't smoke anymore; he said that my health couldn't take it. Yet he knew that the moment I went home I would start smoking again. So he kept me in the hospital for a great many more days than he normally would have to ensure that I would get past my nicotine withdrawal.

They doped me up. They sent me home very doped up. I remember running into my furniture and into my walls. I felt like I was going crazy. I finally called my doctor and said that I couldn't take it anymore. I wanted off the drugs. He told me that since I had an addiction, he was afraid of what was going to happen when I stopped my medication. He did not want me to start smoking again. He had a really good point, because as soon as I went off the medication, I wanted to light up a cigarette.

I would give anything to have a cigarette at this very moment. I know there are people out there who say, "Gee, I quit cold turkey and I've never wanted a cigarette since then." And I just say, "Gee, that's wonderful for you. But that's not the way it worked for me. And it's not the way it worked for some of my friends, who say that they miss a cigarette every day." I guess it's like an alcoholic. An alcoholic is always recovering.

However an alcoholic has twelve-step programs that they can go to. People who want to quit smoking cigarettes don't have programs. I went everywhere trying to find a program. I literally went everywhere. I called everyone. I knew in my heart that I had to be locked away in order to stop smoking. I knew that I couldn't be trusted. I knew that I would cheat. There was no doubt about it in my mind. And the tragedy is that there was no place for me to go.

So what I really have to say to people is that if you find yourself saying, "I have to have one," and then take one, don't beat yourself up about it. If you have a cigarette once every three to four days, you are not going to kill yourself. Rather, you are on the road to recovery. I'm sixty-six years old and I smoked five packs of cigarettes a day. I have been able to stop smoking because I stopped putting pressure on myself to quit. Rather, I congratulated myself for discontinuing smoking my five packs a day. I found that the easier I was on myself, the easier it was for me to finally give it up.

When I was smoking, I never thought it would kill me. I thought I was invincible. I guess you could say that I applied that same mentality to sex. I really believed that I could have sex with the person I loved and I would not get pregnant. Boy, was I wrong. I'm a good girl and I've always been a good girl. I'd always done what my mother and father told me to do. I was very responsible. I was a very hard worker and had been since I was a kid. So I just thought it would never happen to me. One day I woke up and it had happened to me; I was pregnant. I was only seventeen and my career was just beginning. I had no money. I was really struggling to make a go of it. I couldn't go to my parents because I thought it would destroy their feelings about me. In retrospect, I know in my heart that they probably would have been understanding. But at that moment in time, I couldn't fathom telling my parents.

It never entered my mind to keep the child. I knew that I was not financially able to have the child. The father took off as soon as he found out that I was pregnant. I knew that he was not coming back. So I borrowed the money and went to a man I had heard about in downtown Los Angeles who performed abortions.

He performed these abortions in a dirty house, on the kitchen table. He didn't use anesthesia. He asked for the money first and got it. When I left, I was in serious trouble. By the time I got home and got in bed, I'd already lost enough blood to barely get me to the hospital. Luckily, my friend came over to check on me. The moment she saw me, she rushed me to the hospital. I know I would have died if my friend hadn't come over. She saved my life.

Many years later, when I got married and wanted to have children, I discovered that because of what I had done, I was incapable of having children. So I adopted. Adoption at that time was very difficult. Since I was a Baptist married to a Jewish man, there was no available adoption for me. We were considered a mixed marriage, and because of that, there was no adoption agency we could go to where we could adopt a child. So we turned to private adoption and were able to form a family.

It is a wonderful choice, but the problem with it is that there are some children who are adoptable and there are some children who aren't. Ninety percent of the time, the children who are not white, blue-eyed, in perfect health, and gorgeous can't find homes. So the people out there who are having children who are not white and blue-eyed have a problem. It's still very difficult to adopt.

Even though I had an abortion, I know that I wouldn't have the family that I have if some women didn't carry their babies to term. Therefore, one could say that I am on both sides of the issue of choice. I am now delighted to be a mother. However, if I had had a child when I was seventeen, I wouldn't have been able to care for him in a way that he deserved. Therefore, I think it is important to have children when you're ready to have them. My children have fulfilled my life in a way that is incalculable.

I was cast in an ABC movie of the week called *For Hope*, about a disease very few people know about called scleroderma. It is a disease that kills more women of childbearing age than muscular dystrophy and multiple sclerosis do put together. It's a common disease that is basically unheard of. Scleroderma is a defect in the collagen production in the skin. It causes the skin to turn to stone. There are two types of scleroderma: local and systemic (which is worse). Systemic scleroderma attacks not only the skin but the vital organs as well. It turns your esophagus to stone, your kidneys to stone, and your liver to stone. It is fatal.

About eight months prior to the film, my sister had been diagnosed with scleroderma. Since I couldn't pronounce it, I wouldn't believe it. How can you have something you can't even say? Yet I became really worried about it, because the more I learned, the more I knew what a serious disease this was. Therefore, it became pretty ironic when Bob Saget, the film's director, called me in to see about a part in his film about scleroderma. You see, the film is based on the life of his sister, who has scleroderma.

When I read the script, I got chills all over my body. The script is so beautiful. It's about this crazy family and how they deal with this terminal illness. Each person deals with her illness in a different way, and they deal with it separately. I'm proud to say that I play the mother of the family.

When I told Sharon Munsky, the woman who is the head of The Scleroderma Foundation, about my sister, she insisted that I have my sister go to her doctor. So my sister and her husband flew out to Santa Barbara, where Sharon Munsky lives, and had her doctor look at my sister. My sister was diagnosed with local scleroderma. My sister was lucky. The doctor assured her that she would never die of this disease.

When I was little, my mom and dad told me that I could do anything I wanted to do, within reason. If I wanted it badly enough, and I was willing to work hard enough for it, then I could do it.

Consequently, everything that I have ever needed to learn, I set out to learn. And everything I have needed to do to perform, or to function, or to get the right answer, or to create the right product, or to package it properly, or to market it properly, I have set out to learn how to do.

I apply this mentality to all aspects of my life. I apply it to my smoking, to my parenting, and to my acting. I believe that however hard the times are, you can fight your way up, and make it. Now, I know that I was extremely lucky. I was in the right places at the right times. But some of it also had to come from my spirit. I am an extremely tenacious person. When I make up my mind, as I've described earlier, I believe that it is very difficult to walk away from me. I am proud of who I am. I am proud of me.

CHAPTER 18

CARROLL O'CONNOR

In January 1971, he strolled onto the television screen, sat down in a ratty easy chair, and changed television forever. As Archie Bunker on All in the Family, *Carroll O'Connor broke all the rules. Despite his remarkable and prodigious body of work as an actor, writer, and director, Carroll O'Connor will forever be remembered for his memorable pronouncements that first made us wince and then made us laugh, like the famous out-of-tune piano that began the show. As Archie, he forced a nation to examine its faults. He took on bigotry in all its colors. He made us look at the fear that comes from ignorance, the rage that comes from misunderstanding, the bitterness that comes from intolerance—and he gave us an arena in which to talk about it all.*

Growing up in the Thirties in Queens, New York, Carroll O'Connor came of age in a neighborhood and in a culture that seemed torn straight from the scripts of All in the Family. *Bigotry, he has said, was so common that no one reflected on it. His father was a prominent defense attorney in a town still infused with the spirit of Tammany Hall, a place where payoffs and kickbacks were the cost of doing business. During the Great Depression, his dad could get anybody a city job—for money. Money greased the palms of political bosses and labor leaders who winked at each other while keeping the town afloat. And his dad made a bundle at it. He even had a knack for keeping the crime bosses out of prison. But in the end, he couldn't rescue himself. Carroll O'Connor's father and his partner were accused of racketeering, but his partner dropped dead in the middle of the proceedings. So Carroll O'Connor's dad took the rap alone.*

He was "sent up the river" to Sing-Sing, and he became a big shot there too. He already knew everybody who was anybody on the inside, including Lucky Luciano. For years, when people asked him about his father, Carroll O'Connor would say, "He was a lawyer, gone now." Though today, O'Connor paints a somewhat romantic picture of his father, calling his criminal bent a "bad habit." He is still making peace with his childhood, and has come to terms with his own role as a father.

It is said that when a child idealizes a loved one, he ultimately denies reality. It is just a way of protecting oneself, and it usually works for a very long time. But at some point, life slaps you in the face, and you are forced to face the truth. Carroll O'Connor's truth was delivered by the sonic boom of a single gunshot. His only child Hugh had just waved good-bye to Carroll, had gone inside his house, called his mother, and then blown his head off.

At that point, I reacted as a parent who is instantaneously stricken by the reality that a sudden malady has just come upon his child. And I mean malady or affliction in the form of a disease, because addiction is a disease. The same sort of thing comes upon a parent who discovers that his child has AIDS or polio or terminal cancer. In fact, Hugh had cancer when he was sixteen, but he fought his way through that. So now, here I am with a thirty-two-year-old child who's in the throes of a disease, and it looks like it's terminal. I felt it. I felt I was going to lose him. Though not through suicide. I was waiting to get a call from somebody who'd tell me that he'd had an automobile accident. But it never happened. He was an excellent driver.

For Hugh, it was suicide. The suicide occurred because he was delusional, which is what cocaine does. It can make you really paranoid. This word is just thrown around these days. But clinical paranoia is a real disorientation. You imagine that people are watching you, that people are talking to you, that people are on the roof across the street. You might think that somebody is trying to take your husband or wife away and you believe you know in your delusional soul who the person is. Then to make matters worse, you try to convince everybody around you that this is reality.

Children, by nature, believe they're omnipotent. We know that they tend to accept full responsibility for any evil that befalls their parents. It's possible that keeping an embarrassing secret, as O'Connor must have done in refusing to discuss his father, can lock a child into a cycle of blame and shame that is difficult to break. At its core, it is a question of guilt. Guilt is one of those burdens that gets heavier the farther you drag it. There should be no guilt in suicide; not for things you did or for things left undone. But Carroll O'Connor lives with guilt.

If you lose a child through disease, a child at the age of thirty-two, whatever it is, you feel guilty. You feel you haven't done everything. Whether your guilt can be justified, whether it's rational, or it's real, doesn't matter. If you lose a child, you probably do feel guilty. I shouldn't have lost that child. I shouldn't be here. I shouldn't bury my child. My child should bury me. That's the correct order of things in life. So there is a certain kind of guilt there, and it does no good for people to tell me not to feel guilty about it. I'll feel guilty about this for the rest of my life. But on top of that, with me, I think that I was guilty of not being vigilant enough. And for me that's what I say to people who ask me about drugs today. I say you must be vigilant to the extreme. You must spy on your child.

There is a remarkably effective twelve-step program for people who love and live with an alcoholic or an addict. It's called Al-Anon. And to the astonishment of many desperate first-timers who limp into one of those meetings, its goal is not to help families make their loved ones stop using. Its goal is to help people live happy fulfilled lives whether the guy that got them into Al-Anon is using or not. Al-Anon helps people understand which of their feelings are codependant, which of their behaviors enable the addict to keep at it. They believe that turning CIA agent, swiping the stash, and punishing the culprit by words or actions not only is akin to kicking them when they're down, but actually perpetuates the substance abuse. Al-Anon helps people to stop trying to control their loved one and instead to change their own behavior, not the addict's. Funny thing though, over time, the new behavior of a parent or spouse or child can result in new and healthier behavior in the addict as well. Carroll O'Connor has heard all of that. But he neither believes it or espouses it.

You have to watch your kids when they are preteen or teenagers. You have to be vigilant, search their room, listen on the telephone, ask your friends to keep an eye out, ask other members of your family to notice any change of behavior. But that's only the beginning. If you ascertain that your kid is running around with some dopetakers, or you know he buys dope from a pusher, or that your kid is actually using dope, this is only step one. What you do about getting your kid off the dope is a whole other problem. But at least you're on your way since you've admitted to yourself that you know the truth. You weren't ashamed of finding out about it. Just remember, there's not a single person in this country who doesn't have somebody in the family with an addiction problem. You just have to face it. Everybody wants his kid to be perfect. Well the kid isn't perfect and neither are you.

On any ordinary day, when I suddenly see a kid go by, it sometimes takes me back. If you've ever lost a kid, it's grief. I have to keep in mind that for thirty-two years of his life he was so much fun. He gave me so much pleasure. Anything I asked him to do he would do, and he would always do it well, whether it was managing a restaurant or being an actor in a series, he worked on it and made himself very good at it. What could be more pleasing to a father? And he was able to kid me along, to make fun of me, to get me laughing at myself, and to make fun of himself too. He was just a wonderful kid who gave me years of fun and pleasure. It is very painful to think of him as gone. But I try to always think of who he was. I'll see some character on the street, some character that he used to imitate, and I have to laugh. He was a wonderful mimic of accents. Sometimes when I hear an accent that reminds me of Hugh, I laugh! Or I'll see some lanky kid running along the beach and I'll remember how Hugh was such a runner! And that gives me pleasure.

We have many pictures from the time he was little. I have some very poignant pictures of him holding his own baby boy not long before he shot himself. Now, to anybody out there who is saying I'll never be able to look at another picture, don't worry about it. You will. Eventually, you can stand to have those pictures around and you can look at them and take some joy and pleasure from them.

It took a couple of years for me to be able to do this, but I now carry him with me all the time. He lives on in my conscious, and it's a very merry place where I recall only the fun. It doesn't mean that I have forgotten the terrible tragedy of the end, but I just don't think about that as much.

Also, I think faith helps you get to that frame of mind. I strongly recommend a little faith. My wife Nancy and I are Catholic. We go to church every Sunday, and follow all the rites of the Roman Catholic church. I find these rites are very comforting! They tell me that this passage through this veil of tears is not the end for the soul. The soul lives on—in what form I'm not quite sure, but it does so in a cogent, intellectual way. There's a spiritual life stronger than this material, corporeal life. Nancy and I believe that. We believe it because it's true—absolutely true!

There are five stages of grieving that reflect precisely the five stages of death. And not one of them is pleasant. The first is denial: This isn't really happening. It wasn't his fault. I was powerful enough to stop it.

Then rage sets in. O'Connor did what every human is hard-wired to do. He got mad. He publicly called Hugh's dope-dealer an accomplice to murder with a nasty public court battle ensuing. The judge came down on O'Connor's side.

The third stage of grief is bargaining. Engaging in a private tug-of-war with God. It can often lead to the next stage, depression.

Depression is a self-perpetuating habit that's hard to break, especially if you isolate. By isolating, you may not become aware that you do always have choices. And these choices have a lot to do with how you spend your time while you are hurting. Finding things to be grateful for can be a big first step. Writing them down makes them concrete. It may be something as small as indoor plumbing, but eventually, it will lead you to the final stage—acceptance.

Acceptance of death means the embracing of life. Yes, it is a long process, but as is said, time just takes time. O'Connor and his wife Nancy took this time, and they got through it.

CHAPTER 19

JUDY COLLINS

You can know a lot of things yet fail to connect them. You can sustain a boxing ring's worth of emotional and spiritual body blows and fail to see the pattern in them. But when you write them down, when you see them on paper or in the blue glow of a computer screen, you can often see clearly stitched together what your heart has hidden from view.

Judy Collins wrote the score to our lives in the Sixties, giving voice to a young and hopeful generation for whom joy and peace and love were ideals as easily grasped as the air that Collins graced with her crystal soprano.

Judy is the firstborn of five children. Her dad, Charles Collins, was no slouch as a musician in his own right, as well as a radio personality in what were then the wilds of Seattle. Charles Collins was also blind. He had been that way since the age of four. His personality was such that he was positively mule-headed in trying to prevent people from knowing his affliction. Charles Collins also suffered in other ways, from depression as well as alcoholism.

The sins of the father did not leave his daughter untouched. Judy also has battled alcoholism and depression. And her only child valiantly fought the same fight, but in the end did not win.

Judy Collins is a writer as well as a survivor. In addition to the song catalog she's been compiling for four decades, she's written four books. Singing Lessons, *published in 1992, is probably the most poignant. It is a meditation on the death of her child, but it is also about the constant renewal of life. As she turns sixty, you can see in the flame of her blue eyes peering from a still-porcelain complexion that she looks at life from both sides now.*

My son was thirty-three when he died. It was terrible. It was unacceptable. It was devastating. But I knew I had to get through it somehow. And so *Singing Lessons* is the story of how I did get through it, or really how I am still getting through it.

I wrote about some very difficult things. I thought I would start by writing about loss, but when I was in that process, I came to realize that I also had to write about gratitude and about joy. I had to write about the things that also came with this terrible tragedy. I had to write about the solutions and the strategies, and all the things that have helped me stay on my course.

It's almost as if her course were predestined. Judy said that she was always terrified of disappointing her father—not out of fear of him, but out of love for a man who'd already suffered too much. She said that her father's greatest gift was that he believed in her. And he also taught her something it takes most of us decades to learn: imperfection is human.

My father was a marvelous man. I think my work, my singing, my writing, is very much a reflection of his model. He had a beautiful baritone voice, and he'd sing a lot. While he was shaving, I'd hear "Grab your coat and get your hat, leave your worries on the doorstep." He'd wash his face and then I'd hear, "Oh Danny boy, the pipes, the pipes are calling." I was mesmerized by this voice!

At fourteen years old, Judy was a musical prodigy, excelling at piano. She studied under the tutelage of the great Antonia Brico, one of the first women to have a successful conducting career in classical music. That pleased Judy's father. It pleased him so much that he encouraged her to play a song on his radio show. She balked. He pushed. She objected. He pushed harder. She was desperate to please him, and the prospect of a simple piano recital led to an extreme cry for help.

He wanted me to play a piece by Paganini. I was listening to something by Paganini that was very slow and drifty today and I thought, Gee, if I had had that piece instead of the one that I got, which was "La Campanella," things might have been very different. "La Campanella" was filled with all these very challenging runs. I had it memorized, but I didn't have it up to speed. And he was a perfectionist—as I am, I'm afraid. He wanted me to play it, and I was caught. I was trapped. I was also just fourteen. In order to escape, I took a hundred aspirin. I felt I couldn't get out of it and there was nothing I could do. So I tried to kill myself. That was a very big sign that I needed a lot of help.

The very next year, Judy Collins found her help in a bottle. At fifteen years old, working with Antonia Brico, her stakes were getting higher. Even her driving superego was no match for the Rach 2 (Rachmaninoff's second piano concerto). It is a work that can crush the greatest of pianists. Staring down the barrel of that performance, she started to drink.

I hadn't started to drink when I made the first (and only) attempt on my life. All adolescents have issues, but probably more so when they grow up in alcoholic households. In my mind at that time, I felt that I had somehow caused it. So I started drinking when I was only fifteen years old.

That was the year Judy met the man who would become her first husband, Peter Taylor. By then she'd cashed in her concert career to become a folkie. By the time she was nineteen, she was pregnant.

I was pregnant, and then married. That's what you did back then in those circumstances. I was nineteen, and at the time I did not have any professional desires. My husband had a job delivering newspapers in the middle of the night. After my son Clark was only a couple months old and we were barely getting by, my husband said, "Why don't you quit that job at the University of Colorado filing papers in the administration office, and get a job doing something you know how to do?"

Believe it or not, his statement was a total revelation to me. I thought Peter was brilliant! So I got a job in a wonderful club called Michael's Pub in Boulder. I started to sing at clubs, and Peter took care of Clark. For the time it was a very advanced marriage in many ways because he was a house-husband and a student, while I was working at night. I'd be with my son during the day, but soon I had a wonderful burgeoning career. Of course, I thought I could do it all.

Judy was a member of the first wave of women to chase that promise. We now know that the ideal of doing it all—having it all—just doesn't work. Judy, like many of us, wasn't aware that we could have what we wanted but not necessarily all that we wanted. We'd have to make hard choices. But that phrase couldn't fit on a bumper sticker. Not catchy enough for a soundbite. And too much of a mouthful to chant at a rally. Peter got a teaching job in Connecticut and moved the family East. While he was home with the baby, Judy was ping-ponging through the clubs in Greenwich Village, playing gigs and trying to make it. The travel, separation, and lonely nights on the road when alcohol was her only constant, took their grim toll. In 1962, as she reached the top with a debut at Carnegie Hall, she separated from her husband. And lost her son.

I lost custody of Clark, which was the most painful. Thank goodness I'd been in therapy for a couple of years already in New York. When I came to New York, I knew that there was something wrong, and I'd better deal with it. My struggle with depression had started very early, and it wasn't getting any better. How did I cope? I didn't a lot of the time. I'd fall apart and then get it back together. I wrote a lot. And I worked. And I sang. At one point I was supposed to have a wonderful trip to the Soviet Union to entertain. I remember saying to my manager, Harold Leventhoid, "I'm going to cancel it." He said, "You can't do that." My natural impulse is always to cancel and bail out, and it was really amazing that up until that time I hadn't actually done that. Harold said, "Well, you can't do that. You're going to let people down. You'll let yourself down." So I called my mom and said, "I have to go to the Soviet Union and Poland for some concerts this summer. Would you let my sister Holly come with me?" She was eleven years old at the time and my beloved. My mother did allow her to come with me, and it was great. Holly saved my sanity that time.

However, I still struggled. I felt that I was "out there" someplace and was always trying to get back in. It's a feeling I've had all my life. When I was a kid, I sang in all the choirs at church. I was not a Catholic, but I remember one time when I tried to confess to a priest. He said he wouldn't listen because I wasn't Catholic. But I was very much a searcher and living with music.

Music is a whole other dimension. So when you're involved with music and art, you're always living in some other place. You're not really on the planet all the time. So I was very accustomed to a more multidimensional life than the material world. I went to see the Maharishi. I went to see Krishnamurti. I would read his book, go to yoga classes, and go to church. I was always looking. My great teacher Dr. Brico had been a devotee of Krishna Yogananda, which I didn't find out until I was much older. But on my own I began to follow an Eastern tradition of meditation. I've done that for a long time now, and that seems to be the right thing for me. I believe it's all different for everybody, and I think there's no one or right or correct way. As long as you know you're not alone.

By 1968, Clark was living with his father in Vancouver. He was already exhibiting signs that there was a problem. He was having trouble in school. He was hyperactive. He became too much for his father to handle. Peter Taylor called Judy and said, "He's yours. See what you can do." So Judy got her son back. He was ten years old at the time and he was already drinking.

It was interesting. Clark said, "I guess you know." And I said, "No, I didn't know it." Later on, I found out that Peter told him, "It's either your mother or military school." At first we were very happy to be together, and that was what I'd been planning for and hoping for, for many years. Things went fine for a while, but not for very long. There were hyperactive issues. Now I realize what happened was going on because at the time Clark was well into substance abuse and drinking. He was very young, and at that point nobody spotted it.

Judy's career and her continuing bouts with alcohol limited what she could do as a mother. For a decade, she and Clark battled the twin family scourges of alcoholism and depression together. She calls them "The Black Dog."

And of course, you have to look at it this way. Some people have cancer in their families, some people have heart disease in their families. You have to be very pragmatic about your own issues. I look at my family history and say, "Well, I've got this and this and this so I better deal with it." For me it means structure—know what to eat, the way I need to exercise, what kinds of things I can take in to my body without doing any more harm to my body. It's pragmatic and for me it makes sense.

In 1978, as Judy was entering rehab, she met Louis Nelson. She credits his support then and now with helping her to maintain a strong sobriety and healthy recovery. In 1978, Judy Collins began to get well. Five years later Clark began to get well too. After a few halting attempts at rehab, he got sober. He married. He had a baby girl. But addiction is a patient enemy that progresses even when it's dormant. It has been described as a baby tiger in your womb. As long as it's not fed alcohol or drugs, it will sleep. But it will continue to grow. Once awakened, it is a full-grown tiger. The Black Dog was still at Clark's heels. After nearly eight years of sobriety, he went back out in 1991 and started using again. He made a halfhearted attempt at suicide. Then on a quiet January day in 1992, he went into the garage, closed the door, turned on the ignition, and inhaled the last killer drug of his life—carbon monoxide.

Sometimes I'm still very surprised when I hear it. It's like news that is always new. But one of the things that helped me get through this tragedy was that I got a call from a friend who is a survivor. She said, "There isn't a feeling of guilt in suicide, so forget it. If you want to take on guilt, that's your business. But there isn't any." I have found that that's very true. It's unfortunately one of those things that society has laid on the survivors. But it's not true. We can't run other people's lives. We can't make choices for adult people. There are so many times I wish that I could, but we just can't do that.

I do have one regret, which is that I didn't know enough about survival to realize that you have to break the taboo of not talking about suicide—to say, "I think we ought to talk about the fact that I attempted it, and that there's a grandfather on your father's side who also attempted it, and that suicide shouldn't be such a secret." But in retrospect, I tried desperately to do everything I could for my son. And though after he died all I wanted was to get into bed and quit, I knew I had to go on with my life. I had to get out of bed, start breathing, eat three meals a day, go to therapy. And I did. I went to individual counseling. I went to survivor groups. I learned something significant there. I found that most survivors suffer from this terrible burden of guilt—this crippling, terrible guilt. And this guilt causes them to keep the secret. They all say at first, I don't want to talk about it. I don't want to deal with it. This is a poisonous part of my life.

But we have to make people understand that they need to talk about it. There were lots of people who said, "Go on and live your life." I really wanted to cancel my concerts for the first few months after Clark died. Joan Rivers said, "You can't cancel your life. Your life is the way you heal and the way other people will heal. By seeing you and by hearing your music." Then of course, the music did begin to heal me. I know now that she was right. You have to find whatever it is you like to do and then do it. I had to do the thing where I had the power to be the most creative. Sometimes, for me though, it was as small as just petting my animals, or calling my best friends, or just showing up for a lunch date. It's hard to do. Other times you just have to sit and cry. There's no two ways about it.

And sometimes there's nothing you can explain. There's nothing you can explain. I wasn't explaining myself, there's nothing to explain. I also did a lot of talking about my feelings, about my fears, about my anxieties, about my absolute devastation over losing this extraordinary person in my life. Clark was extraordinary. Sometimes he would show up in my dreams and he would say things like, "Mom, this is not such a big deal." Or he would say, "You know, death is not the ending." Those were the kinds of messages I received from out there. I happen to believe in "out there." However, I also believe in "in here." So I listened to what was being said in my dreams, and I wrote down my dreams.

I don't think it's the end. I certainly have a wonderful relationship with my son. I've had such insights and such joy in these years because of what he's left behind and what he's said to me.

I took the time, in terms of my friends, to be with and talk to them. I used to hate it when people would say, "Oh, get over it, you know? It's enough talking about it, it's a year already. You should be through with that!" Well, as far as I'm concerned, grieving is on its own timetable. I'm grieving as fast as I can. And in the way that I can. It's tough to have to get out of bed every day, but you must. You must get dressed, brush your teeth, and call a friend. I believe that setting goals for yourself is a very important step in the healing process.

In fact, during this time, I set many goals for myself. I used to wake up and say things like I'm going to get this song written today. I'm going to go to the hairdresser's today. I'm going to go see my friend. I'm going to read a book. I'm going to do some writing.

I began to write about my life. I was struck by what came out on the page. I not only wrote about grief, but I wrote about joy and about experiences, and about getting married, and about going to Bosnia, and about my singing lessons. I wrote about my treasured experiences.

They say that you have to be careful when you get rid of your demons, because your demons can lead you to an inspiration. They say even the devil works for God. You go through some very dark times in life. We all do. I'm not sure we were put here to avoid those dark times. There is no perfect situation, but most of what happens in life is usable in some way. It's useful and it leads you to the center. And then, when you come through the journey of the prayer, you wind up saying, "Thank you God for giving me this, because I've learned so much."

I am very grateful for where I am today. I drank for twenty-three years. Fortunately for me, in spite of that, I managed to accomplish a tremendous amount. I had good training and I had very, very deep goals. I have been able to confront my fears and express my hopes; I feel very lucky. It's a glorious thing, to be able to be alive, and to have survived this.

CHAPTER 20

DINA MERRILL

You can't guess the mettle of a human being, and you can't predict how it will be tested. We lower-crust mortals tend to imagine a shallowness in those who've been raised in privilege. Often, we're wrong. Imperially slim, impossibly beautiful, with a sweetness and grace that belies an incredibly strong will, Dina Merrill is purebred American royalty; but no princess she. The daughter of E.F. Hutton and Marjorie Merriweather Post was not reared to preen her way through life dispensing noblesse oblige at whim. Decades before the women's movement had opened a single door to power, Dina Merrill was tutored to govern. Her father envisioned a law degree, even Congress for his daughter. She followed his path, until she decided to follow her own. When she dropped out of George Washington University to enroll in the American Academy of Dramatic Arts, her father feared she had become a fallen woman. No one so well-bred would be caught cavorting on the stage. Heaven forfend! Dina Merrill brought her aristocratic bearing to twenty-two feature films, more than a hundred television programs, and countless Broadway performances before she started running the show. Now, as vice-chair of RKO Pictures, she and her husband are working to bring back the glory days of the movie studio that was home to Orson Welles, Cary Grant and Katharine Hepburn, and Fred Astaire and Ginger Rogers.

Hers seems an unlikely path for a thoroughbred to take, until you get to know her. She has devoted her offscreen life to a myriad of charities dedicated to lifting people from poverty, ignorance, and disease. But she is first and foremost a mother. A mother whose son fended the physical and emotional sucker punches of juvenile diabetes—and lost his life.

Juvenile diabetes is a terrible disease. The minute they're diagnosed, it's twenty years off the back end. For a teenager to realize his mortality at a very young age is a scary thing. In talking to doctors I found that other kids are the same way, they try to pack so much living into what they have. And they do too much too fast too soon. In my son's case, that's what killed him.

It was a motorboat accident. He had a boat and he souped up the engines beyond their capacity. The manufacturer even told him that, but he didn't care. We live on Long Island and he'd taken it across the Sound with a friend to visit some friends on the Connecticut side. But the engine broke down in Providence. Later he had to go over to pick it up, and he took his best friend with him. The two of them came back across the Sound, and Jonathan, his friend, later told me that they came back very slowly because it was rough and they didn't want to push it. It was still a hard, bumpy, tough ride. When they got into Three Mile Harbor in Long Island, there was no wind at all, and the water was like a mirror. It was absolutely flat. My son Dave looked over at Jonathan and grinned. He hit the throttle. At that moment, the shearing pin broke between the two propellers, and the boat flipped over on the driver's side. Dave was hit by the steering wheel and he was forced down into the water. Jonathan was thrown out of the boat and was knocked out by the force of it. He became conscious underwater, and he kicked his way up to the surface. He found one of the cushions floating around and used it as a life preserver. Meanwhile, the boat was just going round and round. Someone from the shore saw this and knew something had happened. He came out and picked up Jonathan, but they never could find David. In the end it was five days before they found his body. It was, needless to say, a horrible experience. Since I had other children, I felt that I had to be strong for them, even though I was deeply wounded by this loss.

At the same time all of this was happening, my mom was also quite ill. We knew she wasn't going to last too long. I remember telling Heather, my youngest daughter who was very little at that time, that her grandmother was very ill and might pass away soon and go to heaven. She said, "I guess you'll be next, Mom."

I said, "Well, in a while, I guess so." She said, "What are you going to do up there?" I said, "I don't know. Play a lot of golf and tennis or whatever." She said, "Play tennis with Jesus. I bet he's very good."

It turned out that Mom died before we found David's body. It was four days after his death and we all had to go down to Washington. I remember the night my mother died, Heather had been sleeping on pillows in between our beds because there wasn't another room. Mom died about three o'clock in the morning, and I came back to bed. In the morning Heather woke me and said, "Mom, time for breakfast." And I said, "Sweetheart, go on down and get your own breakfast. Mommy's got to go back to sleep again because Grandma died last night." Heather said, "Oh. Oh. Well, then I guess she'll see David." And I said, "Yes, I guess she will." She said, "That's good." And off she ran, happy at that moment knowing that her grandmother and her brother were going to be together.

Even though she was only four, she and David were very close. Dave used to put her on his shoulders and say, "It's not your kid, Mom, it's mine. I'm taking her home." They were so cute together and he took so many photographs of her that I still have—beautiful ones when she was a little girl.

To complicate matters even further, it was Heather's fifth birthday. All of David's friends had been gathering at our house and we were all looking, trying to find him. Maybe David had gotten some help by some miracle, or by some miracle swum to shore someplace. And here in the middle of all this was Heather, who deserved to have her birthday party even though she knew in her heart that David was gone. We didn't know then that he was dead, and we were still hoping to find him. All the kids rallied around and said, "Okay, we're going to have to smile and have balloons and cheer for Heather." And that's what we all did. That kind of made us smile, made us kind of make an effort to get out of it a little bit. Later on, his friends said that the biggest help in getting over all of this was Heather, because you had to smile around this little girl.

Of course Heather went to the funeral with us. Her father really didn't want her to go, but I had read a book that a woman doctor had written about yearning in families, and how young children who lose parents or siblings, if they're not allowed to mourn with the family, take this thing inside them and feel that it's their fault that the person died. So since I certainly didn't want this to happen to Heather, we brought her to the funeral. The poor little thing didn't really understand. There we were, all of us in tears, and it was all very solemn. And this little face looked up at me. She was trying hard to squeeze a tear out and couldn't quite make it happen. But at least she was made to be part of whatever went on, and I don't think she ever felt that she had anything to do with Dave's death. My husband told me, interestingly enough, that his father died when he was just four. His mother told him that his father had gone away and she never told him where or when he was coming back. He couldn't understand why all these women were hanging around in black dresses, patting him on the head. Here he was, this little four year old, and he couldn't understand it. It was a good several years before his mother told him that his father was dead. In the meantime, he did feel that in some way he'd chased his father away—that he was guilty of loving his mother too much and that was what caused his father to leave. So I do think there is a lot of help in allowing children to mourn. The mourning process is a way of getting through the pain and the anguish, and letting the love and the memories and the humor take over again.

A lot of people wrote to me—people I didn't know. Just people who'd read about this in the press. Many of them had had the same situation happen to them. They'd write, "I can't talk about it. My life is falling apart. I don't see my friends anymore." And, "How do you deal with it? What do you do?" So I would share with them what I had learned. It helped me enormously to get it all out, to talk to people about Dave, and to be able to think about the wonderful memories I had of him. We had great fun times together. He was a rascal sometimes, and I'd laugh about it. It did make me feel better to think about these times and have those memories come back into your mind and into your heart.

I always thought that when a person dies suddenly there may be many strings left untied. If there is a way to contact that person, perhaps you could make him or her feel more comfortable if you could tie up some of those loose ends. So about a year after David died, I was put in contact with a parapsychologist called Dr. Vincent Ragon through a friend who was very impressed with him. When I went to see him the first time, I used my married name, not my professional name, and I was late getting there due to a snowstorm. When I finally got there, he said, "Mrs. Robertson, while I was waiting for you there was an old woman who kept tapping. I think it was with her cane. Could it be your mother?" And I said, "Well, it might be." My mother didn't have a cane but she did used to rap on the table when she wanted to get our attention. And he said, "Yes, I think that was her." But I said, "Dr. Ragon, I didn't come here to get in touch with my mother. I came to get in touch with my son." He closed his eyes for a moment, then he said, "You'll get in touch with your son through your mother. She has him in hand." That just cheered my heart because that was the reaffirmation of exactly what Heather had said—that Grandma and David had found one another.

I had brought along pictures of my other children for him to look at. He put his hand on each of the photographs and said, "Well, I have to tell you something that you're not going to ask me. Your children are safe. You're not going to lose any more children." When he put his hand on Heather's photo, he said, "Oh, this is a very old soul. She has been here many times before and she's going to help a lot of people." I thought that was one of the loveliest things I'd ever heard. And through all her life, Heather has been a very kind and helping person. All through school, she would go to the child that was in trouble and try to help her or him. I love her. I love them all.

Ten years passed. I called Dr. Ragon to see if he could help a friend of mine who had multiple sclerosis. Dr. Ragon had told me that he'd had some success in treating patients with "laying on of hands." So I thought maybe he could do something for her. When we spoke however, he said, "I haven't seen you in ten years. How is everything?" I said, "Fine." He said, "Is there anything you'd like to know?" I said, "Yes, how's my boy doing up there?" And he said, "He's doing fine. He's found your brother." I said, "I don't have a brother." He said, "Just think about it a while."

I did have a half-brother who was killed seven years before I was born. I'd never known him, and in fact, I'd really never thought of him as my brother. There was no way that Dr. Ragon could possibly have known about that. When I realized who he must have been referring to, I said, "Oh." And he said, "Exactly. He died a little bit younger than your boy did, so they found each other." I just think this is incredible. I do believe we go to another existence and there are souls. I don't know what this other existence is, but it's comforting to know that perhaps people do get together in whatever life there is, waiting for us. I like to believe that when I go someday, I'll find my boy, and the brother that I never knew. I'll be with my dad and my mom again. And it makes me happy in my heart to believe that.

CHAPTER 21

RICKY SCAGGS

Ricky Scaggs cradled a mandolin like a baby in his arms, and during our entire conversation, he never put it down. Its owner had died the very year Scaggs was born, 1953. It was shut up in a gun case and went untouched for forty-three long, dusty years, prevented from making the music it was created for. Then Ricky rescued it and made it sing again. Sounds like the story line to a country ballad, don't it? And no one could have sung it sweeter.

Ricky Scaggs, the tenor from Tennessee, did more than anyone in two decades to rescue country music from the ravages of amped-up rock and bring it back to its roots. His backwoods sound is unapologetically Appalachian, and without his fealty to it, George Strait, Reba McEntire, and the Judds may never have prospered with their mountain harmonies.

Ricky Skaggs was picking and singing when he was five at churches, schools, and pie suppers. In his twenties he was transforming country music. In the Eighties, his records went gold and platinum. He racked up Grammys, and country music's top honors, and every accolade to which a singing, string-pickin' country boy might aspire. And he was the youngest person ever inducted into the Grand Ole Opry.

At the height of his popularity, he was brought face to face with mortality. It was 1986, long before anyone had coined the term drive-by shooting. Scaggs' wife Sharon and their seven-year-old son Andrew were passing a tractor-trailer rig on a darkened Virginia highway when the truck driver pulled out a gun and pumped a bullet into the Scaggs' car. Andrew was hit in the head. Scaggs raced to the Roanoke hospital where Andrew was being treated.

Andrew said these words, "Dad, we really need to forgive that man 'cause he don't know Jesus." It was like a dart. It was like an arrow that had been fired into my heart. I knew I had been smitten to the core. When you hear something so full of truth you have no comeback but, "Yes, that's it." I did have to forgive that man. However, it was very difficult because for a long while I wanted to hang the guy up by his thumbnails.

That would've been a good start. But I know from my own heart that Jesus said, "unless you forgive your brother, I can't forgive you. And my Father in Heaven will not forgive you if you don't forgive your brother." This man was obviously not my brother. That violent act was not the will of God. But we've got to forgive in order to be forgiven. I don't want sins held against me for not forgiving somebody else. When you hold hate, when you hold bad feelings or bitterness toward somebody, it holds those people in bondage, too. It absolutely holds those people down. They can't get free until you forgive them.

I asked the Lord one time, when is it okay not to forgive somebody? The Lord said, "Well, I can tell you one time that you cannot forgive: if that person has sinned against you more than you've sinned against me, then you don't have to forgive him." I am a sinner and I deserve to burn in hell.

That kind of pronouncement can be grating to people unaccustomed to evangelical Christianity. Zealotry tends to create more enemies than advocates, and anyone who preaches "one true route" can be a turn-off.

Scaggs is an evangelical Christian. On his tours, he increasingly promoted his beliefs. He has admitted that his zeal for promoting Christianity hurt his career. He's right, it did. The music stopped. It wasn't just that his music was ignored by DJs and music stores. It was. And in the process, he was virtually made a nonperson. One day he heard someone on the radio giving Randy Travis credit for what Scaggs, along with Emmylou Harris, Reba McEntire and George Strait, had created. By the end of the Eighties, Scaggs had fallen off the charts and found . . . peace.

When I was driven and worried about my next record doing well, I was a totally different person. I didn't like myself, and I didn't like the people I was dealing with. I was surrounded by people who didn't care about me. They were people that didn't want to have a relationship that went deeper than the skin. They were people who didn't want relationships that went into the heart.

I am a different person now. However, in order to become this person, I had to dig up my compulsion to succeed and tear it out by the roots. It was a difficult process because I was addicted to this business. This business is like a drug. You can literally be so hooked on this business that it's like you have to go to Betty Ford or somewhere like that to get detoxed out of this thing. I feel so much better inside now that it's gone. Now I try to surround myself with Godly people that I trust. And none of them are in the music business.

I was able to find the strength I needed to get out of this business through prayer. God speaks through me. I hear Him. I hear His voice in myself. If I can't hear him, He'll speak through my wife and my children in order to get His message across.

Record labels would tell you that my Christianity was the problem. However, I don't think that is true. Back in the Forties and Fifties, early Sixties, most country artists always did gospel albums. And bluegrass music was birthed out of gospel. I never really did do cheating-drinking songs, even when I wasn't as strong a Christian as I am now. I just figured I would be better at doing music that uplifted and encouraged people. That's what I've always tried to do; I've tried to find a subject matter that I felt proud of.

***

The perception was that Ricky Scaggs went on hiatus in the Nineties and took a few years off to be with Sharon and their four children. The reality is that he never stopped working. With a scaled-back band and scaled-down expectations, he rolled through every county fair and Christian festival from Tennessee to west Texas.

I've got two bands right now which is a great deal of fun. My country thing is still happening, playing country dates with a ten-piece band on the road. Then I've got a six-piece bluegrass band which grew out of the country band. All of the guys in the country band grew up playing bluegrass. And when I get back to what I grew up playing, talk about watching me smile. What I love in my heart more than anything musically is bluegrass music.

I've cut my schedule back. I'm working a lot in Nashville now, which is great, because that keeps me in town a lot more. People think you have a life when you're out there on the road, and you've got three-hundred-days-a-year sold-out shows. You have no life. What kind of a life is that? People read about the glitz and glamour in the magazines and think, Oh man, if I could just have that! And when I was out there, I was saying, Oh, man, if I could just be home. I'm glad of that because I'm getting to see my kids grow up. I'm getting to go to baseball games. I'm getting to go to my daughter's chorus and piano recitals.

We're doing well. I'm keeping my tithe paid, and that's the main thing for me. If I believe anything about the Bible, I have to know that God wants my money because He knows my money wants me. He doesn't need my money but He wants whatever I want more than Him.

No one's on top forever. It comes in cycles. Every now and then in life you see a Michael Jackson that kind of stays, to a point. Few people maintain a very high profile and are able to sell tickets and records. But by and large, there are not a lot of people that really are able to do that. One of the things that I've tried to do with my career is realize what success is, what really makes success happen. Any time someone gets credit for something that you did, you have to look at it and say, well, do I really want credit for that? Do I really want to stand up and fight for that? In my heart I know the truth.

A lot of people ask me about my Christian life. How can I be a Christian and play in country music? I say, well, wait a minute, how can Reggie White play football and be a Christian? There are no Christian football teams. There's no Christian NFL. There are Christians in the NFL. And there are Christians in country music. And there is Christian music. I feel like I'm supposed to do exactly what I'm doing. It's to be a Christian in this world and be a light and be a help and be someone to encourage—to be an example that it can be done.

Scaggs has done it, at a price. Sometimes, proclaiming to the world who you really are has a down side. But proclaiming it to yourself is essential. That's my "one true route": Know yourself.

CHAPTER 22

PATRICK DUFFY

He's a boy right out of the golden West. He grew up surrounded not by the golden garnish of Bob Mackie gowns and Kenneth Jay Lane faux jewels that decorated the decayed values of TV's Dallas, *but by the raw landscape of a tiny frontier town called Boulder, Montana. Still, Patrick Duffy's man-against-the-sky rugged individualism, and ultimately his salvation, came not out of the American West but from the mysticism of the East—a set of core values that snuck up on him over the course of falling in love, nurturing a marriage, raising two boys, and weathering all that humans fall prey to.*

We know Patrick Duffy best for his portrayal of the good brother Bobby Ewing in the television show Dallas. *Juxtaposed against his evil brother J.R., Bobby Ewing almost appeared to be an angel. As Duffy is quick to point out, however, humans are not wholly good or bad. They are a combination of both attributes.*

Duffy really sees the good and the bad coexisting in each of us. He sees the coordination of yin and yang that forges our decisions. This understanding of good and bad gave him the serenity to survive a real-life true-crime catastrophe. It gave him the tools to look at a wasteland and find acceptance, if not forgiveness.

In the middle of the night in 1986, as Duffy slept safely off the set of Dallas, *two young kids fueled by revenge and too much alcohol, swaggered into his parents' saloon and blew them away with a shotgun.*

The circumstances were bizarre at best. I didn't find out about it until the next morning. I remember the phone just kept ringing and ringing and ringing. I finally got the message. My parents were dead.

The director of *Dallas* at the time woke up to a newscast reporting the incident. "Patrick Duffy, Dead in Montana." He missed the first half of the broadcast which explained that my parents were dead, and as a result he thought I was dead. Needless to say, he totally flipped out.

The entire production company of *Dallas,* and Lorimar in general, were more than helpful to me. I remember the first phone call I received was from the president of Lorimar. He said, "Whatever you need, let us know. If you need to fly home, we'll give you the plane. We will do anything to help you out." They were so great. Almost instantaneously, they transported me from Los Angeles to Montana, which is no mean feat. They assigned a publicist to take care of all the media, because there was quite a lot of buzz about the incident. But we weren't really prepared for the amount of worldwide attention, which immediately overwhelmed my parents' little town of 600 people. It was bizarre to see people doing news reports in front of my parents' bar. It was a week of real adjustment time for everybody.

My parents owned a bar. My grandfather was in the bar business. My mother inherited the bar from him. Then my father took over. I grew up in a tavern basically, and formed a mentality that I would call a bar personality. For me, it has worked out well. When you grow up in a bar, you see all types of characters. Therefore, I believe that it has prepared me for any situation or character that crosses my path. I also think it is a benefit for young people to interact with adults, which is something I was fortunate enough to do from the time I can remember.

We moved to Seattle before I graduated from high school. My parents returned to Montana after I graduated from high school. However, they did not return to our bar, but instead went to another place. When they heard that the person that they'd rented the bar to wasn't taking care of it, they immediately returned and took over. Sadly, it was at that point that they were killed.

Two young kids killed my parents. My dad threw the drunk boys out of the bar for being rowdy and then resumed business. Just before closing time, the boys re-entered the bar and shot my parents. As fate would have it, after they shot them, they ran to the cash register and grabbed some money and a couple bottles of booze before trying to get away. Had they not committed the robbery, their punishment for the murders would have been less. They're both serving their time in prison, probably for the rest of their lives. Their lives and the lives of their families are ruined. It was such ridiculous and stupid behavior.

However, since I believe that good and evil exist in everyone, I guess I look at this incident differently than most. I can't understand the people who say, "I just don't understand how that could happen. I don't understand how that person could do it," because I look at that mentality as being extremely naïve. If I had just a moment with you and said, "Now, just let your mind go as bizarre as you want; I want you to think of the most dastardly deed you can," I believe that it would take you only fifteen seconds to conjure up some terrible thing. Therefore, to me there is no difference between you and the person who did the dastardly deed except for the fact that you didn't do it. The mechanics are there. You have the intelligence to figure out how to do it. So, what's the difference? The difference is you didn't do it. Good and bad are present in everyone, and it is up to you to decide what you are going to do.

It's not my job to forgive them. I still think what they did was wrong. I don't have to forgive them. I don't have to feel anything about them. The justice system worked. The tragedy is that everybody has a choice every time they do something. They made the wrong choice, and that choice affected my life, my sister's life, and everybody who knew my parents. However, it also affected their families' lives as well. I find the negativity generated from this act distressing.

They are being punished now for what they did, and I want them to continue to experience the judicial system's decision. Since they caused this to happen, they must deal with the effect of their actions. The cause and effect relationship is very strict, you know. I guess that's the tragedy of this entire situation. All it takes is one split second to make a decision. Had they not made that decision, the cause and effect relationship in their lives would be completely different.

When my parents died, I had been practicing Buddhism for

fifteen years. My belief in Buddhism has really helped me get through this tragedy. To me, Buddhism in a nutshell says that life is eternal. Life is comprised of a succession of dormant and manifest periods. Dormant. Manifest. Dormant. Manifest. The same life condition travels forever. Therefore, my parents are not dead to me. They are living their lives to the fullest in my heart.

However, I can't help feeling a bit guilty about their deaths. When my parents were alive, I was so busy living that I would let an enormous amount of time go by before I would communicate with them. I remember thinking, Oh yeah, Mom and Dad are in Montana. I should write them. But then six months would go by and I wouldn't have contacted them. Therefore, it is up to me now to make sure that their lives don't end up dormant in my heart.

I practice Buddhism in the morning and in the evening. Through my practice, I can communicate with my parents. In fact, there is not a day that goes by that I am not in communication with them. Now, I know this sounds crazy. I promise it is not. I should explain to you that I am not communicating with my parents in a conventional sense. I don't sit there and ask my dad how he is doing. Rather, I communicate with my parents by responding to part of their lives. I feel very good about my ability to communicate with them, and I believe this ability has really helped me with the tragedy of my parents' death.

I have been accused of being very cold and very unfeeling since I don't display the grief that other people think I should. However, what they don't understand is that my concept of life and death is not based on the general Judeo-Christian concept. I believe that I am not without my parents. Rather, I am with them now even more so than when they were alive.

When I was in college, my belief in Buddhism also came in handy. I was an actor in college. One day, I ruptured both of my vocal chords. When told that I would never speak normally again, I was devastated. How would I be able to act? I didn't know what to do, so I decided to turn to Buddhism. I began to whisper the practice of Buddhism to heal my throat, which really helped it.

Buddhism also plays a huge role in my relationship with my

wife. I was not always a devout Buddhist. In fact, the reason I became interested in Buddhism was because I had the hots for a woman who was a Buddhist. She told me that in the form of Buddhism she practiced, one would achieve whatever it was that they chanted for. I immediately began chanting for her. And I guess it worked because I've been married to that same girl for twenty-six years now.

When anyone asks me what the secret is of twenty-six years of marriage, I always reply that it is just complete acquiescence. If you have a problem and you assume that it is your problem, you can solve that problem. If you assume it's your wife's problem, you can't solve it. You can't change anything outside of yourself; you can only change what is inside you.

Now this does not mean that I don't get totally p.o.'d every now and then. What it does mean is that if my wife had a certain problem that was causing me distress, it is my distress that I need to address. If I change the fact that I'm distressed, I believe that my environment will change to reflect that.

It's very easy not to get upset on the freeway now. It's very easy to take direction from somebody at work. There are a lot of things that are a lot easier when you just assume complete responsibility for how you feel. It is easy.

I attribute Buddhism to making me feel better about myself. When my parents were murdered fifteen years after I began practicing my belief, I realized that subconsciously the inconspicuous benefit of practicing Buddhism was to truly understand the depths of my life. Through this experience, I have realized that life and death is a single thing to me, and this single thing is life.

I think the reason why Americans have a hard time understanding Buddhism is that they've been taught to be afraid of it. Buddhism is one religion that is not based on God. In fact, it has no God involved in it. So in essence, there's nobody to offend, nobody to wonder how you're feeling, no son of anybody. I think that's why most people are reticent to delve into it, because there are a lot of differences that make it difficult for people to accept.

If you want to put a personal aspect to Buddhism, then you

are a Buddha. That's different than saying you are God, or you have a God's nature or God's self. You are as good as it gets. You control everything, including the environment and the universe. Every individual does. By changing something in yourself, by virtue of your own volition, you change your environment. You are your own "governing spirit."

Buddhism has really helped me in my life. I do believe I am a better person today because of my belief.

CHAPTER 23

BONNIE FRANKLIN

Bonnie Franklin is a cross between your college roommate and your mom, with a face that simply sparkles and a demeanor to match. Her clothes are oversized and float around her frame. Her smile wiped the klieg lights out.

Bonnie is a believer, one of those people who does nothing unless she believes in it fully and can jump in up to her armpits. She has spent her life on too many airplanes, in too many bed-and-breakfasts, dazzling too few people with her acting ability in theaters around the nation. I wish everyone had the chance to see her strut her stuff. But for all the characters into which she's breathed life, the one she's most famous for is Mom. For years, we watched Bonnie Franklin take life One Day at a Time. *It was breakthrough television at the time because it had the temerity to actually reflect family life as it's lived on the ground—unvarnished.*

A show based on single motherhood was very reflective of the time. However, it was the first time that a show dealing with single motherhood was on television. The show touched many people's lives. People still come up to me and tell me how they grew up with our show. However, I was a make-believe mom. I was just an actress playing a mom on television. I had it easier than their mothers. I had writers creating stories for me, solving or not solving problems for me. And I had writers who would dictate my path through the stickiest of situations.

We were a very successful show. We were almost always in the top ten. I would receive fan letters that were forthcoming and very heartfelt. So I knew that we were striking some kind of chord with our audience.

The show taught me a lot of things. I was thirty-two when I began the show, and was playing the mother of two teenage girls. I was an actress from New York—not a writer, not a man, not a creator. Our first episode set up the storyline and then we did twelve other episodes that were really quite awful. I remember crying to Carroll O'Connor about the quality of our show. I wanted to make our show better, but I did not know how. He told me that I had to take the responsibility of the show on my shoulders, and if I didn't like what was going on, it was up to me to change it. So when CBS asked us to do shows fourteen and fifteen, I literally put my foot down. I said, "No, not unless it's about what the show's supposed to be about. Not unless these episodes are about divorce and about kids dealing with divorce—about all of those desires and wants and fears and insecurities that single parents and their children feel." I told them that they had to be shows about a woman trying to say, "We're going to try." The result was better than I could have imagined. Shows fourteen and fifteen were terrific, and it seemed we had found the right path for our show.

At the time, our show was radical. We dealt with a lot of important stuff. Norman Lear always said, "If you can entertain then you can deal with other issues, but our first job is to entertain." So we were able to make people laugh and still deal with teenage pregnancy, and epilepsy, and heart disease, and hearing loss—essentially things more important than "who will I go to the prom with?"

It is a delicious irony that Bonnie Franklin's offscreen experiences with the meaning of the word family are more fascinating than anything an army of writers could have dreamed up.

In the closing days of the century, she has an old-fashioned, dependable nuclear family, forty-strong, most of whom live in the immediate neighborhood. To hear her speak of it, her family life seems too idealized and too fragile to exist in today's world. She's one of five siblings, born to a dynamo of a mother who, approaching ninety, still jets around—far too busy to get old—and a father whose death from a stroke has given Bonnie new purpose.

I have a great family. I was fortunate enough to be able to tape a special called *Bonnie and the Franklins.* It was a tribute to my family. I have an extraordinary mother. My father died a year and a half ago, which is a story in and of itself, but he was remarkable. I have four siblings, who have their own children. I hear the stories from friends about the dysfunction in their families. I did not experience that. Rather, I guess the dysfunction my family had was reverse dysfunction. They were incredibly supportive, present, loving, and believed that I could do anything. I didn't realize how remarkable they were and are until I started living my life outside of my family. I realized that they are very special people!

We all live in California. Some of the grandkids are starting to make their way in the world, and some of them live in New York. But even when they go away they end up coming back. There's a real strong sense of family that's just important to us.

The miracle that made it happen was my mother. It was very important to my mother that her kids be very close. That was the focus in her life. She had a large family herself, and it was very important to her that she have a family that was close—who loved each other and cared about each other. As a result, her life was always about that. Some people may say, "I can't spend that much time with my family. I've seen enough of my sister today!" However, my mom made sure that those feelings were kept to a minimum.

Of course we had fights. We threw things and we yelled. There were times when we hollered, "I hate you! You're not my sister and I'm probably adopted!" But those feelings would soon pass. About fifteen years ago, my two sisters, my mother, and I were having a Mother's Day lunch. As we sat there that day, something happened. I have a very clear image of sitting there for hours. I don't know if it was timing or where we were in our lives, but we all called each other after our lunch and told one another how much we truly liked one another. A great bond was formed that particular day. We knew we could count on each other, and we knew we were there for each other. I don't know what it was, but it was as if there was something in the air that day that made us bond. I love my brothers, but my two sisters and I are really kind of neat ladies. We really like and respect each other. We admire what we've done with our lives and how we've brought up our children. We know that we can converse about our achievements and failures and that we care about what's happening in one another's lives. We understand how lucky we are to have one another, and we don't take our relationships for granted.

Just hearing her say that forced me to think about my own family of five siblings, an aging mother, and a dad who died too young. She's right. You don't take what they've given you for granted. Bonnie, like me, is part of the sandwich generation. What she learned in nursing her dad into death may give life to a lot of people she'll never know.

Dad had a major stroke in 1987, when he was eighty-four years old. He recovered magnificently due to his stubbornness and his determination. There was kind of a Harry Truman thing about my father; he was really stubborn about getting better. He always had a positive mental attitude, which, coupled with the support of the family, became essential to his recovery. I'm very grateful for that time with my dad because I got to really know my father. It was a gift to us that he allowed us to be there for him. It was wonderful. I found humor in my father that I never knew he had. In retrospect, no matter how difficult that time was, it was a great period in our lives.

During that period of time, I became very involved with stroke survivors and their families, and with the Stroke Association of Southern California. I say strongly to everybody and anybody who is reading this, pay really close attention to the warning signs and to the signs of a stroke itself, because there's new information, new techniques, and new treatments that can be life-saving. If you have a weakness on one side of your body or blurry vision, or a really bad headache, immediately get yourself, or have somebody get you to an emergency room. The first three hours are crucial. If it's hemorrhaging, there really is very little that can be done. But eighty percent of strokes are clots, and there is a new clot-busting drug called TPA, which has been used to treat heart disease for a long time and which can erase all the debilitating effects of stroke. So it's really important to know what the signs are, and to get to the hospital right away.

Stroke is really, really hard. It changes your life in a split second. It changes your life and everybody you know—your family and your loved ones and your friends—in a split second. That's how fast it happens. And you need to be aware of all of those symptoms that you're aware of for heart disease: high cholesterol, high blood pressure, diabetes, and weight, because all those things affect it. You need to pay attention. Sometimes you get little warnings. We tend to think it's nothing. Just pay attention because it's hard to come back, and if you can avoid it or if you can stop it in its tracks you're home free.

One of the most important campaigns we've launched with the Stroke Association is an education campaign. Stroke is the number-three cause of death in America. It's the number-one killer of African-American males and the number-one cause of adult disability. Twice as many women die of strokes as they do of breast cancer. So we want to make sure that the hospitals and their emergency staff deal with a brain attack as they do with a heart attack.

We're going out this year and making sure that every hospital has a team in the emergency room that knows the right questions to ask. But that is not enough. Families also need to know what to do. The families have to know the patient, because sometimes the patient will lose the ability to speak. So it's just terribly important.

The rehabilitation from a stroke is toughest depending on where the stroke hits.

When you're in the middle of it, you can't be objective about it. I would go to rehab classes and to occupational therapy classes with my father every week. The different manifestations of stroke went from something as small as a person's hand not working to the entire side of one's body being paralyzed. Speech might be fine, but the left side of the body is in trouble. You look perfectly okay, and yet there's something that's not computing.

In rehab, people like my darling father are made to get on the floor and have to learn how to get back up, because if they're alone and they fall, they have to figure out how to get themselves up again. So you see people really struggling. We don't realize how hard it is to push yourself over, to be able to get up on a knee, to be able to grab something, to crawl over to something, and to be able to hold on. These are people who have led very independent lives and now have to relearn how to do the simplest things, like sit up and shift your weight. It is hard, hard work. They are the most courageous people. And I admire the caregivers almost more than the stroke survivors because of the love and the support they give.

My mother's life changed in an instant. When my mother became the primary caregiver, she'd never balanced a checkbook. She had to take over the driving for a man who didn't want her to drive. I moved into that house when my dad had his stroke (I was lucky to be able to do that) and made my mother start driving again. I made my mother learn how to handle a checkbook, because I knew my dad was not going to be able to do it.

You must learn to change your expectations. You have to live for what you've got that day. And maybe it will get better. And maybe somebody's going to be able to walk without being in a wheelchair. But you have to live for right now. It's a huge lesson.

I was doing *Annie Get Your Gun* a year after my father's stroke, and he flew out to the East to see me in it. It was nighttime and his brain got tired and his body wasn't working well. It just threw me. I was having a very tough time. I was in tears when I talked to a fellow castmember whose grandmother had had a stroke. He said, "Bonnie, get rid of your expectations. You need to just get rid of them. You need to appreciate who and what he is now, not what you hope he's going to be a year from now." Talking to my friend changed a lot of things for me. It was a very good lesson.

I think what held us together and what made it work for us was the strength of the family. We just lucked out. Our strong kind of love and support had a great deal to do with my dad's recovery and the gift of having my dad around for nine more years. Mom always calls that time our bonus years. They really were bonus years. My dad went to plays that I was doing and attended bar mitzvahs and weddings and graduations. We had a wonderful time.

Nine years later, my father had another stroke. It left him nonverbal—unable to communicate, unable to do anything on his own. In my opinion, he shouldn't have lived that last nine months. It was very, very bad. I talked to God. I screamed at God, "This isn't fair, this should not be. Let him go. This is not good." On the day he died, I was out of town and my little sister was on one side of him and my mother was on the other side of him. He always had a lot of strength in the nonstroke side of his body, and he was holding my little sister very tightly, but he was really gone. He had been nonverbal for a long time and he was kind of in and out. The aide was in the room and they were saying all of those wonderful things, "We love you, always know that. Go with God." My dad opened his eyes and he said as clearly as could be [to my mother], "Always." That was his shorthand that he used all the time to tell her what he felt. "I love you with all my heart. Always." And then he died. Over and out. Talk about a gift!

My own father always said, if you can't accept and appreciate death, you can't really understand life. His cancer had progressed too quickly and he was in a hospice unit by the time we had all gathered to be with him. It was the longest day and night of my life. We spent it pulling up favorite events embedded in our family lore. We spent time talking about the difference between giving up and letting go. We had cake and ice cream to celebrate my little brother's birthday. And even though Dad was hooked up to life support, he ate some too. And then his breath rattled and he died. I whispered, This is so terrible. And my baby brother said, "No. You'll cherish this day for the rest of your life." He was right.

CHAPTER 24

CELESTE HOLM

It was one of those experiences so emblazoned in my brain that I remember what I was wearing. I was just eighteen, fresh out of high school, very serious about my grave responsibility as a cub reporter in Minneapolis, and utterly clueless. The very first real TV interview I ever did was a major disaster. The subject swept in, changed the entire lighting schematic and proceeded to castigate me for being ill-prepared, asking uninformed questions, and not listening to her answers. I finished the interview, ditched into the ladies' room, and burst into tears. It was the greatest professional gift I ever received. The great Celeste Holm had raised the bar. She wasn't being rude. She was right. And I never, ever went into an interview unprepared again.

She is very funny, and witheringly bright, and punctilious to a fault. The kind of dame that makes you pull your socks up if you want to match her stride. She actually is a dame, having been ceremoniously knighted by the king of Norway. She takes the subway, shops only at sales, and speaks her mind, for which she's been arrested by the mayor of New York. (She was demonstrating against the proposed demolition of classic Broadway theaters. The Mayor was Ed Koch. The theaters were razed.) And over six decades, she's been honored with Hollywood's highest awards. In spite of her stature as one of American theater's blue-bloods, she still relishes being crammed into a trailer with five other actors, a camera, and full crew to play the grandmother on the TV series Promised Land.

I can't imagine a family without grandparents and parents and grandchildren. It's very hard for me to understand that because my grandparents were so much a part of my daily life, and they were such a glorious part.

I had the most wonderful grandmother. How I adored her. She was so much fun. She had done everything. She'd never heard of women's lib, so of course nothing ever stopped her.

She was an orchestra conductor, and her husband edited a newspaper. He died when my mother was six months old. So my grandmother took over the newspaper. Nobody told her she couldn't, so she did. She also taught drama and English, which means that I am stuck with grammar that will not slip. Which means I'm on the script all the time.

When I was only two and a half, my grandmother, always my source of inspiration, took me to see Anna Pavlova. I didn't know I was going to see magic. But that day I saw a woman change a whole audience. Before it began, I looked at the people in the theater, and they didn't look anticipatory the way I was. I thought this was going to be wonderful. I knew it was wonderful because everything she ever took me to was wonderful. But I didn't know it was going to be magic. And then when the house lights came down and the curtain warmers came up and the curtain parted (I remember that particularly, you don't see that very often anymore), this magic began. Oh, the dancers were so beautiful. They were so strong and they were so sure of themselves.

Pavlova danced so easily that you wanted to be right up there with her. And then, when it was all over, the whole audience had changed. They suddenly on some level seemed to have been made to realize what a gift it was to be human. So I came home and flung myself to the table to the chair to the mantelpiece and said that was what I wanted to do for the rest of my life.

Nobody seemed surprised. My mother was a painter, and my grandmother had done everything. My father was a Norwegian. The reason I mention that is because coming from a climate of nine-month winters and three-months just plain cold, you've got to be interested in everything. And he was. But he was the only one who dared to suggest it might be difficult to be a great dancer. But I said, "It looks so easy." He said, "Exactly." That is true of every art. It has to look as if it sprang perfection at once.

When I was fifteen, my grandmother insisted that mother and I take this tour of Radio City Music Hall. We were led around there by this gorgeous young man. He was really quite something. Tall, dark, handsome, and wearing the most beautiful navy-blue suit with a lot of gold buttons, gold epaulettes on the shoulders, and white gloves. Those were the days of radio and so NBC was very tidy in those days, before television came in and just mussed it all up. We were shown where the Rockettes took their naps and ate their lunches and how they could turn the stage into ice in twenty minutes. Perfectly marvelous stuff, there's no doubt about it. And at the end of the tour, my grandmother, never shy, said, "Tell me, young man, you're not going to do this for the rest of your life, are you?" And he said, "Certainly not. I'm an actor." "Oh," she said, "I am so glad. You have just the right equipment. Now tell us your name so we can keep track of you." I didn't listen.

Two years later, I found myself on the back lot in Hollywood, being taken by Mr. Elia Kazan to meet my star. And he took me into Gregory Peck's dressing room. The first thing I said was, "Do you remember when my grandmother asked whether you were going to be a guide at Radio City for the rest of your life?"

The name of that production with Gregory Peck was Gentlemen's Agreement, *one of the groundbreaking postwar films on anti-Semitism. For which Miss Holm, at the age of eighteen, won an Oscar for best supporting actress.*

Zanuck was short and he wanted everybody to think he was tall. So he made wonderful pictures. He had the courage to make pictures that I think he wouldn't have done if he hadn't been short. But it worked. Because everybody respected him for his judgment. And he made this picture, even though Louis B. Mayer called up and said, "Don't do it, don't rock the boat. Please." But he did it.

And she did the film The Snake Pit, *another groundbreaker that for the first time exposed the widely accepted practice of treating barbarously the mentally ill. She wasn't cast for the film; she demanded to be in it. In fact, she volunteered to be the electric shock machine.*

I would be anything. I just wanted to be part of it because I thought it was so important. They used to control people institutionalized with mental illness with chains. It was inhuman. I thought it was important that people be made aware of this. And it was. It was a question of kindness. Another person is being treated inhumanly. Help them. That's all. You can. I just try to make people aware of the potential that is going to waste unless they are helped.

To that end, Celeste Holm works tirelessly with organizations that bring the arts to people with mental disabilities: Arts Horizons, which is an outgrowth of the Creative Arts Rehabilitation Center, and also the Festival of Music. Do you know that every time you ask her for an autograph, she charges you fifty cents and sends it to the United Nations Children's Fund, UNICEF? She can be tough when her motives are true.

Celeste has two children of her own, from two different marriages. She blew through a third and then met and married fellow actor Wesley Addy. That one had a staying power of thirty-six years. He died on New Years Eve, 1996.

When my husband died, he suddenly turned white right in front of me, and then he was gone. Gone. This was not real. This was not a man. A spirit that I'd been talking to and loving and laughing with all those years went away. One that I touched and felt and reacted to all the time isn't there. And that's what's so difficult. I was just so stunned by it all. Just wondering how to take my own next breath. Still, I can imagine how he would react. Often I feel that he would have loved being with me at such and such an occasion. Or I think, God, he'd have hated this.

I'm still not used to it. One time I was coming down the stairs, he was being interviewed in the living room. I heard somebody say, "How do you account for your great success in your marriage?" Suddenly I thought, maybe I shouldn't be hearing this. Then I heard my husband say, "We just belong together." I was the rib, I guess. Adam's rib.

It's very hard going on. I don't know how to describe it to people. I try to remember all the beautiful things that we shared and laughed at. That helps. Of course, work is a wonderful antidote. And the kids are lovely to me. Everybody is. They're so kind, they really are. But it's just not the same. I'm just lonely. They say you get over it. I wonder. But I try to behave the way he would want me to and do what I have to do. Laughing. Reading. Music. Crying.

I can laugh now. But there are many levels of one's being. You don't realize how many there are until you've lived a long time. You can be looking at something terribly funny, and at the same time you don't lose track of something else that is much deeper.

We all are spiritual, whether we're aware of it or not. Because all we are is spirit. What we regard as the most wonderful thing in life is the essence of God. That is the best that any of us can conceive of, that is in ourselves. The first word that comes to mind is kindness. I think that's essential. We all have it in ourselves if we look. We all have a concept of what we regard as wonderful. What happens every spring all around us reassures us of being part of some kind of rhythm. When artists put together something which expresses what seems wondrous to us, like the sense of the value of life in *The Lion King,* the sense of the harmony of those animals in the jungle, that's it. All of us are lifted up by this reassurance. That's what I wish for my grandchildren, the sense of wonder. The sense of the unexpected. To be ready for realization that can happen so unexpectedly at absolutely unforeseen moments and enjoy it. I think they're born with it. I don't think we have to give it to them.

Celeste Holm says the first time she knew she was at home on the stage was in a play called Papa's All *when she suddenly realized her toes were uncurled. She wasn't holding onto the stage with her toes.*

She says the only way you control an audience is by totally controlling yourself, as Pavlova did so many years ago. Celeste gave us her Pavlovian turn. But there's a lot that none of us, not even the greats, can control. They say it takes about two years to really be at home with the loss of a beloved spouse. And widowhood still appears to make her toes curl. Time just takes time.

CHAPTER 25

NEIL SIMON

He has packed more people into the theater than William Shakespeare (which is quite a feat considering that Bill had a head start). Playwright Neil Simon has never been very comfortable with his celebrity, even though he wears it well in public with a slightly bemused elegance. He keeps his private life inside his heart and allows only small well-considered parts of it to bleed into his work. Simon says he's always considered himself to be two people: the writer and the man. He says that there was one woman who knew them both. Her name was Joan. He saw her across the lawn at one of those resorts in the Catskills that were summer hot spots for New York singles trying to escape the asphalt of New York. It was love at first sight. She was engaged to be married, and Neil's heart was broken. But he held onto the memory of her, and the following summer, she was there again. Unengaged.

They married and had two beautiful daughters and started living the life struggling playwrights write about. It was a life built on absolute honesty and absolute trust. He allowed her inside his soul and she may have been the only woman who really knew him completely. She was the genuine certified love of his life. Joan Simon singularly informed Neil Simon's writing. It was when he lost her that he learned she still informs his life. Maybe that kind of major league love gives one a sense of immortality. Maybe that explains the eternal quality of his work.

~~~~~~~~~~~~~~~~~~~~~~~~~~

I don't think you can write a play without starting it with anger, because all plays, comedies as well, are about conflict. Sometimes you think that the subject matter of the play is something that you've just arbitrarily picked to write about because it's a
~~~~~~~~~~~~~~~~~~~~~~~~~~

good idea. But if you start to search inside yourself, it's your rebellion against something that you don't believe in, that you think is wrong, even if it's marriage. It's not that I don't believe in marriage. I know that all marriages have their problems, but the audience will leave after five minutes if you write a play about a marriage that's perfectly happy.

There aren't many. But there are some that are happier than most, and those are the fortunate people in life. I did have that primarily with Joan for nineteen years before she died. It sort of spoiled me for anything else that came along in my life, but I don't want to idealize it and say it was the perfect marriage. We fought all the time because she was so interesting, there were great things that she wanted to fight about. She wanted to push me into certain areas. Not about the writing, only about the living. She would say to me, "Let's live in England for a year." And I'd say, "I can't, I have work to do." She would say, "You can do it there." So we did. And then we did it in Italy, and then we did it in Spain. They were the best years I've ever had. I needed someone to do that for me, for my life, to push me, because I was so busy doing the other stuff.

We would have dinner, and then I would go upstairs. We had a little townhouse and I'd go up to the second floor, where my office was. She was doing something else and I was looking over the pages I wrote. I'd pick up a pen and I'd cross something out. Then I'd sit down, and I would write another thing, and she would say, "Neil, the day is over. We don't do writing now." She'd pull me away from the writing, which is exactly what I really needed, and then we had a life.

The two of us to went down to San Antonio to play in John Newcombe's tennis ranch (John Newcombe, a few-time Wimbledon winner and U.S. Open winner). And he said, "Joan, I don't like the way you're limping there, so you better go see a doctor." We did the day afterwards and they took an X-ray. They saw a tumor there. They were going to do a biopsy, and when they took her upstairs they found out that it had already metastasized. It was in the breast, which was where it probably originated. But he told me exactly how long she would live, which would be a year and a half; and that's how long she lived.

The worst moment always is when you hear it. You can't say to the doctor, "No, you're wrong. You have to check this over. You're wrong." He took me into the worst possible place in Lennox Hill Hospital, which were the back steps, the steel steps. I thought if he's taking me here, this isn't good news. And he said, "It's metastasized. She's got a year, a year and a half," he says, "and that's it. There's no way to save it." And the minute he said that, I felt that I was falling into a well, and trying to grab the sides, but I just kept falling and falling and falling, and waiting to hit the bottom. You don't really hit the bottom.

Then, it was the dealing with Joan herself. Joan never mentioned it. The doctor told her on that day that she had the cancer, but they got it and it was going to be all right. I think it was proper in those days. I don't even know what it's like now, because I wouldn't like to know what it's like now. But he said to me, she will discuss it with you when she's ready. She never did. In the year and a half, she never said, "I have cancer and I'm dying." Never.

She knew. I knew she knew. Especially when it went into remission, because the radiation stopped it, and we were playing tennis again that summer, and I thought we were free, and then it started to come back. I knew she was going to go, but I never knew when. You hear of people living years and years, but the year-and-a-half prediction was an accurate one. And it turned out to be a strange kind of nightmare. Most nightmares are the terrible things you dream. My nightmare was everything was wonderful. Joan was well, we were doing everything we wanted. And then I woke up in the morning and looked and said, "No, she's going to die." So it's a reverse kind of torture in a way. But her own bravery and courage and ability to keep things as normal as she possibly could, especially for the girls, was astounding. The girls never knew. I made a decision not to tell them because I didn't want to disrupt anything in Joan's life, or I was still guessing maybe she was going to be all right. So I waited until almost the last possible minute. I spoke first to Ellen, and then to Nancy, who's younger, and told them both. I said, "Mom is not going to live." And they knew it. I didn't have to tell them. They said, "We know, we know." But they didn't know that it would be that quickly.

I did something after Joan died, because when Joan was ill, I needed something to turn to. Not someone, something. I was not religious in my own religion. There was no place I could go to talk. I didn't want to talk to an analyst, so I decided to talk to Joan. I had a picture of her that I put on a desk, and I sort of sat in a comfortable place, turned out the lights, put on two candles, and talked to her at night. A lot of people, I've learned, do this, sometimes. And you think that you are making contact with someone in another place, in heaven, or whatever you choose. That wasn't it at all. I was talking to myself, through Joan, who was filtering the unnecessary things in my life, and telling me what to do. I knew I was telling it myself, but I needed her to go through it. Her. She was so honest. That was her greatest attribute. She would always tell me the truth, so I couldn't come up with a lying answer. If I'd say, "If I do this, I could really have a better time doing it," in a sense, she would be saying, "No, that's not the right way you should go." But it's me saying it to myself. Because I knew that's how she would probably answer. So when I thought about the question of how do I become a mother and a father to these girls, I woke up in the morning, and the answer was there. You don't become a mother, you just become a really good father.

I wrote a book called *Rewrites,* which is my memoirs. The book ends on the day of Joan's funeral. The second book begins on the morning after that, when I wake up, not wanting to get up out of bed, to go face the girls. I was not going to ask the question, "What do we do now?" I was going to say what we should do now. I gave them options. I said, "I don't think we should just hang around here. We should see some people who want to come and pay respects. But, if you'd both like to go to Europe, I think maybe we could just go there, and I don't know if we'll have a good time or not, but we'll be together." Ellen said she wanted to. Nancy was in camp, and she said, "I want to return to camp." So I felt very good that she had a sense of knowing what it was she wanted to do, that she'd be better off being with kids her own age. Ellen was older, five years older, and Ellen suddenly started to do things that Joan did when Joan and I would travel to Europe. We'd be walking and Ellen would say, "Dad, that would really be good for the kitchen, we could use that." And, "I think we need some new dishes." She just suddenly was taking over. It was terrific to see that.

I think what complicated it is when Marsha Mason came into it. And they both embraced her, saying, "Dad, this girl [in the play that I was doing, *The Good Doctor*], she's terrific, you ought to take her out." And I finally did, after great persuasion on their part. They all liked each other, and eventually Marsha and I married. Then, Ellen sort of lost her position there. Marsha was coming in as Mom.

That's bound to happen; there's nothing out of the ordinary there. Things were going well enough as it was, that we were all so well-adjusted with each other, the two children and myself. I didn't have rebellious kids that I had to get in line or something. We've just gotten closer over the years now, so now it's twenty-five years later, and I'm closer to them than I've ever been.

For all of his sophistication and erudition, Neil Simon is at heart a hearth hugger. Virtually every play he's written, every belly laugh and every tear he's passed on to us through his work was born in his family. If we've seen his plays, we know the strength and sassiness of Joan. We know his devotion to his daughters. We even know his mom. There's a scene in Broadway Bound *in which he dances with his mother. And he didn't make it up.*

My mother told us for years and years that she once danced with George Burns. When I wrote it in the play, I made it George Raft, because he was more provocative, you know, being the tough guy. It made it more romantic in a way, because George Burns we think of as a comic. But to my mother, George Burns was like a god, because he was a great ballroom dancer before he met Gracie, and he went to the Bronx, and he would look around these ballrooms, and look for the best dancer, just to dance with them for the night, and then say good-bye. The fact that it happened to her made her the queen of that area for months and months and months. They said, "There's May, she danced with George Burns." She always felt that I didn't believe the story. After I wrote *The Sunshine Boys,* and George won the Academy Award, there was a birthday party for me, and my mother just kept looking at George Burns down at end of the room. And I said, "Come on, I'll introduce you." She says, "He won't remember me, it's fifty years ago." And I said, "Well, just say hello. Remind him." And she said, "No, no." So George made his way down the room, and he got to my table, and he said, "Hi, Neil, I want you to stick to what you're doing. You're going to make it one day." And everybody laughed. And then he said, "And who is this attractive lady?" And I said, "George, this is my mother, May Simon." And out of nowhere he says, "Would you like to dance with me Mrs. Simon?" And without a beat, she said, "I would love to." She got up, and there were other people dancing, and they danced around the room, and people started to move away, like this was staged. They were just dancing and they were reliving fifty years ago. She went around the room, and as they got towards where I was sitting, his back turned towards me, but she was facing me and she said to me, "What did I tell you?" She got her wish.

I could feel the tears welling as they are almost now, because it's such a perfect thing to happen for somebody. That's like a great reward for doing something wonderful in your whole life.

As a kid I would save my wishes. I would never wish that the Yankees would win. I'd say, "Let some other Yankee fan use up his wishes." I felt you had a certain amount of wishes, but it wasn't like three wishes or ten wishes; it was only major wishes. It had to be something really important. Like that it didn't rain on my graduation day because I had a little white suit that my parents could hardly afford, and I didn't want to get it wet. Silly things like that.

I love working. I love moving on. I hate the waste of talent for the wrong reasons. Play out all the years that you can still be great. I feel that I still have the capabilities, the talent, and the drive to want to keep writing. I imagine one day it will stop. It may be slowing down a little bit because the theater is changing so much, so I have to choose my ideas a little bit more carefully. I still enjoy it. I am enjoying writing this book. Sometimes, it doesn't matter what it is I'm writing. I just love the art of writing.

My life is separated into about twelve parts. Into the plays. Into the relationships. Into deaths. Into births. There is always a new sense of life all the time. Optimistic and prolific life.

The book that Neil Simon is writing about his life after Joan is called The Play Goes On. *It does go on for all of us. When someone who's been part of your heart dies, the idea that the sun will rise the next morning is almost unimaginable. That's the way it's been for me. But the darn sun rises and the sorrow that fills your soul moves out over time to make room for joy and memory and your own prolific life. Only it's better this time because it's informed by the fact that you were lucky enough to have been given love. That's the real legacy.*

CHAPTER 26

JOMARIE PAYTON-NOBLE

Having the dream of being an actor is dicey stuff. Overlay that with poverty and racism, and your chances of making it are pretty darn dim. What does it take? Attitude. Maya Angelou once said you can't liberate yourself without liberating a whole lot of strangers along with you. JoMarie Payton-Noble has pulled that off, whether she knows it or not.

You know her as Harriet Winslow, who sassed her way onto national television as the tart-tongued elevator operator on ABC's hit Perfect Strangers. *After a two-year-long tour de force, ABC gave JoMarie her own spin-off,* Family Matters, *where she ruled for a decade.*

JoMarie came up dirt poor in Opalocka, Florida, the second of nine children. By the time she was eleven, she had all the responsibilities of a grown-up and all the opportunities of a nobody. She wasn't just bucking up against racial bigotry. Class prejudice kept her down. But the girl could dream. Her toughness disqualified her for an ingenue role by anyone's standards. But her acting was electric. She won her first Award as a senior in high school for her depiction of Mama in A Raisin in the Sun. *She worked her way through the University of Miami as a waitress, club singer, and then in an accounting office, where she heard they were casting for the road company of the Broadway musical* Purlie. *With no resume, music, headshot, or car she talked her way into the audition and sang a cappella. She got the part and got to Los Angeles, and then* Purlie *closed. JoMarie Payton-Noble was left flat with a twenty-year-old car named Betsy, an economy size jar of peanut butter, and day-old bread. She made some hard choices. Then she made good. And she's spent her life since trying to make it right for her mother and for other people's kids who grow up in the violence of poverty.*

Coming up in the segregated South, the eldest daughter of nine children whose father split, is enough to knock the wind out of anyone. Not her.

My father split when I was eleven. My mother was left to raise nine children (six boys and three girls). She ran the house all by herself. I helped her out because I had to, but it didn't bother me. I had to cook, wash, clean, and go to school at night. Sometimes, however, I would have to forgo school for baby-sitting my younger siblings. Going to school was never an issue in my family. We all were allowed to miss one day of school a week. I'd miss Monday, my brother would miss Tuesday, and another would miss Wednesday. Since my mother couldn't pay for childcare, we understood that missing school was a necessity. I did not have time to be a child. Even though I wanted to play like the other kids, I knew that my mother needed my help. It was hard, and it toughened me up.

I think I probably always had self-reliance. I think I was born to be a little bit tough because life was not going to be easy for me. I'm real tough. I'm glad I'm tough. I had to be, coming from where I came from.

I think what made me the toughest was the first Christmas after my dad left, when I was eleven years old. Around five or six o'clock that day, somebody sent a basket of food. That helped, and I was grateful for that. But there were no toys.

We lived in a very small two-bedroom house, so we slept two and three in a bed, depending on how big we were, and my mother slept on the couch. And oh God, I remember that particular Christmas it was really cold, too. I made them all get in the bed. I got in the bathtub, took a bath, and went to bed. We didn't have enough blankets. So my mother took the sheet and put it over us and then what blanket we had, she put over us. And then she took the clean clothes and she laid the clothes on top of us.

I was up in the bed with my hands pressed together, I remember, and I said, "Oh God, please, just let twelve o'clock come for me, twelve o'clock." Because twelve o'clock was the next day and that was Christmas. I remember praying real hard that night, Christmas Eve, praying real hard for twelve o'clock to just get there and go away. Because I knew we weren't getting anything. I didn't particularly care whether I had anything or not. But I wanted my brothers and sisters to have something. They wanted skates and they wanted toys. I didn't care if I didn't get anything. But I wanted them to have something.

The reality set in real quick that there was going to be nothing. When twelve o'clock happened, I cried, and then I said, "Okay, we're at Christmas, we're not getting anything, that's just the way it is."

So I got up that morning with my brothers and sisters. They said, "What are we going to do?" And I said, "Oh, we'll be okay." We had some kickballs. So we went outside. But with so many of us that was a plus. There's always a balance to everything. We all had friends. Each one of us got one friend. That was eighteen people. Our friends had toys, so they came over. That in itself made everybody feel good about the fact that, okay, we didn't have Christmas toys but then Vernon has something, and Janice has something. And my mother was able to go and buy us one game. One game that six players could play. So God makes it real good for you. He evens out the score. Thank you, God.

I thought it would be enough to flatten me. I'm surprised that it didn't.

I've never resented it because I saw how hard my mother actually worked. My mother worked seven days a week. Monday through Saturday she worked cleaning houses, a different house every day. And on Sunday she'd sweep the hair out of beauty salons because they were nonfunctional on Sunday. Then she'd call me up and say, "Jo, meet me up at the Winn-Dixie grocery store." I'd meet her up there on the bus because our car had failed years before, and we'd bring the groceries home on the bus. I remember asking her one day, "Ma, why do you have to work seven days a week?" She said, "Well, we need the money." I said, "Ma, we don't need that much money. We can eat beans. Seven days a week? Everybody should have one day that they rest." And I said, "Ma, I will never work seven days a week for anybody for any of my money. Never in life." She said, "That's why I'm doing this, so you won't have to work as hard as I do."

Acting was my way out. I didn't know it was going to be so

tough, though. In first grade, I did my first play. I was Little Red Riding Hood. I didn't want to be Little Red Riding Hood because I didn't like the red cape that Little Red Riding Hood wore—in fact, I hated that red cape. All my friends got to wear little tutus because they were the flowers in the forest. Larry Wade and Johnny Wooten (the cutest boys in class) liked the girls who wore the little tutus. They didn't pay attention to me; and I wanted their attention, too.

So I began to protest about my role in the play. My teacher would not budge. She said, "You're going to play Little Red Riding Hood and that's all there is to it." I think that was a good lesson to me. In my life, I have never been the flower; I have always been Red Riding Hood. When I was younger, I wanted to be the flower because I wanted the outfit. But, as I grew up, I realized that the role of the flower was boring. I wanted to stand out.

Yet it was hard for me to stand out in acting, since I was so discriminated against in school. Because my mom was a maid, I wasn't allowed to take drama classes. The kids that got drama classes were the kids whose parents worked in the library or the cafeteria, or their Dad owned a gas station or had a profession. Maid was looked down on, and my mom was a maid. So I was looked down on, and I was poor.

I wasn't allowed into the drama department until I was in the eleventh grade. My first acting teacher wanted me to star in a play. He thought I had the ability. But I couldn't do it because of school politics. So he devised a scheme: He created a talent show and made me in charge. I was the emcee.

The show became my baby. I organized the show so that I was the star. At the time, the Supremes were extremely popular. The girls in the show wore the cutest Supreme-inspired outfits. While I was extremely excited about my role, I began to panic because I was too poor to buy a Supremes costume. I became so embarrassed. I remember saying, "Oh God, I'm the emcee, and I have nothing to wear." So I asked my mother for money. I said, "Ma, do you have some extra money? I have to buy something because I'm emceeing this program." She said, "Oh, baby, I really don't have that much money." But she knew how much it meant to me so she gave me $50. She gave me $50! That's a lot of money. So with the $50, I went to one of the most expensive stores you could go to and looked on the sales rack. I remember, I bought a silver Lily Rubin dress that had been marked down from $250 to $35. It had a little dirt on the collar, but I didn't care. It was silver and it was marked down to $35. So I bought it.

My friend Ernie Bettencourt worked the lights for the show. He knew how important it was for me to feel special during my big performance, so he came up with a plan. He said, "Jo, don't worry about a thing. You're gonna shine like nobody's business that night because, baby, when you sing this song you're going to have on a red dress. And then when you sing the next one, that dress is going to turn blue." Oh, it was phenomenal! I was magic with that one dress on. That dress turned a different color every time I sang a different song. It was fabulous. It was fabulous!

I've never resented my childhood. I saw how hard my mother worked to keep us afloat. She sacrificed her life to give us ours. She was a really special woman.

My difficult childhood gives me an understanding of underprivileged kids that most people don't have. Therefore, I feel that it is my duty to try to help those children that don't have the money to seek professional help. That's one of the reasons that I travel around the country and speak at drug rehabs. I go into the jails; I go into the schools. I'm not afraid of these kids. I just want to help them.

When I speak to these kids, I speak to them about suicide. Sometimes things get so tough for these kids that they want to kill themselves. I tell them that God doesn't forgive you for committing suicide. One should never feel that they have to take their own life. Somebody will help you if you ask for it. I have the ability to talk to these kids honestly, because I too have contemplated suicide. But then I remembered what my mom, dad, and grandmother said. They said, "God doesn't forgive you for killing yourself. That's the one sin that He won't forgive." At first, I didn't understand it. Why was suicide the unforgivable sin? Yet, then I realized why. For every wrong thing you do in your life, even if you kill or you steal, you can say, "God, please forgive me. I did not mean it. Please forgive me." You can say that if you are alive. But if you're dead, you have no voice. You have no heart. You have no conscience. You have nothing with which to ask for forgiveness.

Sometimes I am afraid that I am not a good mother. My number-one job is to be a good mother to my child. I want to be there for my child so that whenever she needs me, regardless of whether she has killed, stolen, or prostituted, I would want her to feel that she could come home. Even though I doubt myself from time to time, I am lucky because I really feel that I am a good mother. I am doing my job. I believe that if my child was in trouble, she would come home to me. I am a good mother.

Twenty-one years ago my life hit rock bottom. I didn't have much money, and I was really depressed about a lot of things, especially the fact that I couldn't go home. I'd gotten my big break in the national tour of *Purlie,* but it closed in Los Angeles after only a two-month run. I had to move out of my furnished apartment. And I had to send money home to my mom and pay off my credit cards. Some friends gave me a car and I treasured it, because my car Betsy was all I had. She was a pink and white '57 Chevy with a 283 engine in her. I learned how to change my oil. I learned how to prime my carburetor. And I moved into a ragged, virtually abandoned apartment complex that was under renovation. My mother always had a roof. Even if it was a raggedy roof with stuff falling down, I had a roof over my head. I didn't even have furniture or even a bed.

I remember going into a drugstore. All of a sudden I saw this little piece of marble sitting on a little metal stand. It was engraved and it said, "If God is your partner, make your plans big." That was all I needed. I immediately turned my life around.

Every time I walk into a new surrounding or a new home, I make sure that my marble is in my hand. God is my partner; that's what keeps me going. I always say I'm grateful for anything that anyone does for me. I'm blessed that a lot of doors have been opened for me. And I feel obliged to open doors for others. That is why I want to help those children who grew up in socioeconomic backgrounds like mine. I want to give them the gifts that my mother attempted to give to me.

My strength comes from my God. I try to pass these beliefs on to my daughter. My daughter doesn't get everything she wants. She doesn't get to go every place she wants to. I make her suffer sometimes because I have to toughen her up. My daughter doesn't go to private school. She goes to our neighborhood school because she needs to learn to grow up with the people that she lives around. I did that on purpose. She was in private school for three years, and I pulled her out. I believe that you need to go to school where you live. You need to know everybody in your neighborhood so that when you're walking down the street, somebody knows that you belong to me. You need to walk. I believe that these things help you grow into a good person.

I think it is important for children to see where their parents grew up. When my daughter first visited the house I grew up in, she was shocked. She said, "Ooh, Grandma's got roaches, Grandma's got rats." I explained to her that the small house she saw is where I came from. I was poor and I had nothing, but I worked hard to get past whatever adversity crossed my path. I let her know that one can always be productive. One can always be somebody with a dime or a dollar.

If I should lose everything I have now, I haven't really lost anything, because what people are looking at and what I have right now is material stuff. Stuff is not what I'm about. What I consider to be my richness I've always had. My richness comes from my heart and soul. I can lose my house. I can lose my Mercedes. But that is not important. I can't lose the life lessons that I have been taught and that I have learned.

My mother had always been there for me. She was always in the audience in her ragged clothes, in her shoes that she had to clean with Vaseline. That's how I learned to do it. You shined them up with some Vaseline, you took a rag, you cleaned them off so they wouldn't catch too much dirt. She'd be embarrassed because she didn't have anything to wear. I said, "Ma, don't worry. One day you'll have everything you need to wear. Don't worry about it."

About nine years ago, I bought the house that I grew up in for my mother. I was doing *Perfect Strangers,* and I wanted to buy my mother a present. My mother had never had anything that was hers. Since I now had an opportunity to give my mother something meaningful, I did it. I had to spend about four or five thousand dollars on the house. I was so proud. I remember saying, "Ma, listen. This house is yours now. You held this house for all these years. You don't have to worry about paying the landlord anymore. Now we can fix it up. You don't really need a big house now because we're grown. You can fix this up any way you want to, make a little dollhouse, whatever you want to do."

My mother was extremely thankful. However, she was still stressed. You see, my brother moved back home with his two kids because he was having problems. My mother took over and basically began raising his children. She turned gray from all of the stress. It was wrong. So I went to my mother and said, "Ma, put your clothes on, we're going to go out and look for a house." We saw ten houses that day. My mother fell in love with the first house that she saw. We bought it right there on the spot. It was a great feeling to be able to give something back to her. I try to give something back to everyone I can. It is a long process, but, I am on my way.

CHAPTER 27

SANDY DUNCAN

She grew up before our eyes. A tiny little girl out of the Texas prairie with a voice as big as the Texas sky and a personality to match. We saw her on The Hogan Family, The Sandy Duncan Show, *and she was the best Peter Pan to hit Broadway since Mary Martin created the role. We thought we knew her.*

Many of those who make it big make it early, but there's sometimes a big price for that. Sandy paid, and paid. She battled two failed marriages, bulimia, a brain tumor, blindness, alcoholism, and depression, but she's still got the pixie in her. When I approached her about her quiet triumph, she asked, "Which one?" It's said that women in their fifties are at their best. They are at the peak of their wisdom and grace and their talents. Today, at the age of fifty-plus, Sandy Duncan is living proof of that notion. She is the mother of teenagers, a playwright, and she owns her own life. But it took an awful lot to get there.

In retrospect, I think I took the path of least resistance. For many years, I was a woman in America "on top of it." I was a celebrity, and I had this public persona, which put me into a kind of automatic pilot where I played the role of the person that people expected me to be. I stopped asking questions, and I stopped changing. I was always the good kid, the caretaker, and everybody's comic relief. It was my business to see that everything ran smoothly and everybody was happy. I ran myself ragged if I gave a party because if somebody wasn't having a good time, I believed it was a direct reflection on me. There's a certain amount of narcissism that's mixed into that. But I really felt responsible. I used to try and sleep with my ears clear of the pillow, like I'm on guard. "I'm covering the west side of the valley and I hope somebody's covering the east side." I was really plugged into all this responsibility. Somebody once said there are guests in the world and there are hosts. Well, I bought into being a host very early in life.

I knew who I was supposed to be. And I knew who I made up to be. That's the trap, you see. That's what I fell into because you never feel you're offstage until you finally just decide to take yourself offstage. Because if you go into a social situation, you're either living up to this image or you're doing things that will damage it, so there's self-consciousness—always. People will come up to you and they will react more to what you represent to them in terms of a persona than who you are or what you have to say. So even if I go up to buy something in a store, it takes me a good five minutes because at first people are going, "Let's see, who is she? Uh, she works at my bank. No." You just see their eyes glaze over, and you have to redo your business two or three times to finally go, "The perfume in the back." So you go through your life with this sort of hyper-awareness of who you are moving through the world. Just this year I finally stopped doing that. I'm so much more relaxed about moving around in the world. We all have our rituals that keep us in our little ruts, and every now and then they break down on you.

Sandy Duncan's breakdown was an avalanche. She was only twenty-four, sustaining the external body blows of a divorce and the internal destruction of eating disorders, enslaved by round-the-clock shooting on her series, suffering searing headaches, going blind, passing out, and carrying on like a trooper. It can work. But not for long. Her doctor told her she was having a nervous breakdown.

He said, "You're having it because you're going through a divorce, and this is the first time you've had this national fame, and you're working long hours. You're just nervous." I kept going, "I don't think so." This was a year before the CAT scan was invented, and the bone behind my eye was masking a huge tumor. They couldn't see it in regular X-rays. So after about six months, my vision was practically gone, but I was still working twenty-hour days. This was with a brain tumor and passing out! It was lunacy. I remember the very last show. I was determined to get those thirteen in the can. I remember my mother flew out to stay with me at the doctor's recommendation, because I was frail. I think I was bulimic at the time because I was eighty-six pounds. Of course I thought I looked fat and insisted that eating cottage cheese and yogurt was what the doctor ordered. "I'm supposed to eat this," I lied. That night I had what was probably a little mini-breakdown. All of a sudden everything turned stark white and I remember screaming from the bathroom. My mother had just arrived from Texas, and I yelled, "Something's wrong! I don't know where I am!" I thought I had flipped. In reality, it was this pressure of a brain tumor pressing on areas of my brain. The doctor arrived and gave me a shot to go to sleep. I saw way off in the distance a little tunnel and my mother and the doctor standing in a doorway, and he said, "Sandy, you've got to get rest." I said, "No, I have one more day of shooting." He said, "No, no, no. They'll do it Monday." I went, "No, no, no." When he gave me the shot, I remember saying right before I went to sleep for twenty-four hours, "You're putting me to sleep, aren't you?" I was totally convinced that they were killing me. That's how insane you can get from illness or from pressures, and it's a horrible thing because you have no control over it.

It was the night before my surgery. I'd never met Lucille Ball in my life, but apparently she was very fond of my work, so she came to visit me in the hospital. She came sweeping into my room with this red hair and black cape, and I remember thinking I must be hallucinating, because I was pretty sick by then. She gave me this little box, and when she put it in my hand, she said, "Now you put all your pain in this box, you hear me?" I still have it. She sat with me a good half hour just holding my hand and talking to me. It was a very sweet thing to do. Later I found out that she said to my dad who had come up from

Texas for the operation, "So you run a gas station back in Tyler, Texas?" And he went, "Yes, yes, ma'am. That's what I do." She said, "Do you have somebody watching out for you there, I mean, covering the business for you while you're here?" I don't know what she planned to do, but she acted like she was going to take care of it if he didn't. When the operation finally occurred, it was going to be "exploratory." In the end they sort of poked around and found a big mass. So they removed it right then and sewed me up.

Mind you, being the "good girl," I spent my entire hospital stay visiting people up and down the hallway, just perky as you can be. I looked like a big Q-tip with a huge big bandage on this little skinny body. When the tumor was gone, an odd thing happened. I suddenly got hungry! I don't know if it was tied directly to the operation or not, but I think after you lose as much weight as I had, your body kicks into some other gear and starts feeding off itself. I'm so grateful that, for whatever reason, I wanted to eat again.

Prior to the operation (and during the filming of the show) the tumor was pressing on my optic nerve and was cutting off the blood supply. So my eyesight was pretty much shot. Now, I'm totally blind in my left eye, and pretty near-sighted in my right eye, so my vision is certainly not the best.

For years her ability to feel emotions wasn't the best either. She couldn't allow herself to feel the terror of possibly losing not only her livelihood but also her life. She took care of the critical medical problem, but she completely ignored the emotional jolt, and there is a real danger in denying your feelings.

At the time there was much speculation about my career being over and that I wouldn't work again. I became determined to reestablish myself as an entity in the world. Sheer will carried me through it, but in the process I didn't pay any attention to who I was inside—my "inner child." I realized just a few years ago that I was traumatized to the core. I didn't let any of those emotions in, I just had to survive.

Survival techniques only work for a while. And when they stop, it can feel like a ton of bricks. In 1993, after nearly a quarter century of burying her feelings, Sandy Duncan crashed into a clinical depression. The good news is, it is not the kind of depression caused by a chronic, progressive chemical imbalance. It was temporary. The bad news is that while you're in it, it doesn't feel temporary and it's tough to see a way of getting up and out.

That's where my kids come in. When there is something going on outside yourself, you just must function and not totally let go. I had periods where I thought I could easily become one of those people that's catatonic, that just sits in a room and is completely nonreactive. I had blown many circuits. I was exhausted, mentally, psychologically, every which way. I just felt like I couldn't function. I couldn't. But I did. I forced myself to because I had to, and there's something to that. On the other hand, I had to sit with it. It was very uncomfortable; it was painful; but I had to sit with it to learn anything from it. In other words, to give me some antidepressants and just pop me back on the horse was not the answer for where I was going with this journey. I wanted to find out why I was there and where it was going to lead. It was about a two-year ongoing process, and I learned that in fact you can be in charge of your own life and you can get off that thing that's driving you, whatever it is. If it's keeping up with the Joneses, as some people do, or if it's having to be famous by somebody else's standards, I just started to really address what my own standards were. I remember going to parties and people saying to me, "Are you ever gonna smile again?" And I'd say, "I don't know. It's my privilege not to." I was so full of rage and anger.

I think that is what happens to you when you think you've lived all these years and you haven't done things on your own terms and you're running out of time. I was pretty much devoid of joy. I felt like I had nothing to live for, nothing to say, nothing to contribute—and it was sobering. I was abusive to myself because this is what comes out of this whole lifestyle of people-pleasing. I let everyone contribute as well to this self-abuse—

"Get in here and kick her some more."

It's like alcoholism. I went through that, too. You have to say, "I'm not going to drink anymore," but there I was drinking again. "I'm not going to drink anymore." Then you finally admit it and say, "Oh, my God, I have a problem." Then you have to take that first step. But once you do, you just keep taking those steps. It's a journey.

I turned to my husband during the time, who had to exercise a great deal of patience and understanding. I do believe that is what long relationships are about, sometimes. But in terms of the one going through the struggle, you just have to make that journey yourself. It's a solitary, lonely journey. I did have the help of a wonderful psychiatrist as well, but ultimately, I turned to myself, and I started listening. When you're in overdrive (I call it Maytag spin cycle), you tend not to listen, and you tend not to settle down to the bottom and observe. So that couple of years, I was so quiet.

I have a real strong sense of a God. I'm not churchy, and I'm not one for organizations. They frighten me. But I'm quietly religious. So all of that helps. I do believe there's some purpose to all this. If you do this, it becomes a quiet faith. It's all about giving up control, and for me that was really difficult since I was such a control freak. But it's all about admitting there must be some order and design, and somebody must know better than I do about what that design is.

As much as I sometimes think I have nothing in common here with the rest of humanity, I do. There is that little inner thing that connects us all. Everybody's everybody, and that includes the bag people on the street. Once you've been through enough things, you are released from judging because you realize that, "That could just as easily be me." And when you really believe that, you tend to want to help people as opposed to judging them.

We're all free-falling up. We're not free-falling down. That's my belief. I don't think it's spiraling in a downward motion. I think it's spiraling up. Let's take this huge leap into the light, the unknown, the whatever it is that awaits us all that we go to by ourselves. You can do it and freak and go the other direction or you can choose to say, "Life's really damned interesting, and whatever happens is supposed to be happening." To think otherwise is silly. Maybe that's fatalistic. I know there are choices in the world and you do reach crossroads. But the other way seems like such a safe, fearful way to live to me. That's not how I choose to live. So many things can happen, like the nice neighbor on the fifth floor shoots himself or you step onto a plane and it blows up. The answer is to give yourself up and to stay open to experience. Otherwise, you'll be hovering in an apartment or a home somewhere frightened to leave.

No threat of that for Sandy Duncan. After two failed marriages, she's settled in to family life for the long run. She now knows what a solid marriage is and the self-examination it takes to make it work. She's living it. She's lived the mind-numbing custodial life of a high-powered career woman turned new mother, with all its joys and frustrations. And now she's got help in defining who she is. She's got teenagers.

Wait till your kids get to be teenagers. It's definitely high maintenance. Somebody just gave me a book, which I think is quite funny. It says, "Get out of my life, but first could you drive me and Cheryl to the mall?" Because that's really what it is. Talk about needing to have your self-esteem intact! Well, I'm the stupidest person that ever walked. It's, "What are you wearing?" Or, "Oh, Mom, your hair!" I'm just grateful I'm fifty with teenagers, because if I were much younger, I'd be a mess. They're pretty tough. But then I never stopped working, even when they were babies. I would haul them around with me, and I've just always incorporated them into whatever I was doing. In turn, I tried to incorporate myself into whatever they were doing.

One of my children is showing thespian tendencies, but why shouldn't he? I think what I've hoped to do by incorporating them is let them see the ups and downs. I used to hang out at my dad's gas station and I'd hand out bubblegum and watch them sweep the floorboards. I knew what running a gas station was, and I chose not to do it. So I think this way they don't just see the limousines; they don't just see the fame part. They come hang out at rehearsals and get damn bored. So you better pick something you love. That's the only advice I give them.

Peter Pan, a leading-edge baby-boomer if ever there was one, has grown up. She is one of 76 million people turning fifty. She accepts the pitfalls of her past with surprising equanimity. And even when she cozies down into an oversized turtleneck that buries much of her face, you can still see that pert, perky pixie—a description she used to loathe.

I hated being described as "pert and perky" when I was younger. But now I'm ever so grateful. I'm doing great. I don't know if it's because I'm part of the baby-boom generation and there are a lot of us out there. We're all talking about how we've grown and where we're at. But I do know that for whatever reason, I've found that in the past two years, I've come to own my life more than I ever have. It's almost like I suddenly woke and realized that it is my life and I can do it the way I want to. At some point you just start to rely on your own life experiences. It's a whole different feeling. There's a relaxation that comes with it, and a pleasure. I feel I could do almost anything. For example, I just wrote a play, I loved working on it. So now I'm back to talking fast again, but it's coming from a different place and a different motivation.

CHAPTER 28

ROD STEIGER

Something in the gaze of Rod Steiger implies danger: the narrow eyes, the jutted chin, the tensed muscles of his cheeks. It is there even when he's laughing. A hint of something long pent-up that will, without warning, blast forth and knock you flat. Even as a little kid, they called him "Rodney the Rock," and he is proud of it. A demanding taskmaster who is as tough on others as he is on himself, Steiger refuses to help just any young actor eager to learn from the pro. He won't help just anyone who wants to act. He will only help those who have to act.

Steiger's powerful performances in On the Waterfront, In the Heat of the Night, *and* The Pawnbroker *cemented his reputation as a virtuoso actor, but his own persona is equally formidable. He is a very formal man. In his business, Steiger is one of a kind; but he shares a condition of many other great individuals: Vladimir Horowitz, Winston Churchill, and Abraham Lincoln. Rod Steiger suffers from depression. It kept him out of work and out of life for nearly a decade. But it has also given him a new mission that he approaches with messianic zeal. He's devoted his years of recovery to fighting the stigma that's often associated with this most misunderstood illness. Even Mike Wallace has credited Steiger for making it easier for him and others to acknowledge their depression.*

I had it eight and a half years. When you're in the depth, you don't think much. You certainly don't think about your profession. Maybe in the beginning of the depression you start saying, "What's happening? What is going on?" With a depression like I had, which derived from a chemical imbalance, this realization comes progressively. You don't wake up one morning and you're depressed. You look at something ordinary, your mind takes it in, and the next thing you know you're looking at it a little longer. You just like to watch a little longer. Pretty soon you're sitting like that.

Experts surmise (that's my new name for science, surmise), they surmise that you go through levels. The worst level is the level of self-pity, which is undeniable. I remember I was being interviewed on a radio in Chicago or someplace, and the man said, "Well, you sound like you're feeling very sorry for yourself." I said, "At one time I was very sorry for myself, which is perfectly natural. If you don't think you're special you won't get up in the morning. You don't go around screaming it, but that's the way it is."

But then you fall below self-pity. I was in a state when I would go upstairs to my bedroom, and my wife could smell me downstairs in the living room. If she hadn't been around, I would have laid there in excrement. I would have never gone to the bathroom. I only went because I knew she was downstairs. I didn't shave. I didn't have any volition. I'm talking about clinical depression, which is a chemical imbalance in the brain in the connections between the synapses. It's different than what I call a social depression. A social depression is the deep sadness when someone you love dearly in your family dies, a lover you've been with for years dies, or your business collapses. You can be depressed for four months, you can be depressed for a year or more. But you can work your way out of it.

My wife saved my life. I was going to kill myself three times. Imagine a girl who at that time is twenty-two and I'm fifty-six. All of a sudden she is handed this aging man with a mental problem. And she saved me. Her strength and her love saved me. It's more than just being indebted to somebody you love. You're honored at their concern and their compassion. I'll never forget it.

My wife was learning things too fast now. There are all these idiots that scream at a clinically depressed person, "Pick up your boot straps!" I love that phrase. One more time, and I was going to kill somebody.

Never, not even once in eight years did this woman criticize me. She never said, "How can you sit there like that? Pull yourself together! What kind of man are you? What's wrong with you?" That's so beautiful. I remember when she would start to shake, and she'd say, "I'm going to the Valley and play handball with the girls." I'm sure, excuse the expression, she beat the shit out of that ball. Because whatever frustration, whatever fear she had, she took it out on the ball. But she never hit me with a criticism. That's love.

Then we went from one doctor to another, from one pill to another, from one theory to another. I remember the turning point. It came from my wife. We were with this doctor after I'd been taking these pills, and she said what the problem was, but I didn't realize it until later. "Will you stop the crap and forget who he is and deal with him like a human being, not a movie star?" she said.

That's another thing. Looking for a doctor. Even to this day, if I go to a doctor or I go to a psychiatrist, the first thing I look at is the office. If it seems cold and bare without plants and few pictures and the people behind the desk are snippy, that's one point against them. Then I go in and talk to him. I tell him a classic joke, and he writes a note. That's two. Then I say, finally, "Have you ever read, *The Little Prince*?" He says, "No." I say, "Oh, that's three." I'm gone after that. I read *The Little Prince* when I was very young and I've been reading it ever since. It is one of the few books that gives you a spiritual uplift without advocating any religious dogma. It is about a little prince who wants to protect his planet and poses one of the great questions through a conversation he has with a wolf he wants to befriend—are we responsible for each other? The wolf says to the prince, "I'll tell you something. If you tame me, you are responsible for me." *The Little Prince* is usually found in the children's section in the bookstore but it doesn't belong there, really. That's not a children's book.

Mr. Steiger wears a large medal that he never takes off. On it is the imprint of The Little Prince. *He wore it for his big comeback in the 1989 movie*

January Man. *After a slow and painful recovery, it was a bigger personal comeback than even he ever expected to make.*

I was so elated that somebody remembered me and that I got the job. Hollywood is merciless. You're a hit on Friday and then if something goes wrong over the weekend they don't know who you are on Monday. I've been dealing with it almost fifty years so I'm used to it. But it was a bit stressful. I was worried if I had any talent left, if I'd remember the lines. But I wanted to see if I had anything left of something I loved dearly to work with. I got this scene where I had to be kind of powerful and strong. This is what I was known for. And, boy, it started to come back. I played the mayor of New York, and in one scene I had to be angry with the chief of police. I went berserk. When I finished, they applauded a little. People were stunned. I realized I overdid it. It's like you find out you can make love again after you couldn't for eight years, ten years. I got so excited to feel the power of it and to celebrate the return of whatever talent I had. But because the audience was looking at a movie story, they thought this is me getting angry with them. It wasn't that. I kept seeing how I could be getting stronger. In other words, I could walk again. "Wait a minute, you don't have to run now. It's just a walking scene here." But once I began to feel the joy of being alive again and being able to do something I love, I'm sure I went crazy.

When I was a kid, people would call me and say, "Your mother's in the bar, she's drunk, we can't help her out." I would come down and physically wheedle her or push her out. The neighborhood had something to talk about. And the kids, of course, were merciless. My mother, by the way, was a member of Alcoholics Anonymous for eleven years of her life and pulled herself out of it. She herself became a very good sponsor and took care of somebody else in AA.

But somewhere inside of me something must have happened that said, "Someday, I'll do something good enough, for the name Steiger will not be laughed at."

Whether or not hard science can link the genetic bullet for alcoholism to the onset of depression is irrelevant to Steiger. It is the stigma attached to the depression and how it is treated that galvanizes his considerable energy. He's addressed the National Institutes of Mental Health, the American Psychiatric Association, and Rotary International on the issue. He has enlisted the support of more than 200 rotary clubs in the cause. He even testified before Congress about clinical depression at the time when it was still not discussed.

You mustn't be persecuted or be ashamed of being depressed. It is a disease like diabetes, and you've got to get the right medicine. You have a chemical imbalance. Everybody is a different chemical machine. Until you get the pill that's right for you . . . well here's the other problem. I went to get my medicine in the pharmacy and I said, "Wait a minute, this pill costs a fortune." I said, "What do the poor people do?" He says, "They die." I said, "Come on, that's a bad joke." He says, "No, I'm not joking." It's a group that becomes suicidal. They can't take it anymore, and for various reasons they may do away with themselves.

What you say is, number one, do not isolate yourself. I have two cars in my family. One license plate says, "Keep Moving," and the other says, "Courage." You've got to get yourself out of the bed. Don't lay there and smell like I did. Go for help. And do not apologize for being human. Do not apologize for being in pain. You have a right to ask for help. If other people who are supposed to be your relatives are members of the human being family, they should help you and there should be no stigma put upon you, any more than it should be for being black, white, Catholic, Buddhist, or what have you. You can't judge a person who is sick like that. I was talking to Senator [Barbara] Boxer and Senator [Arlen] Specter and I said, "We don't talk much about the children. We should begin to emphasize to the public that the person who's depressed is not at fault, and it will affect the family and child."

Despite Steiger's awareness that depression will be the enemy against which he will struggle for the rest of his life, he and his wife committed an act of profound hope and optimism. They had a baby. Michael.

He's giving me a tremendous education. He taught me one thing when he was two months. We had to fly from Los Angeles to New Zealand, and we took him. Behind us, there was a man and woman with their child, about the same age. They were having some kind of disagreement, and instinctively, of course, their child picked it up. He cried the entire seventeen hours. Our boy didn't make a sound. Now I'm not bragging about him. He doesn't even know language yet. But the parents' moods, whether it's depression or anything else, influence that child. Our child felt secure. He never heard his mother and father take after each other in public.

Without mental and physical health, you can't be successful. You can call yourself anything you want, but without mental and physical health, there is no such thing. To me, a successful man or woman is someone who works at something he or she loves. They get paid enough to have clean food and a clean place to sleep. And they have enough; this is the most important thing. This puts you in the smallest minority of people in the world because I don't think 100 percent have it.

You do have control over the major chunk of your life. And we have to gradually work our way through it. I was lucky. I became an actor. It fit my personality. I had some kind of a feeling for it. I know what it is to go to work. I have also worked in a leather factory. I learned to drive on an ice truck when I was thirteen. I worked in the icehouse. When I came out of the Navy, I went into civil service because I had one year of high school. I had nothing to give this society, and they were taking veterans. If you had the IQ of a decimal point, you got into civil service. I was mopping floors and cleaning things. My generation believed there was no such thing as "macho." Being a man meant you made your own living and paid for your own food, for your own place to sleep.

When I used to take the train from Newark, New Jersey,

where I grew up across the swamps and mud flats of Secaucus into New York, I used to imagine our first mothers and fathers covered with mud, slime, and nothing to protect them but their teeth and nails. I'd look up at the skyline of New York and I'd say, "We have a lot of good. We have more good than bad." If somebody said, "Why?" I said, "Well, look at that. Why do we take these miracles for granted? We did that. Look at it."

I want to thank all you people who've been wonderful to me for almost fifty years. You've fed me, you've clothed me. You got me through a depression. Now I have a wife and a child. Bless you.

I wrote once that pain is a teacher that must be understood. Tears are the instant release, but to cry and not to gain from the combat with pain is complete defeat. You must learn from your pain. And you must not be condemned for being in pain when it is part of the evolutionary process of nature. It is part of being alive. I refuse to be labeled or stigmatized for being ill. I'm lucky because I can talk about it on television. I can try to help people.

CHAPTER 29

WILLARD SCOTT

Willard Scott admits it. If Vaudeville were alive and kicking, he'd be the king of the Orpheum circuit. He calls himself the last cornball in America. But if he's a cornball, there's never been another with his abundance of grace and class. Willard, for as long as I can remember, was as much a part of America's morning ritual as alarm clocks and coffee. As the weatherman on The Today Show, *this true son of the American soil has consistently celebrated the values, the hopes, and the traditions that have defined the American experience, even as he was playing the role of class clown. He comes by it honestly. Willard Scott was a real Bozo—Bozo the Clown!*

But when Bozo hit the big time in network television, the giants of dogmatic journalism weren't laughing. They were too busy trying to retrofit their square-peg recruit into their round hole. Or was it the other way around?

I don't know who's the round hole and who's the square peg! Larry Harman, God rest his soul, was the creator of the TV Bozo that the kids knew thirty-five, forty years ago. I was the third Bozo in the country, but I was the first Ronald McDonald! That's right! And Ronald came out of Bozo. What I did and what I learned working as Bozo the Clown, working with a camera and being intimate and having fun with the camera, is what I carried over into the weather act that I did in Washington and on *The Today Show.* You can create a warmth, you can create, hopefully, a love between you and the audience because you're not reading a teleprompter. You can be really very intimate and very friendly.

Doing the Bozo show gave me that background. It was wonderful.

This sounds like I'm being really syrupy, sickly sweet, but I say this with some humility. I wasn't smart enough to realize what the odds were that these people at NBC gave me for surviving. I think there's a great advantage in not being too bright, because if you're too bright you worry about things. And I didn't really worry that much.

I would see my colleagues' and bosses' reaction to me. I'd do my bit or make some off-the-wall remark, and they'd say, "Hmmpf, Hmmpf." Either somebody would do that at the anchor desk or one of the engineers would say, "Hmmpf, Hmmpf, Oh, my God, this man!" And this is wonderful! Talk about triumph. About six months later, one of the engineers in the elevator said, "You know, I was in the studio the other day, you were in there, and I thought you were crazy. But my mother loves you in Brooklyn!" Ha! I said, "Oh boy! I'll buy an apartment! If I've won over his mother in Brooklyn, I'm in business. I'm ready to rock 'n' roll." I swear to God, I never worried about it too much in the very beginning because I wasn't aware of how tenuous, how thin that little thread was. Everybody thought I'd be gone in three or four weeks. Everybody! I don't think there was any money on me at all. I used to say, as a gag, that I was forty-seven years old and moved to New York and did the network TV show before I ever found out there was anybody in the world that didn't like me. I always thought everybody loved me and adored little sonny, because I had this incredible love from my parents and my grandparents. And I had cousins and uncles and aunts—and I never knew anything negative!

\~\~\~

Until, that is, the mid-Eighties. The affliction started small at first, then mushroomed, then threatened to destroy his livelihood and render him terrorized for life. He first noticed it as a mild fear of heights. Then it became a fear of performing. Then it became full-blown stage fright. Then frightening panic attacks. There are an estimated 50 million people who suffer from phobias of some kind. They don't have to be disruptive. But when phobic anxiety interferes with a person's ability simply to function, it can be very serious indeed.

Willard's was very serious. He had the courage to get help. And he's spent a good deal of time traveling the roads of America urging other people to get help. You don't ever beat it, but you can overcome it.

Years ago, when I was crossing a bridge, a real narrow, high bridge, in Charleston, South Carolina, I had a little problem with the bridge. It just came over me. But it didn't bother me that much, because I don't make my living driving across bridges. Thirty years later, I was about forty-eight, I was on *The Today Show,* and I was being careful. Thirty seconds to air, the countdown came, and maybe by eight . . . seven . . . all of a sudden, I started to hyperventilate. A couple of the crew looked at me and said, "Are you all right Willard?" And instantly there's sweat all over me. It started to pour sweat like somebody had turned a hose on, and then I turned ashen white, and everybody thought I was having a heart attack. I got on the air, and the only way I beat it was to make a fool of myself again by saying, "Oh boy! Man! Let me tell you folks, that weather out there, I mean it's cold! Up in Nebraska!" And I was dying. I was dying. And when I got off, I was literally shaking. I went for treatment with the psychiatrists, with the doctors, and it didn't happen again for another couple of months! But then, the second time it happened I knew I had a problem. So I got help. It's a real problem. It doesn't make a bit of difference who you are.

What I found was that once I had the second one, I was waiting for the third and the fourth. And did I anticipate! I kept waiting for the next and the next. And a couple of them did come along.

I've tried some pretty bizarre treatments. For a while, I'd take a hatpin with me because I thought maybe shock treatment would help. Just before I went on the air I gave myself a couple shots of the wacka wacka. One doctor was so funny, because he suggested to me, "Willard, what you do is you take a paper bag, and you put it over your head, and you breathe into that paper bag." I said, "Doctor, I'm getting ready to do a network news show on television. Aren't they going to think it's a little strange that I have my head in a paper bag?"

The truth is, and I want to stress this so strongly, you never do this without a doctor. You never do this on your own. You must get some help. What I tell everybody is don't be afraid to seek help, you're not alone.

What the doctors would help me do was to say, "Look. Don't be afraid to take something that will help you break this cycle." Because once you realize that you have the confidence of a little pill in your pocket, it was a Valium in those days for me, I swear it helped.

I had a half of a five-milligram Valium pill under my tongue, and I took that for almost a year, just to make sure that something would work. But I stress and urge no one to ever do that without seeing a doctor, because that is an addictive drug. Today it's become a huge thing, but when I started my problem, people didn't know as much about phobias as they do now. In those days a lot of doctors would just say, "Oh go home Willard, you're just tired. It's all in your head."

I was getting ready to put one doctor up against the wall because he was destroying my confidence. He said, "Willard that half of a Valium isn't doing you any good. It's all in your mind." And I wanted to strangle him. I said, "Wait a minute! God, I've been trying for three years to find something that would help me, and whether it's in my mind or not, who cares? Don't tell me that!" I don't believe it was just in my mind. I know that for a fact, because I could go on the air now.

I'm convinced it's chemical. I'm convinced that it's a chemical deficiency in your system. It's a depression. Phobias and things like that are so common among people today. I'll bet you there's probably more medicine dispensed for manic depression than anything else. It's a real problem. I don't think you're ever over it. That's one of the things that the doctor told me. You learn to live with it.

I think back, and I say this with great respect for my dear father, but my father drank a lot. All of these things do tend to run in the family, don't kid yourself. A macho man like my father would never want to admit to being depressed or to being phobic. I'm not sure they even had the word. It wasn't that common in those days, back in the Thirties when my dad was coming along. But he would get a little rough when he drank. I'm convinced in retrospect that that was part of the weakness that I really inherited, not the drinking so much as the drinking to cover up. He did that to compensate for his depression or his problem.

I don't want to ever think he was an alcoholic. He was so good and sweet and I can say that he was the best father, and he was best man at our wedding! He only drank weekends; but when he drank, he drank enough so that it got to him.

He did it, I believe, to cover up his depression and his anxiety. I guess all of those things tend to lead to basic insecurity. People fear that they're losing their mind. You're not losing your mind. You have a chemical imbalance, and you need a little help. There are so many doctors, thank God, who understand now. They don't just pat you on the head and say: Sonny, you're just tired, or you're nervous, or you're just feeling sorry for yourself. (Excuse me for the soapbox here. I'm doing a little proselytizing.)

Talking to people about panic attack is one of my missions in life. I run around the country doing speeches, and I went public with that. It helps. I tell you, not only does it help the other people who have panic attacks to know that they're not alone, because there's so many, but when I help you, if you happen to have the problem, by going public, I help me. It's casting your bread on the water.

Willard is deeply Christian and uses prayer as a source of power. Maybe that's where he gets his resilient humility. But he also gets it from the earth. Willard says Scotts have been farmers since they first climbed out of the trees. He was the first Scott not to have been a farmer, but he took the lessons of the land with him all the way.

My father was the first one to ever leave the farm. My grandmother and grandfather on my mother's side made their living as farmers too. They had cattle up in Maryland, and they sold milk to Western Maryland Dairy. Anybody who knows dairy farming knows that it's work seven days a week. If he got 350 or 400 dollars a month in cash, that's all they had for money.

It's hard work, twice a day, seven days a week. Tennessee Ernie Ford was one of mine. I used to love Tennessee Ernie Ford. He had a song called, "Milk 'em in the morning, feed 'em, milk 'em in the evening blues." Everyday you had to milk them twice a day! My grandfather went away for only three or four days a year, and his neighbor would take his cows, and he would reciprocate. It was a lot of work.

One thing you learn is to take a bath every night. I couldn't do it. But there's such pride in it. A lot of my friends are dairy farmers. I don't know which comes first, the cow or the egg, but there is in the type of person who goes into farming something true blue. There's honesty, there's a love of the land, there's a love of family, there's a love and respect of God that's tied in to that pastoral job, that noble job of being a dairy farmer. Simplicity. That was the joy of living.

I think that for me, the lessons of faith and the lessons of the land become one and the same. As the lessons of faith and the lessons of playing a violin do for a great musician, or the lessons of faith and the lessons of dance are to a ballerina. It's probably whatever you love and whatever you are in concert with. I think that's the combination for me. There's a little thing for people to have in their gardens that says you're never closer to God than you are when you are in a garden. When you work outside and when you see nature, and you're a part of it, and you love it, there's a definite correlation.

I'm basically happy, but I find there is a problem, which has to do with depression. As we get older, our bodies aren't the only things that sag. I've got to be perfectly honest, I think that as I get older, I worry more. I worry about things that I never even gave a thought to before. I worry about saying stupid things. I'll say something and then about an hour later or a day later, I'll think to myself, Why did I say that? Whether it was on the air, or to somebody, and then I become obsessive about it, to the point that I will worry for a month about saying something stupid, to the point where sometimes I've called people back up.

I've always been blessed with having some religious training. And I wish I could give everybody a touch of it. I'm a good Christian. I pray a lot, but the older I get, the more and longer my prayers get. It's a conversation. I'm sure a good psychoanalyst can sit down and make it probably very cut and dried, which is okay, but it really is a conversation between me and my maker. It's a conversation that shows humility by the fact that I am having the conversation, because I am acknowledging that there's somebody better and bigger and stronger than I am. And that I'm not alone! That's what is so terribly important.

But you don't always get what you pray for. I very rarely pray for anything material. I pray for my family more than anything now. And for me. For me, I say thank you, God, thank you! I've had a wonderful family, my mother and my father, and when I was a kid I had both grandparents as well, who lasted until they were almost eighty years old. In my day—and for the most part I think it's still pretty darn popular—if a child really feels cared for, which I did, the kid's going to be okay.

My prayers get longer every night. One night I fell asleep, and I only had half my prayers said. I woke up worried, because I hadn't said all my prayers! It was three o'clock, and I finished saying my prayers! It is a conversation that offers peace. It's not going to solve everything instantly, but I think over the long haul, it gives you a base, and I think it humbles you. There's nothing like being humbled. Especially when you're humbled before God. Then you know there's something better than you are. I hope and pray to God there's something out there better than I am. I take great strength in humility.

I have my teeth. I have a little bit of brain left and two brand-new thirty-thousand-dollar knees. And I'm eighty pounds lighter. The doctor told me if I didn't lose weight, I'd break my new knees. Actually I bought Hugh Downs' old knees. I got a bargain!

CHAPTER 30

DEBORAH NORVILLE

I like Debbie Norville, though at first I didn't. In retrospect, our relationship was a setup from the start. When I arrived at NBC News, my new boss actually told me before I'd met her that everyone at NBC was thrilled at my arrival except for Debbie Norville. She would hate me, he said. Heaven knows what he told her. No matter how genuinely warm I was with her, she'd ignore me. She'd lounge on the set of The Today Show *during commercial breaks, cruising a newspaper and behaving as though I were one of those motes that fly through the air of TV studios catching the light only at inopportune times. As I said, I didn't like her much. I had no way of knowing then that Debbie was already living in a buzzsaw that was cutting her through and through. It wasn't that she was being mean. She was just sheltering herself. And I don't blame her.*

Her rise was meteoric, her talent exceptional, and her future seemed limitless. She had led, in her own words, a charmed professional life. But when that charm deserted her, when all the bright lights flickered and failed, she was forced to look deep within herself, confront the demons of her own depression, and find the strength to survive. If the old phrase "golden girl" had been coined specifically for her, it couldn't have been more appropriate. Before the age of thirty, she had conquered every challenge of television news and stood poised on the brink of a brilliant network career. Then the golden dream became a nightmare, unraveling in the most public and painful way possible. By the same boss who had set me on guard against her upon my arrival at NBC News, she was put in a position to be the "other woman," shrewdly edging "the loved one" Jane Pauley off the couch of The Today Show. *The story was a natural for all the columnists who lacked both the mental acuity and the imagination to make more of it than a cat fight. In the debacle that followed,*

Norville came to represent the All About Eve *monster and in her own words, "damaged goods." The boss caved to mounting pressure from the Nielsen ratings, and Debbie was the perfect scapegoat. She was pregnant with her first child and, as they say in the business, on the beach.*

Deborah has said we all learn how to deal with emergencies—such as a grease fire in the kitchen—but that she had never learned how to deal with crisis. She was slammed with a public relations, internal, political, and plain old identity crises that she was not equipped to handle.

Deborah was shocked to find herself in a state of real depression. Twenty-five percent of Americans suffer from depression and eighty percent of them are women.

What she did to put her life back on track is worth considering. She began simply by making herself busy. She broadcast a radio program from her apartment, clinched a new job as a traveling correspondent for CBS, and when her son Niki begged her to come home, she found a new home as the anchor of Inside Edition *and had a third baby with her husband Carl. Then she wrote a book. Writing it down and then looking at your life, or even a piece of it, on paper is tremendously instructive.*

I did have a hard life. I think what made it so hard for me was that my life had been a success professionally. However, my personal life was another story; it was really rough. When I was growing up, my mother's chronic health problems ruled my universe. When I was eight years old, she had spinal surgery and had to relearn how to walk. When I was ten years old, she was diagnosed with rheumatoid arthritis. By the time I was fourteen, she was confined to bed. That's when my father walked out and my parents were divorced.

Life without my dad was strange. Yet my sisters and I knew that we had each other, and we knew our parents loved us. Despite our parents' problems with their marriage, and certainly my mother's problems with her health, they were always very careful to make sure that we knew we were important to them.

When I turned twenty, my mother died due to complications from being bedridden with arthritis. It was very traumatic. However, we managed to keep on living. In retrospect, I think my sisters and I weathered our personal traumas very well.

My mama used to say that my sisters and I were her hands and feet. She ran the household, and there was no question of that. But she told us what to do. If we were going to have roast beef and mashed potatoes for supper, then she would dictate our responsibilities. "Debbie, you do this to the beef and Nancy, you peel the potatoes, and Kathy, you open the can of green beans." We all had our jobs. We did the dishes, we set the table, we did the laundry, and we folded the laundry. I don't think she trusted us with the iron, but we pretty much did everything else. I don't remember watching cartoons as a kid. In fact, I don't think I watched cartoons until I was old enough to have a sleepover at somebody else's house. Saturday was chore day at our house. Everybody else looked forward to the weekends, everyone except for us. "Oh, man, we have to make the beds." It was that sort of thing. It made us grow up.

It was really hard for me when my parents separated. I was only fourteen. I was going through puberty and experiencing hands-on how difficult adolescence could be. And if that wasn't bad enough, my dad started dating the chorus teacher at school. Imagine that—there I was, extremely awkward, having to deal with the fact that my father's car was constantly stationed in the teachers' parking lot. It was really hard for me to deal with.

My sisters and I were never given instruction on how to deal with our parents' separation, yet we seemed to manage. I think one of the things that we had going for us was our deep personal faith in Christ. We're all born-again Christians, and I think our faith in Christ helped us have the strength to move on.

Unlike the crisis in my childhood life, my crisis in my professional life was *my* professional crisis. I couldn't say, "That's Daddy's problem or Mommy's problem." Rather, it was only Deb's problem. I probably should explain. NBC had named me to be the new newsreader on *The Today Show,* working alongside Jane Pauley and Bryant Gumbel. It was great. I'd filled in many times on the show, and I was told by both them and by the bosses that they couldn't be happier to have me on board. But by the end of the first week, there was an article in *USA Today* that put a negative spin on my presence on the show. I'll never forget the first words of the article; it said "Watch out, Jane Pauley." It went on to say that I looked awfully comfortable on the set with them—almost too comfortable. You see, they had me sit on the sofa with them at the end of the half hour, which in retrospect was the dumbest thing they could have done. I didn't ask to be center-stage. I was just happy to be there. In fact I would have sat on the floor if they asked me to.

The *USA Today* article was only the beginning. Every day I would see negative articles in the newspapers. They would always start off with things like, "fastest rising star." Meanwhile, I saw my star falling. I saw the golden girl get awfully tarnished. I didn't know what to do to make it stop. I certainly wasn't equipped to handle it. I looked like the other woman encroaching on Jane's turf. I fell into a state of real depression.

My depression was devastating. I was unable to conduct my life the way I had done normally before. I didn't leave the apartment. I had just had a little baby, so it's conceivable that part of my depression was postpartum depression; but I really don't think so. I have had two children since that time, and my postpartum was nothing like what I experienced when I left *The Today Show.* I saw myself as a television journalist; that's who I was. When I left *Today* (I resigned before I was pushed off the show), nobody begged me to stay. I wish I could say otherwise. When I realized that no one would hire someone who was so unlikeable to be their anchor, it was really tough on me. My whole identity did not exist anymore. I felt I was no longer who I thought I was. I was no longer a journalist; rather, according to newspapers, I was now a hideously awful person.

I had to search inside myself to find an identity that would cover my entire being, rather than one that was defined by my profession. I started from scratch. I began to look at my successes outside of television. I went back and did an exercise that I hadn't done since I entered the Junior Miss Pageant when I was seventeen years old. I wrote a one-page essay titled, "Who Am I?" Through my writing, I realized that "who am I" had nothing to do with what I did for a living; rather, it had to do with what I was, and what I believed. It's all about what's at the core of one's essence. Writing this essay really made a big difference in my life.

I got in touch with who I was. And knowing that has enabled me to make choices in my life that are right for me.

In my book, *Back On Track,* I describe both the steps that I went through to get back on track as well as the steps that ten or twelve other women went through to get through their own personal heartache. I won't lie, compared to these other women's stories mine is a day at the beach. For instance, the book describes the story of a woman who was raped at the age of twenty-five when life seemed filled with limitless possibilities. She worked in television. She changed her career. She ended up marrying the man who rushed to her side afterwards. And as she says in the book, "The episode is still there and it still plays itself over in my mind. But each time it replays, it gets quieter and quieter and softer." This is a woman who's gotten back on track after an unfathomable event in her life.

There's also a woman in the book who had breast cancer; everyone in her family who'd ever been diagnosed with cancer died within two years. So the first thing she did was prepare her will. Well, she didn't die; she beat it. Her daughter just got married, and she's praying for grandkids any day.

Yet even though our stories were vastly different, all of the people in the book went through a process that mirrored my own. Maybe we all didn't take the same steps, but we went through a very similar process that I had never seen articulated in the same way. My advice to all is as follows: First, acknowledge you've got a problem. It really does stem from the whole AA type of thing. Then take tiny baby steps, make small goals for yourself. My first goal for myself was to get dressed. I knew that if I got good at getting dressed, I would begin to put on my makeup. And if I could do those two things, then I'd leave the house. As you accomplish each baby step, you pat yourself on the back. You revel in it as though you've just won the Super Bowl and scored the winning touchdown. You say, "You go, girl! That's great! Man, you didn't think you were gonna get dressed today!"

In my book, I wrote down thirty-seven nice things to do for yourself, because a person who is in crisis cannot think of a single positive thing to do. My personal favorite is, "Send yourself flowers three weeks from now." When you get them you'll forget that you had sent these to yourself three weeks ago, and you'll say, "Oh, this is so great." Then you'll see the card, "To me from me," and you'll laugh. If you were having a bad day, it will change your trajectory and put you on a more positive track. If you're having a good day, it'll keep you there because you've just pulled a great joke on yourself.

Research shows that those of us who are in a negative mindset—which anybody who's gone through a depression as I did or anyone who's had a life crisis is—find it nearly impossible to conjure up any kind of positive image. So one of the exercises in the book is to make a list of your happy memories. Think back to the times in your life, and go back as far as you like, to those times when you felt good, when you felt loved, when you felt on top of the world. My list of happy memories are as bizarre as the first time I filled in on *Sunrise* at NBC and word filtered back that the fifth floor (where the important people were stationed) liked me; or the can-can skirt that my mother made when I was eight years old. That skirt was extremely important to me. In fact, I still have it in the dress-up box. I loved the fact that my mother, a woman who had so many other problems in her life, had taken the time to make my skirt. It was wonderful. Those types of happy memories help you get out of the doldrums of depression.

However, it is important to realize that if you do need someone else to help you through your depression, it is nothing to be ashamed of. In my case, I knew that it was going to take me a long time to feel better. In fact, it ended up being almost two years before I went back to television. As the time ticked away, I became more and more anxious to get better. It seems to me that we as a society have a problem with immediacy. Since we live in a microwave society where everything happens instantaneously, we expect our cures to happen just as fast. Of course, it doesn't work that way. I guess it is like breaking a bone; if you've ever broken a limb, the break happens instantaneously. However, the recovery takes much longer. The physical therapy that comes along with the break is time-consuming and very boring, and sometimes it's downright painful. But it is extremely important to be able to give yourself the time to be strong enough to walk on that broken leg again.

It is said that twenty-five percent of Americans suffer from depression and eighty percent of them are women. I think the reason for that is that women sort of take ownership for everything that happens in their little sphere of influence. Cornelia Otis Skinner said women have in their hearts a capacity for sins they never committed. I think it's so true. We women have a lot of hats that we wear. I have help at home, and yet I still feel responsible for every single aspect that happens to my kids. Today my son put on some jeans and there was no snap on the front (the snap was lost somewhere). I felt responsible for my son losing his snap. I was sure that someone else noticed that the snap was gone, too. For me, when those things add up, my bottom falls out.

I got back on track without going to a counselor or a therapist or any kind of "expert." Since the "experts" had not handled things so well at NBC, I tend to have this bit of a distrust for them. Frankly, I think that's where most women come down. I think we all suffer from the "I can do it myself" syndrome partly because there's no one else we can rely on. When everything else crashes around you, sometimes the only constant in your life is you. I have a husband who is great, but at the time it didn't help. I had to realize that no one can make you feel good about yourself except for you.

That's really why I wrote the book. Women put themselves so far down the list of priorities; there's the husband, there's the children, there's the house, there's the job, there's the volunteer work, and somewhere way down the list comes, "there's me." We're not likely to go out and get that professional help that we might need.

I think it is important to reach out to other people. In fact, in the book I wrote a letter which says, "Dear Blank, things have been tough since (fill in your crisis). It would really be great to see you again/talk to you again/hear from you. I know you're very busy but if you could call/phone/write/whatever, it would be great." By reaching out to others, you have the ability to feel better in life.

I think there's a purpose to everything that happens in life, and I think there was a purpose in what I went through at NBC. The purpose for my crisis was that I was able, in a very quiet way, to show people that yes, life can deal you a hand that you wouldn't have chosen, that you didn't expect, and that you didn't know how to deal with, but it doesn't have to defeat you. It taught me that I'm a strong person, that I have, I think, a gift for helping people. I have been able to reach out to people. I have hugged people. A woman in Colorado with tears in her eyes told me she knew she would be able to get through her painful divorce after hearing what I had to share. A man whose daughter slid under the lawn mower while he was driving it read my book the night that they were in the hospital while he waited for news of his daughter's recovery. He read my book on the floor of the room and used the bed as his light source. He told me a couple of days later that my book got him through that night. Before reading it, he thought he was going to kill himself for what he did to his child; after reading it, he realized that he too would be able to get through his crisis.

I guess my spirituality comes from seeing where God has made a difference in my life, where He has enabled me to see lessons in life events. Where God allowed me and my son Niki to find a turtle on the side of the road and examine him. We noticed how when the turtle stuck his neck out, he took a step. It was only when he stuck his neck out that he got anywhere. And the light bulb went off. God was telling me, "If you don't stick your neck out, Deborah, you ain't going no place." I've seen God work in those kinds of ways in my life. I've seen the way people have responded to what I've learned in my own journey of getting back on track. And I've seen where it's made a positive difference in their lives. I've seen where I have found a purpose in my crisis, and I think that purpose is to help other people who similarly feel as I did that life will never be good again, that those wonderful times are all behind me.

Through all of this, I learned that defeats happen in life and that you can't be defeated if you choose not to be. I can't dictate what goes on in life. But I can decide what happens inside myself. Now, I can proudly say that I have chosen to see the problems in my life as opportunities rather than setbacks. And for that, I am a much better person today.

CHAPTER 31

ALAN ARKIN

Alan Arkin is as intense, intelligent, and compact a person as I've ever met, but he's still one of those males who appears to prefer earned run averages and geopolitics to anything approaching tree-hugging. Hardly the type to launch himself on a journey of the soul—or so I thought.

Ever since I saw him up there in The Russians Are Coming, The Russians Are Coming, *I've been fascinated by his versatility and artistry—or maybe I just like short guys. He's won us over in films as diverse and as honored as* Catch-22, The Heart Is a Lonely Hunter, The In-Laws, *and* The Rocketeer. *But to know him through his roles misses the man completely. To know him through his talented kids, including Adam of* Chicago Hope *and* Northern Exposure, *is to see only a fragment of him.*

Two decades ago, he was at the top of his game, considered among the top three actors in the world. He had a great family and awards galore and was perfectly miserable. It is one thing to define a character. It is quite another to identify your own character. For Arkin, it wasn't as simple as an "Is that all there is" question. It was the question of "Who am I?" that became his continuing nightmare. This New York tough brought up in a Judeo-Christian mentality couldn't find any answers.

Then Arkin met a man who faced him Eastward and launched him on a journey into the recesses of his own soul. While he had help, in the end the journey he took was a solitary one, not altogether comforting at first. But on the path he has discovered the value of pain and a new definition of success.

Success is not a word that applies to everybody in the world in exactly the same way. Success is achieving what works for you inside. It has nothing to do with what the world thinks.

I decided I wanted to act at the age of five for what I think were pretty neurotic reasons. I said, "I'm going to become a successful actor and no one can stop me. I'm going to be an actor. That's all I want to do, and that's all I want to know about."

As I grew up, I held onto this same dream. I put most of my life on hold. But then one day I reached it; I was a successful actor. And suddenly I became depressed. I realized that I wasn't happy. I had achieved everything I had set out to achieve, yet when I wasn't onstage or in front of a camera, I was nobody. When I became a successful actor, all of the things that I had thought were going to take care of themselves didn't. I was still just a guy, facing the same problems and fears that I had had all my life. It was a big slap in the face. Success wouldn't and couldn't make my fears go away.

There are plenty of people who bury themselves in their work twenty-four hours a day. It's a cozy hiding place, but I couldn't do it. I desperately wanted to find some degree of happiness with my family and with myself, when I was alone, but I couldn't do it. So I said, "There's got to be something more than this." I began my search for something else. It was not as if I was pursuing any kind of a spiritual path. Spirituality just presented itself to me and seemed the only thing available offering help.

I remember my turning point. I met this guy who was my stand-in for one of my films. He seemed really happy. Because he generated a good aura, he got a respect and attention and peace and joy out of his life that I had never experienced. I didn't understand how or why he was able to experience happiness and I couldn't. As a result, I got angry. I said, "What the heck has this guy got that I haven't got?" So I decided to study him in order to find out his secrets. As I followed him around, I learned that he had been meditating for years and followed a specific philosophy or belief system. This belief system gave him the strength to be content. I began to work with him. He taught me about his beliefs in this particular form of Eastern philosophy.

The philosophy begins by introducing yourself to yourself. You sit in a room and do nothing. You say, "Well, I'm just going to sit here and not do anything for ten minutes. If the phone rings I'm not going to answer it. If somebody bangs on the door I'm not going to answer. I'm going to sit here and find out who I am without any kind of agenda, without any kind of reference to the outside world in any way." Initially it's terrifying because I didn't want to be with me. People fear that they're not going to find anybody in there. They feel that there's not going to be somebody in there. They want to have an intermediary. They want to have some external reference to who they are. You find terrible horrible things out about yourself. But what you find if you do it long enough is that there is somebody in there. There's somebody you can make reference to, that you can pay attention to.

It's not as if a moment arises where you say, "Oh, this is who I am." It's a continually unfolding process, as anybody who's worked on themselves in any area will know. Even if you want to become a pianist, there's not a moment at which you say, "Now I'm a pianist." In the East, if you ask a Chinese painter, "Oh, you're a painter," he'll say, "No, I am not a painter." He'll say, "I paint." There's a very strong distinction.

Through my meditation, I have learned a great deal about myself and my goals. I think anger is a necessary thing to acknowledge in yourself because most of the time anger covers up fear. I thought that once I got in touch with my anger I'd be a lot happier person. But what I started to find out was that anger was a lethal weapon. Once I found that it was causing a lot of pain and destruction around me, it's not that I didn't want to feel it again, but I didn't want to unleash it again. There's a difference.

I am now able to acknowledge when I'm really angry about something. If my anger is directed towards somebody else, I'll try to say, "What you said now made me very angry. I don't know whether it was intentional or whether I'm misreading what you said. Can we talk about it?" It is an infinitely healthier way to deal with anger. Then you have an opportunity to take down defenses, discuss, and resolve the issue. But while it sounds easy, it isn't. It takes a lot of work.

I don't know anybody who walks through life with a sense of perfect serenity, but one of the things I can do at least part of every day is to say, “I am right here right now.” It just makes everything infinitely easier.

Most people’s behavior indicates that they’re not here right now. They’re projecting that in twenty minutes they’ve got to get in the car and do something, so they’re not entirely present. I’ve recognized that the more present I am in what I’m doing right now, the more I can enjoy almost anything that I’m doing. When you’re really involved in and engaged in the moment, it almost doesn’t matter what else comes next. I’ve reached the point now, and this is not voluntary—it’s happening to me and it’s scaring the hell out of me, frankly—is I cannot plan anymore. I can’t plan ahead.

I’ve become very efficient with what is in front of me and take care of that. If that’s taken care of, I know that the next thing I do in the next hour will also be taken care of.

Many of my old beliefs have gone by the wayside for me, because a belief system, to me, is what I would like to be true. Most of the time I couldn’t substantiate a lot of what I believed and would get enraged at people who challenged me. Now, I believe in the possibility for infinite change, including infinite growth. And I believe in the interconnectedness of all things.

I no longer have to take responsibility for everything that’s happened around me. The pain that comes is not retribution for anything. If you like yourself, you can accept something difficult that happens for what it is rather than saying, “Oh, look what I’ve brought on myself, this substantiates what a horrible person I am.” Pain is a wonderful thing. It’s the great teacher. When you have pain that you don’t credit with having a reason, you might say, “This is a terrible misfortune that’s befallen me.” But if you recognize the reason for that agony, it doesn’t bother you. Almost all of us, at one point or another, have had the experience of deciding to get in shape. Well, what happens when you get in shape? For the first week you’re in agony. If you worked out for a week and didn’t expect pain to come, you might say, “What a horrible misfortune that’s come to me.” An athlete would recognize that pain as something that strengthens him. I believe that all pain is a way for us to strengthen ourselves.

Periodically, life gets murderously hard. It is part of the human condition. Nobody ever said that your life was going to be a picnic twenty-four hours a day, seven days a week. It just can't be. Things happen. But while things happen, having an approach to your life and a trust of yourself and a comfort with yourself gives you infinitely more material to deal with it.

It didn't take any kind of courage for me to launch myself on this journey. I felt like I had to do something because nothing was working. I didn't feel like I had an alternative. While I am forever glad that I have reached this point in my life, the journey here has been extremely difficult. As I grew on my journey, my old self started dying. My belief system, essentially everything I believed in, started leaving. I began cutting the strings to my past life. Cutting the strings took courage because I really thought that I was going to die. Well, in truth, something inside me did die; and I'm forever thankful that it did.

God is part of my lexicon now. But, to me, He's not a guy up in the sky that's giving out favors or punishments to people. Rather, he is a matrix of living thought. Scientists believe that the universe is made up of matter which becomes nonmaterial and then comes back with information. The universe is a matrix of living thought. To me, that is the perfect definition of God. Therefore, since we are all a part of the universe, we are all a part of that matrix. I find our association with the universe and God to be extremely comforting.

The idea that we are part of something so vast helps put your personal potholes in perspective. At least it does mine. But the notion of being alone with myself routinely terrorizes me. Beyond the fact that there are things I fear exhuming from my own soul, I fear taking the time. When there are kids to raise and bills to pay and laundry piling up around my knees, the very idea of taking time for myself comes hard for me. But I have learned this much: Arkin's notion of living in the moment has miraculous consequences. If I'm facing backwards, wallowing in the past, I am going to trip over a pile of wet laundry. When I'm focused forward into the future, I fall back on my old trick of trying to control what hasn't happened yet. And that's defensive. It's living in fear. Fact is, today is all I have. It's all any of us has. When I'm completely focused on right this moment, I can relish the hours spent reading to my children and the extra hours it takes to prepare dinner when they help. Instead of becoming woefully inefficient, as I feared, staying in the present really does ensure that the future will take care of itself, carpools and kid logistics notwithstanding. Someone said to me once that yesterday is over, tomorrow is not promised, but today is a present. A gift. That sounds right.

CHAPTER 32

F. MURRAY ABRAHAM

In the film Amadeus, *the bitter broken composer Antonio Salieri curses the fate that failed to touch him with greatness. The actor who brought him back to life has been touched with greatness, I think, and has gone through rough road to get there.*

The day we spent together in black-clad New York (everyone in the arts wears black—it sets off the street soot so nicely), F. Murray Abraham wore red. How's that for confident? His Syrian-Italian roots project from his cheekbones, and his dark eyes miss nothing. He is tactile and keen-minded in the extreme. I have never met a man who picks up on subtlety with more acuity. There was electricity in the air between us.

Fahrid (in Arabic it means "one and only"; now you know what the F stands for) Murray Abraham is a Pittsburgh native, son of a Syrian Orthodox garage mechanic who immigrated to America and married an Italian. They moved the family to El Paso where Murray caught the acting bug. At UCLA, too frightened to even audition, he worked as part of a two-man stage crew. The other man was Francis Ford Coppola. (Everyone has to start somewhere.) Once in New York, Murray accumulated a long list of off-Broadway credits, and parked cars, and played Santa at Macy's, to supplement his income. Small parts in big films followed, but the Salieri role had been coveted by the likes of Jack Nicholson, Ben Kingsley, and Al Pacino. Absolutely nobody expected Murray to get it. But get it he did, and for his efforts, an Oscar, a Golden Globe, the Los Angeles Critics Association Award, and the Albert Schweitzer Award for classic film acting.

There's a line in the film world that goes, "Nobody who wins an Oscar ever goes hungry again . . . unless you're F. Murray Abraham." It's not entirely true. Murray has worked steadily, but none of his roles have come close to matching Salieri. For a while, he took it as a personal rejection.

Maybe he just gave himself too hard an act to follow. Or maybe he just lacks the temperament for the glamour and dollar-driven Holly-world. Or maybe he just didn't play the game. He calls New York theater his polestar and its quality a lot more gratifying than face-time on ET.

Amadeus did not start his career, but it certainly launched his celebrity—at a price.

Amadeus was the most important project of my entire life, because it's a continuing success. And it was also successful in Europe in a very big way, so I began to do films all over the world. I was making a very good living and finally seeing the world that I'd always wanted to see, first class. The other good thing is that *Amadeus* is an annual event, so my success from that film continues. That's not true of every Academy Award winner. That's very lucky. But the funny thing is that in all the years that have passed, when it's shown on TV, young people come to me—really young people—and they say, "Oh, you're that guy in *Amadeus.*" One of these days I'm going to look like the old Salieri, and they're going to say, "You were terrific but you were much better than that guy who played the young Salieri." They won't know it's the same guy.

That was the good news. The bad news is that it does test your friendships. You can't discuss which role you want to take for many thousands of dollars with your core group of serious actors when they're trying to simply get an audition. It's very difficult.

It tests your family relationships. I became really involved in my own fame for a while, and my family suffered for it.

It also tests your sense of who you are. I began to believe all of the nonsense that people told me. It was dangerous. I can understand how some of these really young kids become disastrous when they become rich at twenty-one. How do they handle that stuff? It takes a real maturity.

People suggest that you are responsible for your failures as well as your successes, and it's really nonsense. It really is. Are they suggesting that I won an Academy Award because I wanted it more than those other people who were nominated? Take a look at their faces. They all wanted it. I was lucky that year.

But then I was disappointed. I really believed when I won the Academy Award for that performance that Hollywood thought I was a real good actor, until I started seeing the material they were offering me. A child killer, a rapist, a rapist of my own children. I said I'm not interested in this. I really am not.

And they wouldn't believe it. They kept offering more and more money. So I just left. I started doing films in Italy and Russia and Istanbul and all these wonderful places, and taking my family. You begin to understand the value of the work by itself, so that when I came back with a little bit of money (I don't need that much), I began doing plays again. That's really where my heart is. I'm still looking for another great movie one of these days. But the fact is that I am very lucky and I have nothing to complain about at all.

You are where you're supposed to be. F. Murray Abraham may have once been caught up in celebrity and all its trappings, but he's caught in another quest now—a private internal one. Though he's notorious for keeping his personal life close to his vest, he seemed to be unfolding it to me. As he talked about his journey from grandiosity to something approaching humility, his face would frequently reflect flashes of insight, as though he'd never quite thought of what he was telling me in quite that way before.

He has spent a lot of time searching around inside of his own soul. He had a glimpse of his own mortality, a jolt that connected him with his spirituality.

I think one of the most important things is the soul and the existence of the soul and the care of the soul. When you get away from it, which I did and still do from time to time as a human being, you lose track of the reason why special things take place.

Part of our obligation in this life is to find out as much about ourselves and our place in this world as we can. That is a spiritual search. It is absolutely personal. I don't mean to say you are the center of the universe at all, but if you want to try to cure the ills in the universe, I believe you have to start with yourself. You must clean up yourself first. That is your first obligation.

Finding an expression of your spiritual center in this world is your obligation. If you have no idea of your soul or whatever you want to call that thing that separates you from every other person that ever lived, you are missing something. That is your obligation to God, to Buddha, to whomever you choose. I think that my higher power is a God, the same God that lives in you. "Higher power" is an interesting term. I like the idea of Quakerism. Quakers believe that God exists in every person. I think Christians and Jews and Muslims think of God as being outside. I believe that God is inside. I don't think I need a priest as an intermediary. My obligation is here, to the God that resides here and in me.

I think that what I'm looking for is the truth in this life. I was almost killed three years ago in an automobile crash. Two drunken kids hit my car. They were going very fast. They were both killed. I was cut out of the car.

After the accident, the fact is that I became extremely depressed. I guess it was the proximity of the two dead young men. They were twenty-five, about the age of my children now. I was one of three kids, and my two brothers have been killed. It's one of those things. One was a victim of Vietnam, the other was killed while in the Army. It's hard to talk about it. It would have been nice to see them have nephews, nieces. I couldn't understand why I was spared, because it was an absolute miracle that I lived.

What it did was remind me how quickly the life disappears. There was no flashing of my life before my eyes. I was alive and then I was almost dead.

I think that what we have to understand about this life is the gift that it is. This sounds like old saw, but really think about what we are here for. It's more than just accumulating money or making fame of your name. It's something else. I don't think that your responsibility is to change the entire world or the universe. You've got to start right here. I'm not saying it's easy. I get into some terrible situations because I'm a selfish, greedy guy. I do things I shouldn't. But I'm telling you that time is running out, because you can be killed any time. You need to ask yourself what do you want to be doing when you die? What is it that you want to be doing? Something you're proud of or something you're ashamed of?

I started to search out why I was spared, and I couldn't understand why. I really questioned it for quite a while until a friend of mine said, "To act!" Acting is my gift and my obligation to God. I believe there was a reason a couple of thousand years ago that actors were regarded as priests. I really think acting can be a channel of grace, but you've got to have the good material to find that channel. You can't do it with soap operas. (Nothing against soap operas, I've done them.)

My work is my prayers. I mean it. I try to conduct my life in a noble fashion, but it's not. It's my work that's noble. Not my life. I do separate my life from my work. I don't know if it's proper, but I do. My work is sacrosanct. I'm a tough taskmaster with myself and with people around me. But the joy that I get back from it is a delight.

Devotion to the work shouldn't exclude your family, which sometimes happens. It's too bad that people now are so devoted to their careers that they forget their family. I did for a while and I almost paid for it. Then I began to realize it and devoted myself to reacquainting myself with the kids. By that time they were saying, "Oh, yeah? Prove it." It took time and diligence, but we're back together again, spiritually and mentally. They're terrific kids. I simply let them know that I was available, that they should pick up the phone at any time if they needed something or wanted to talk. I didn't care. I said, "I'll leave the rehearsal, I'll leave opening night."

Saying, "I'm sorry," is hard at first. I have plenty to be sorry about, and apologies roll off my tongue. But I mean them. I'd begun getting in touch with people I insulted many years ago. A lot of them didn't get back to me, but I tried. It's important. It's a little like the twelve-step program. It's a very good program. At least you made the attempt. Don't walk around feeling guilty. Say you're sorry. If they accept it, fine. If they don't, that's fine, too. You tried. Get on with your life. Do something, that's the point. And don't compare it to somebody else. Don't be like Salieri. Do your best because what more can you do?

I think that success is fine. I've had it; I've tasted it. It was a lot of fun. I spent all the money. Now it's time to get on with the important things.

I am devoted, and I really do love acting. It's an interesting phenomenon after all the years I've been in this business to still have a remarkable passion for my work. I mean really a passion. But there was a point not too long ago where I began to feel smug. I really felt there was nothing I couldn't do. It may be difficult, it may take some training, but I can do it. That's what I felt. I'd done the classics; I'd done Shakespeare. I had done the greatest roles ever written. You've got to put yourself on the line from time to time. I think that the moment you get smug, you find yourself in a situation where you get pulled up short. Some people really don't want to see that kind of thing because it's difficult to face it. But we must put ourselves to these tests.

I've been together with my wife for many years now—thirty-seven years—and the crises still happen. You really must face the fact that you're changing. Both of you are changing. There is no guarantee you are going to get through that change together. I think that you have to trust that love within each other. I think it's a renewal. That's a serious thing. I think it is an exciting renewal, a constant test.

When I was working on the part of Roy Cohn in *Angels in America,* I wanted to dedicate the performance to some friends who had died. The list got so long that I was devastated all over again. I had forgotten how many. So I dedicated it to all my friends who had died of AIDS. It was a long list. It took a while to get over that, to get back into the rehearsal.

But the most devastating thing and, I think, the cathartic thing about the play was coming out of the theater afterwards and being greeted by people from the Midwest and all over the country—parents of these homosexual men who had died of AIDS, who had been so intolerant and who were there with apology in their eyes. They wanted to thank us for what we had helped them come through, to realize the validity of their son's lifestyle and choice. That was the value of the theater. And that was the value of our work and my work as an actor.

• • •

I don't know who I did it for, but I know I was driven. I know I still have a lot of ambition. But I think I'd like to channel it someplace a little bit happier. I want people to come out of the theater feeling good. I think that's important. That's what I'd like to do for the rest of my career, if I can. Because I'm funny. My early career was all comedy. Then it became all tragedy. I think it's time to get back to all comedy again. Life is serious enough.

It is this day and your obligation also to tomorrow that is most important. There is a tomorrow for this civilization, and that's our obligation. It is not just us. There's a whole world out there. And we do affect the world. There is providence in the fall of a sparrow. I believe it.

CHAPTER 33

ROLONDA WATTS

Rolonda Watts has been looking up and out her whole life. From the time she was a North Carolina kid picking salamanders out of the creek and gazing at the blue Tarheel sky, she's been headed for the big time. She wears on a chain around her neck a New York City subway token. She made it there as a local television anchor, and then she got her own syndicated talk show. Television, especially syndicated television, can be bloodsport with a propensity to reduce all things and all people to a common denominator. She fought that, and won.

Make no mistake, Rolonda didn't come up poor. Both her parents were professors, and her great-grandfather was the founder of Bennett College. She was raised in an all-white neighborhood and sent to the finest schools.

Still, being black in the Sixties in the South had some bearing on her life. When she talks about it, it is with compassion for racial division and a breezy attitude that makes it sound easy. Maybe it was.

The high school that I went to, Salem Academy, is an all-girl preparatory school founded in the 1700s, and I was the only black in my school. I never recognized a real difference. I guess kids don't do that. You had a best friend; you go to the creek; you meet on the corner with your bicycles; and you spend the night over. The only time that I think we really recognized a difference was when *Roots* was aired and for our U.S. history class, we all had to sit together and watch *Roots.* The character Kizzy, who helped tell the story, was a girl about our age at that time, so some of the girls really connected with this young girl living in slavery. When the tragic ending came, the girls were crying, and then all of a sudden they looked over and recognized I was black! And they said, "Was that true, what we just saw?" And I said, "It's only what they could show you during prime time!"

One of the girls was from a Southern city where her father was mayor, and where one of the tourist attractions is still the auction blocks. What that allowed us to do was to talk about our history. You can't talk about slavery without talking about American history, black and white, and what I loved was being able to be in that situation. I was able to open some minds a little bit.

I was very, very popular in school, president of the glee club, and on the field hockey team. I never felt different. I will say that when we went to the boys' schools I didn't get asked to dance very much; maybe race had something to do with that. There was one incident though at the senior prom. The junior class gave a surprise theme to the senior class. The theme was Southern Comfort. I walked into the gymnasium, and I remember the murals had all these southern scenes, and on one of them was a cotton field with some pickaninnies in it.

My date looked at me and he said, "I don't believe they did this!" And I said, "You don't understand. These girls love me, I don't think they knew what they were doing!" To which he said, "I don't understand how you forgive people for this, because I don't get it." I still believe to this day that racism does not always have malicious intent. Sometimes it's just ignorance. I think that was the case at the prom.

But my French teacher, who was from Belgium and Jewish, called an entire school meeting and talked about how hurt she was. She began to talk about what it felt like to be a Jewish girl in Belgium, and if she had walked into her prom her senior year and seen swastikas, she would have been concerned. It opened our minds. It could have been a perfect opportunity for a race war. Somebody could have gotten upset, but instead it was talked out. I think in situations where there's already division, there's no need in fanning the fire. Let's find out how we can make it a gentle hearth, so we can sit by it and tell stories and learn about our differences.

I thought I was smart enough to cut corners. I learned I couldn't. I'll never forget this. I was in this African-American literature class at Spellman College. One of my assignments was to do an oral book report. My book was Ralph Ellison's *Invisible Man.* I was editor of *The Spellman Spotlight* newspaper; I had the lead in *Guys and Dolls;* I was dating a guy who was helping me with the mayoral campaign. I was busy, okay? I didn't have time to read the book! So the night before the oral report was due, I turned to my roommate and I said, "Let's get in your little rickety car and go down to the bookstore and pick up the *Cliff's Notes* for this thing cause I can talk through it!

I learned the abrupt lesson that night that you can't buy classics like Ralph Ellison's *Invisible Man* in *Cliff's Notes!* I said, "What am I going to do?" And she said, "I think you better read the book!" So I was reading the book, and reading the book. The first chapter was the battle royal. I got into it and the next thing I knew the alarm was going off and the sun was coming up; I had fallen asleep. But I knew I could talk! So I would talk my way through it. I got up in front of the class and I said, "This is the greatest book, the imagery, the similes, the metaphors, but the best part of the book that describes all of it is the battle royal." I described chapter one and I thought I'd won them over.

Finally the teacher asked me, "Did you read that book?" I said, "Yes, I read the book. You know I read the book!" She said, "I know you read the battle royal, did you read the book?" And I said, "Well, no." And she looked at me across a sea of desks, and she said, "How dare you cheat Ralph Ellison!" Here is a man who had to be invisible so one day I could be seen on television! Here's a man who had to be silenced through a pen so that I could use a pen and my mouth and write a book and be on television and be visible and invisible, too, if I want to be! He gave so much so that I would have an opportunity. The least I could do was read the man's book!

Ellison made me miss summa cum laude. I graduated from Spellman in three years magna cum laude because of the D I got in that class. But it made a point. You have such a responsibility to your visibility, and a lot of it is a responsibility to my ancestors and the people who came before me in my field. The women who blazed ways for me, all the changes that have happened because someone could not do what I'm doing today, allowed me to do it, and the least I could do was study that. It has been an important lesson for me. Every once in a while, I will go back and read *Invisible Man,* because I can understand a lot of the feelings there. But I also learned a lesson that your mouth can't always get you out of trouble!

Rolonda's mouth, along with her intellect and ambition, got her into television—and out of her hometown. Something happened there that she does not choose to share. Whatever it was, it caused a schism in her family that is not healed. When she returned home to accept an honorary doctorate from the University where her father chairs the fine arts department, her parents didn't show up. When I asked her if she felt lonely, she said, "But I love being alone."

The issues she hasn't been able to work out at home, she's worked out at work. She's used her role on television to talk about families in crisis and explore resolutions, always drawn to little girls in need of rescue. Maybe she herself is looking for ways to be saved.

Her happiest days with her family were those during which they allowed her to dream big.

At the end of every summer, after the kids had finished summer school, and summer jobs, and summer visits to relatives, my family would get together and come to New York City, to go to Broadway and see the big city. That was a big deal for a little girl from the country! My brother and I would ride the subway all day long. It was better than a Dixie Classic fairground.

To me the subway token symbolized dreams because with that one little token that said "New York City" on one side, and on the other "Good For One Fare," I could go anywhere. People walked as fast as I did, talked as fast as I did. Down South where I'm from I had a lot of energy when I was growing up! But being different fit in here. I'd always said, "I'm going to New York!"

That was my dream. I used to take that token and shine it with steel wool, and it would shine like eighteen-karat gold. My dad gave me this little chain, and I wore it around my neck, and I held it onto it. My parents were very big on having dreams, and I think that was the beginning of this little girl's dreams.

It was a happy time with my family, and I think that was a time when my parents were helping me with my dreams. That's why they brought me to New York, to be able to think bigger than just picking salamanders. And my dad helped me shine.

I don't know if I'll ever know what really happened. I think that many times in families we all come to the table with different issues, and unless we're able to work those issues out, they can be a problem. I love my family very much. There is no question that there is a tremendous amount of love in this family. I just hope that one day we will be able to sit down and resolve a lot of the issues. Sometimes when you're estranged, you don't even remember what the real problem was.

I come from a family that doesn't like to talk about anything. As a kid I was never allowed to express anger. So how could we talk about something that made me angry, because I wasn't even supposed to be angry? I was allowed to talk, but we didn't talk very much about how we felt. And there were things, difficult things. I know that it's tough. It hurts. I'm not going to act like I'm superwoman. Sure it hurts when you don't have your family's support. Sure it hurts when you haven't been able to resolve some issues that are still affecting your life.

I had a suicide in my family, and it was something that the family could never talk about. It was embarrassing to say somebody killed himself or herself. You can't say that, because it was never discussed. Those feelings of abandonment, those feelings that I could have done something, those feelings that naturally come with a suicide in a family, were never addressed. Our family had really no place to turn except each other. But we couldn't because they came from an era that said, "You don't talk about your family!" If you don't talk about yourself and your issues that come from within your family, then you cannot be a full completely healed person.

So I can connect with the woman who got on my show, and

talked about suicide. I could understand what she was talking about. I could understand when a family got on and talked about having a missing member of their family. I understood what that felt like. Those were the types of things that have given me great purpose. I think there's a tremendous responsibility to your visibility on television. If I have one hour, it's going to be for families and people who love them, whether they're talking to each other or not!

That is one of the reasons why I did *The Rolonda Show* with so much focus on families and crisis. We had a marvelous series that ran for four years about families in crisis. I applaud an industry that is promoting something worth talking about. We were acknowledging the fact that some things that go on within families and relationships are very difficult to talk about. But we also acknowledged that you aren't alone and that there are programs out there and people out there to help. We talked about issues—not in a sensational way, not in a way that would make people tune in to watch car wrecks—but we tackled issues that were difficult to talk about for families.

My feeling was that there was a tremendous need for some type of respect for people's life stories on television. I have problems with my family, but I don't want to make a show out of it. I don't want people screaming at the audience and my mother.

So if people are going to scream and yell, let it be a passionate voice that says I want to save something I love! People were on our show fighting, but they were fighting for the things they love. Many of the folks who did the show had never been on an airplane before, never been to New York City before, but trusted us enough to come on that stage and tell the world that it can be better, and you can make a difference, and I will share my life story, so that you never have to be here or so that you know you're not alone. Those folks gave me courage.

I know that one day we're all going to be healed, or at least we're going to come to some kind of agreement to sit down and discuss what hurts us so much. I don't think it's anger so much. I think there's just been so much hurt, whether that's imposed by each other, or imposed on us as little kids, or when I was a kid. Those are things that take time and healing. I've seen it on my show. I've seen the most courageous people in the world who have walked on that show and changed their lives and changed mine by touching me!

I did the talk show for four years, and my parents never came to see it. They never saw my set, which is really sad.

But I've been really blessed in my life to have tons of very special people in my life who are all different kinds of people. All different races. All different beliefs. I'm very proud of that. With that comes an ability and an opportunity to be able to really flesh out things that they didn't talk about ten years ago. Adoption used to be a bad word. Now it's something that I may even be considering doing one day. But in my parents era, to be talking about adoption, and on TV! And say somebody in your family was adopted! Lord, have you lost your mind?

I said on TV one day that my mother and I had had an argument, and my mom got really mad. She just went off! I think that I tend to be a lot more open about things. We just have different ways of approaching issues that are sensitive and difficult to talk about. It's the very thing that I think has made my family so estranged.

But I don't have to just depend on my family. I have wonderful people around me. I have a professor who has come to visit me. She was the one who said, "You are special, there is something special about you," and who gave me my first opportunity. And she is here to support me and to help me with some of my acting. I have dear friends who I call family who are here to support me. So we build our own support systems.

My parent's favorite saying is, "If you're going to pray, don't worry. If you're going to worry, don't pray!" And it's just that simple, I believe. I say five words, "Let Your will be done." He's in control up there. God, help me see the purpose behind the things that you are sending me to live with, because I know it's all right, I know I'm going to be fine, you're not going to send me anything I can't handle! He's got me. I'm with Him! I think you do have to have faith. You have to believe in things that you can't see in front of your face. I'm still trying to figure it all out. I believe if you try really hard to do the right thing, and you admit that you're human too, that He will look after you. I believe God believes in matching grants!

Pain a lot of times is a catalyst. After you say "ouch," it makes you say "What am I going to do now?" It gets you moving. I've got a long time to live, I've got a lot to work out! But I know that time heals. That's the beauty of life.

CHAPTER 34

ED ASNER

Back when the letters CNN, strung together, meant nothing to anyone but the zealous few who started it up and the insomniac souls who were mesmerized by it, my bureau was a glassed-in cage in the lobby of New York's World Trade Center. Strangers would regularly peek in to see the news hounds in their natural habitat, and I would regularly try to avoid their stares while delivering some event of major import to a camera that stood between us. Every so often, one of those strangers would attempt to enter. Ed Asner was one of them. He strode in, charged like a bull, and swept me up in a crushing bear hug as though I were the girl he'd been chasing in his dreams. I was smitten.

Ed Asner, I've come to learn, is an inveterate flirt who works very hard to please everyone that crosses his considerable path. He was born into an Orthodox Jewish home in Kansas City, the youngest of five children, with a patriarchal father and a mother who took care of them all. He is a dreamer who really wanted to be an adventurer, laying pipelines in South America, being a cabin boy on an Alaskan cruiser. By going into acting, he got to play them all. He's got a shelf-full of Emmys and a credit list in film and theater longer than these pages will hold. He is at once learned and distinguished, a social activist and an unapologetic liberal—as well as the kind of basic guy who you could easily imagine would smash beer cans on his forehead and put cigars out on the walls. He is a news freak who never got to be a newsman but played one on television.

It is said that television is reactionary. It only reflects what is already out there in society. Every once in a rare while, television can lead. Just before the end of apartheid in South Africa, the highest rated show there was The Cosby Show. *And in America, a year before women were admitted en masse to television newsrooms, among the highest rated shows was* The Mary Tyler Moore Show, *a woman who could make it after all.*

The Mary Tyler Moore Show was a success because it was beautifully written. Mary is a stellar personality. She was the hub around which we all turned as we performed. We all nicely dovetailed into each other. Norman Lear was on the scene at the same time with Archie Bunker, tackling huge ideas and problems and situations. We were milder. We dealt with traditional problems and situations. We were a gentle show. But what we were doing still mattered.

I grew up in the Midwest in Kansas City. Kansas City was a gentle place to grow up compared to the stories I've heard about other places in the country. It was the same with *Mary Tyler Moore.* When we dealt with problems, we had a gentle way of dealing with life and its problems and the world, with some beautifully written characters, some great situations. When we ended our last show, the famous critic for *The Washington Post,* Tom Shales, who I'd taken issue with at other times, wrote a column on it, and he said something beautiful about us. He said it was seven years of a wonderful bunch of losers. I think that's what we were. In our own way, in our respective characters in their little lives, we were losers.

We were the fourth- or fifth-rated station. Ted Baxter was the biggest dodo that ever lived. Murray was the failed writer. Sue Anne hopped from bed to bed and cooking show to cooking show. Georgette? Georgette was a winner in her own way. But Phyllis lost Lars in the course of the show. Her daughter was more intelligent than she. Lou had gone from the *Detroit Free Press* and all that old newspaper glory to the fifth-rated station in Minneapolis, and even got fired a couple of times during the course of the series. And his wife divorced him to find herself.

These were losers—wonderful losers—and I loved every one of them. And when Shales wrote that, I think even he was admitting that because of what we achieved together, we were winners.

In trying to make the transition from half-hour to hour, comedy to drama, three-camera live audience to one-camera dead crew, the character of Lou Grant almost broke me. It was an enormous strain. Nobody involved had ever done an hour series. They had done movies, they had done features for television, and half-hour specials. Nobody had ever done a long string of hour-long running shows. We were all trying to find our ass with both hands.

The producers and director were the team from *Mary Tyler Moore*. I was given the dictum, "When you get out there with Lou Grant, just remember who you are. You're the one who has to keep the flame alive." I was in therapy at the time. After we went on the air, I went to the therapist and said, "What do you think of the show?" He said, "Why do you grimace so much?" I realized I was doing so much body-English because there was no audience. I was trying to punch up those laughs for the laughter I wasn't hearing. So I got a grip on myself and buckled down. I'm proud of the shows we did that first year, but we spent it looking for the light at the end of the tunnel. It took a year, and an enormous change in personnel, to make it work.

To know Ed Asner only as Lou Grant, the grumpy boss with the heart of gold, is to miss the duality and the yearning in the man. I think he sees himself as both saint and sinner, good guy and bad guy. Sometimes it's hard to strike a balance. He's a guy who likes being in control and relies on neither psychiatry nor spirituality to lighten his load. He's always felt an obligation to speak his mind on controversial issues. During the Reagan administration's El Salvador initiatives and the partisan political brawl that tarred the Screen Actors Guild, Asner remained an unbowed leftie. For a good while there, his outspokenness came back to bite him where it hurt most. CBS canceled Lou Grant. Asner considers it the price of principle.

Number one, I approved of extras being covered by the Screen Actors Guild. And number two, I believed in providing medical aid to the people of El Salvador who weren't getting it from the government, while our government was supplying that military government with arms to kill those peasants. I declaimed against that policy.

For those two acts, I was branded a traitor. Richard Scaife Mellon wrote an editorial in his weekly paper that in any other country I would have been taken out and shot. Two boycotts were initiated in Congress against *Lou Grant* because of those two, in my mind, humanitarian positions. For somebody to wrap himself in the flag and attack those positions, or that Scaife should have been bitter about the American electorate's ability to hear those opinions and make up its own mind, or that he would depict such acts as unpatriotic and revolutionary, to me, was scandalous.

I thought my outspokenness about what was happening in El Salvador was mild, but evidently it got a heavy reaction. And I was branded a troublemaker.

Nobody will maintain the blacklist existed, even though you could open any drawer of a casting director or a producer and there was a list in there. Even at the height of the blacklist, you didn't know the blacklist. I know of two instances where I was blacklisted, and if I know of two myself, then I gather that there had to be quite an extensive list. It has nothing to do with partisan politics. "This is a conservative, he won't hire me," or, "This is a liberal." It's business. When one becomes suspect, as I did at the time, even your liberal won't hire you. Too hot. I'm not good for business. I may hurt the box office. And they never admit it to themselves. As I said at the time, the liberal who blacklists you will say, "No, he's too fat." Or, "He's too bald. He's too old." One casting director I had done favors for told my agent, "I think he's overexposed." He had never given me a job, but I had done favors for him. And he considers himself a liberal.

It was a phenomenal learning period for me. At the time I was bitter, but I'm not bitter now. I'm not bitter because I survived. I finally weathered it. If I had never worked again, then I'd be bitter.

I had giving parents. Though Orthodox Jews, they certainly weren't West Bank orthodox. They weren't the kind that would kill Rabin. They'd probably treasure him. I had two brothers and two sisters. Both my brothers were handsome and dashing and liked the ladies as well as they were liked in return. My sisters were lovely and beautiful and became social workers, at least for a short while. So I think that social work aspect of my sisters and the benignity of my parents created the liberal aspect of my character.

My father was uneducated. He was illiterate in English. He knew his Yiddish and he knew his Hebrew, although he couldn't translate Hebrew. He had chopped shingles in the woods of Lithuania from the age of twelve on, and came to this country as a teenager. After working a year in the sweatshops in New York, he moved to Kansas City in 1900. He had the resources to get himself a pony and a cart and went around collecting junk, and he built up a fine middle-class family.

I was about the only kid he never whacked. I was the youngest and by the time I came up, of course, he'd mellowed. But when he whacked, he had no idea of another recourse. Nobody did at that time. God knows as a parent I wanted to whack plenty of times and have a couple. But no more. He knew nothing about child-raising. He regarded my mother as his mother, practically. He was her sixth child, so that in terms of rearing kids, he was unknowledgeable, but still a good father, a loving father.

As a parent myself, I try to learn from that example. I just try to bite my lip. Wait it out. Try not to be so abrupt. I try to remember that this too shall pass. If you're responding out of anger, then all that's going to come across is your anger. You should really open your mouth in retaliation and/or response if you think the other person will be helped and is capable of being open to the retaliation and response.

I think most of the time I went into therapy, it wasn't because I felt I needed it. I think I went into therapy to help people who suffered from me to better understand me. So I went in to get a clear understanding of myself so I could explain it to them. But it just didn't work that way. You have to go into therapy believing deeply in it, wanting to be helped. I think I just didn't want to be helped enough.

I interpret "you don't have to control anything" as being out of control. Being out of control is a frightening prospect to me. That's probably why I was a failure at therapy, because I would not be out of control. And it's probably the reason why I just don't get too spiritual. When you're busy surviving, most of the time you try to not get bogged down in spirituality so you can be light on your toes and dance away from the jabs, I think.

I suppose spirituality, if it's done right, is a minimization of ego, of recognizing one's minor stature in this vast universe, which is probably one of many. Spirituality probably relies on doing good more than if you didn't rely on spirituality. If we are influenced to always try to do the right thing, the good thing, then I would say that automatically we're spiritual. But on the other hand, I'm sure Cotton Mather thought he was doing the right thing, the good thing. Even Hitler probably thought he was doing the right thing, the good thing.

When I find out I've hurt someone, I'm aghast. I'm amazed. Very often it comes from having to be too warm, too jocular, too cute in trying to make them feel good. Trying to make them feel good, I hurt them.

But "I'm sorry" is used so much. It's like "thank you" and "please." Nobody really knows the depth of the value to "I'm sorry." You can only look into the pit of the eyeballs and try to gauge. Most of the time we're embarrassed by the person telling us, "I'm sorry," and we want to make them feel good. So you say, "That's all right." Then we look away. "Never mind. Let's pass on. Let's move on." So you don't examine the situation. I've been there many times.

It was a wonderful, wonderful victory when the day finally arrived that I realized I wasn't the saint I thought I was. I thought that was enormous growth. After that, I try to live that fine line of not letting the sinner overwhelm the saint. I know I can't get rid of the sinner, but I try to give the saint a leg up every now and then.

CHAPTER 35

CLIFF ROBERTSON

A man's gotta do what a man's gotta do. It's an age-old cliché. But after what happened to Cliff Robertson, because of his own bravery, it's an adage that rings true.

Hollywood is a company town. According to author David McClintock, in his bestselling book Indecent Exposure, *Cliff Robertson had always been something of an outsider in Hollywood—an East-coaster who preferred good work to glory. Since he usually played a handsome leading man, like the young bold Captain John F. Kennedy in* PT 109, *or one of the FBI's* Untouchables, *or a cult sci-fi star in the* Outer Limits *and* The Twilight Zone, *it is ironic in the extreme (considering what was to come later in his real life) that Cliff Robertson was also the man who played Philip Nolan, the exiled* Man Without A Country *in the classic* Playhouse 90 *production.*

Cliff Robertson was thrust into his own kind of exile—a work exile—simply because he did what he thought was right. He saw corruption and he gave it a name. In so doing, he exposed a web of conspiracy and intrigue that threatened to undermine the entire film industry. But through this experience, he also emerged as the conscience of an entire industry.

It began innocently enough. In 1977, Cliff Robertson received a 1099 tax form that indicated Columbia Pictures had paid him $10,000—money he'd never collected for a show he'd never done.

When Robertson decided to dig into the matter, a wall of silence closed him out. The resistance did not just come from the studios, nor the film industry, but it came from the legal community—even law enforcement. Robertson had stumbled upon an embedded system of embezzlement, fraud, and financial chicanery that was de rigueur in Hollywood, and the whole town wanted any scandal surrounding it to go away.

At that time, the head of Columbia was David Begelman, who coincidentally had been one of Robertson's former agents. Begelman at first blamed the forgery on a temporary employee, and then on a low-level clerk. As time wore on, his explanations became more unconvincing, and finally it was revealed that the person who had forged Robertson's signature was Begelman himself.

If you want something kept quiet, you don't mess with the IRS. The FBI was called in, and soon Hollywood staggered under the twin titans of media scrutiny and government inquiry. In the end major careers were ruined, and the power-mongers in Hollywood would neither forgive nor forget that Robertson was the man who started it all.

So they effectively shut Robertson down. His unofficial blacklisting was quiet, subtle, and devastatingly effective. He was humiliated, isolated, and shunned by those he considered friends as well as by anyone who could provide work for him. And that was the least of it. He kept getting furtive phone calls suggesting he could own the world if he would just keep his mouth shut. When he didn't, he was almost killed.

In terms of opportunities lost, there's no way to calculate the price Robertson paid for his outspokenness. But he was never intimidated enough to refrain from talking about it. In fact, his New York Times *article warning that corporate corruption could ultimately destroy the moral fabric of American industry and American life was deemed worthy of inclusion in the congressional record.*

I thought a computer had made an error. I didn't think anything was wrong. But I said I'm not about to pay taxes on money I didn't earn. I simply gave it to my attorney and said, "Let's find out what's going on." So he proceeded to check it out, and we found all the evidence.

We've had Wall-Street-gate, and Watergate—now it was Hollywoodgate, where there was some corporate corruption on the highest level. In this case it was the president of Columbia Pictures, David Begelman, who forged my name on a check. It turned out he'd done others, as well. He had a system, and he thought it was foolproof. But it wasn't.

David Begelman was never my close friend; he was an acquaintance only. In fact, he was one of twelve agents that represented me in our agency where there were six agents on the

West coast and six on the East, and any one of them could represent me. He was known to be a rather slippery character, but he was a charming guy and I think this enabled him to get away with this for years.

When my accountant and I discovered what was going on, I gave it to my attorney and asked him what the law says I must do. He said, "Unless you give this evidence to the authorities, you become an accessory to a felonious crime. Double parking is one thing, but this kind of thing is heavy." I certainly didn't want to be an accessory to any crime.

But the unwritten commandment in Hollywood is, "Thou shalt never confront a major mogul on corruption or thou shalt not work." And that's been endemic in our business for seventy years. I broke that code.

I was aware that there could be and there might be [a contract out on me], but I wasn't aware that there was. When I was in England filming, the FBI got in touch with me and I was told there was a problem and that I was not to say anything while they were investigating. From then on, we took a different route to work each day and I'd ride to work lying down with a blanket over me. I'd arrive at the back of the studio, and I'd get out and act as if everything was cool.

Of course I had the support of my family and friends. At the time, there were some writers, directors, and actors who did say to me, "Bravo, somebody has finally confronted this creative bookkeeping, and somebody's confronted this corruption." But then many times they'd end it by saying, "Oh, by the way Cliff, don't mention my name, okay?"

An awful lot of good people are afraid. That's the word that keeps coming up. I even wrote the article in the *New York Times* about this fear in Hollywood. They are brave and bold and wonderful about pointing fingers at what's wrong in our society and in our world, but they're very reluctant to turn the finger back where they should, back at themselves. This is fear of self-examination, fear of saying, wait a minute, maybe we are wrong here. Maybe with all our power and our money, we've gotten too acquisitive. Maybe we're only measuring our values on the dollar. Maybe we have to think about the human condition more.

We've confronted a lot of realities that we pushed under the rug in some ways. But we have a long way to go. And I'm nobody to preach.

I was asked by my union to speak, so I spoke. I was also asked to write an article in the op-ed page for the *New York Times*. It kind of corroborated what a lot of people already knew. There were many other people whose names had been forged, but they chose not to say anything.

The message was being sent loud and clear: "Don't do what Cliff did or you might end up just like Cliff—not working."

The FBI said to me at one point, "You know, Cliff, possibly the only thing that kept you from wearing lead shoes in a bay was you're too high a profile." They said, "We're dealing with a very few people who couldn't care less about Cliff Robertson." What they were concerned about was that what I had done, which was in effect confront top authority moguls, they were afraid that I might be setting a precedent.

They were right because within twenty-four months, Laurence Olivier, Michael Caine, Sean Connery, Richard Attenborough, James Garner, and other actors started coming out of the closet and confronting creative bookkeeping. Not necessarily forgery, but creative bookkeeping, which is also embezzlement. They started coming out and talking about it. The first guy always gets hit a little harder.

During the following three years, I wrote a play and I directed a small movie, but I didn't work as an actor.

I'm sure my cat got tired of listening to me, but I have some great friends in this business, and they were all there for me. Happily, I'd worked a lot up until that time so I wasn't destitute.

There were times when I wondered if I'd ever work again, but having started my career in the theater, I felt a little more secure. I felt I could always do a play. I also knew I could write, and I thought I could direct as well. When Doug Trumbull finally put me in one picture, it broke the ice. Other producers and film studios said, "Hey, we want to use him," and I was back working again.

Through it all, I never felt betrayed, but I did feel I was being tested. I was brought up to recognize that we all have obstacles in life, and we have to overcome them. I've tried to tell my kids to treat each obstacle as an opportunity in disguise. It's a way of the good Lord testing you.

I don't want to sound like Don Quixote, with or without portfolio; I just think we're all brought up with certain kinds of values, and some of them can be pretty strong. I was brought up in a fairly religious Presbyterian family, and we were taught to try to adhere to certain values. And they've stayed with me, in spite of my working in a business that is not known for its spiritual values. I made it through this experience really treating it like any dilemma. It was a day-by-day kind of acceptance and an ultimate philosophy that eventually it will get better.

Class did win out in this case. Cliff Robertson's talent was just too big to ignore for long, and his film career got back on track. But he's continuing to stick by his values. While still being paid handsomely as the spokesman for AT&T, when the communication workers union staged a job action, he sided with the union.

Through all of it, Cliff Robertson has handled himself with dignity and a quiet modesty. In a corrupted business known as "Hollywoodgate" he chose to pursue what was right, refusing to accept business as usual. Though he didn't have to do it, he fearlessly went ahead and did what he knew in his heart was the right thing to do. And that is probably a very good definition of an honorable man.

CHAPTER 36

MORLEY SAFER

Morley Safer is one of the good guys. In the TV world of tabloid prattle and pandering info-tainment, he is the rarest and most valuable of commodities: a good reporter. He was one of my childhood heroes when, as a kid, I was bent on being a war correspondent. When other giants of journalism publicly ridiculed our little band of crusaders who were trying to launch CNN, Morley gave me a hug and said he thought it was a brilliant idea—and I vowed to hero-worship him forever. He is affable and intelligent, he talks straight and brooks fools not at all, and he still has to be reminded to snub out the cigarette before the "on-air" light turns red.

At the end of this century, Morley Safer still looks like he's stepped out of its mid-section—the Forties. Picture Edward R. Murrow's postwar London, a rumpled gentlemen's club of reporters bonding over bottles of diminishing alcohol with cigarettes balanced on the sides of their smiles.

London is where Morley launched his career, first with the Reuters news agency, then the BBC and CBC simultaneously.

It's been a career decorated with Dupont Awards and Emmys and Peabody Awards during which he developed into a droll and deliciously skeptical social critic with a knack for puncturing the gas-filled balloons of the pompous and pretentious. He's one very important reason why Americans have for almost three decades gladly given 60 Minutes *of their time to TV on Sunday nights.*

Too young to have caught World War II in the teeth of his typewriter, the upholsterer's kid from Canada was hired by CBS in 1964 to catch an undeclared one in Southest Asia.

Vietnam's explosive and depressive effect on America is well known. There is no point in rehashing the war or the conduct of its players, including the reporters. But it's worth remembering the conventions of war and of the times.

America, back then, was a nation ill-informed about what the stakes were, and irresolute about its commitment there, and still harboring the attitudes of the last war—America, right or wrong. In 1964, reporters on the ground in Vietnam began filing stories increasingly critical of United States involvement. Back home, editors, publishers, and producers were routinely spiking those stories, killing them so as not to appear unpatriotic. They say that truth is the first casualty. Morley didn't know at the time that he was about to risk his career, his reputation, even his life to tell the truth.

In 1965, a single report by Morley Safer marked a turning point in the public's perception of the war. It represented the end of innocence about America's power and God-given moral rectitude. Arguably, that report cocked the trigger for the antiwar movement. Americans had been told its troops were sent to save South Vietnamese villages from the Communist incursion. And then, Morley Safer showed us Cam Ne.

Cam Ne was a Marine Corps operation. The mission was to destroy a village. They destroyed it with flame-throwers and cigarette lighters. It was simply a punishment operation. They weren't trying to evacuate the people. As a human being, I was deeply affected by what I saw.

I had some understanding of how people regard land, particularly the ancestral land in Vietnam. Vietnamese hamlets, in a very particular way, are little self-supporting units with people's parents buried right there on the land. The U.S. troops came in and just devastated it—for no apparent reason. I was just appalled.

There was an infamous line, "We had to destroy the village in order to save it." That is not a logic that many people can quite get their brains around, but the destruction of Cam Ne was part of the policy. We had to destroy this village in order to win the war. And I was outraged. The sight of American troops engaged in that kind of operation is, mercifully, a very unfamiliar one in the history of American arms. But when it happens, it brings to mind that long list of dreadful sights that we all have seen during the last half-century.

CBS, to their credit, went with these stories. I would have been shocked and outraged, and really disbelieving, if I had heard that my stories had been spiked. It just wasn't in the cards in those days, and I don't think it's in the cards these days in CBS either. I think that CBS had set a standard for how broadcast journalism, at its best, should work. I was part of a group of men and women who felt a responsibility to tell these stories.

I figure if you're in this line of work, you really have to live your professional life by the same standards you apply to other people. And cry foul when foul should be cried. If you're going to accuse someone in government of being a coward because he does not do the right thing, and you don't function by certain standards, you don't have much left as a journalist.

As the country grew more and more restless, more and more uneasy, quite apart from what they were watching on television, it became more and more outraged by the war. I don't think it was a question of our becoming more popular. But I think it depends on who you asked at that time. The government did not like us; and a good part of the military did not like us; and there were vast stretches of the country that also didn't like us.

It got to the point where President Lyndon Johnson called me a Communist. Then somebody in his office said, "No, he's a Canadian!" Johnson is alleged to have said, "Well, it's the same damn thing!"

I wasn't threatened by Johnson so much as investigated to some extent by the White House. The bigger problem was with his version of patriotism. I don't think there is anything wrong with patriotism, but I think when patriotism is put to the cynical use of a few brass hats, that is the sort of patriotism that is the last refuge of the scoundrel.

It went farther than that. President Johnson called CBS demanding Safer be removed. And his administration put out the word that Safer was a KGB agent.

A suggestion of treason is personally damaging anytime, anywhere. But in an environment bristling with M16s it can be deadly. Fragging, the elimination of a detested superior officer by his own troops under cover of battle, was not unheard of in Vietnam. Fragging might not apply to a war correspondent, but Safer was in danger of being shot by "friendly fire" twice.

You should not regard the military in Vietnam as being monolithic in any way. There were a lot of good very decent men certainly among the grunts and among the officers as well. Some within the military establishment in Vietnam were very pleased with me. But others were not. The Marines were not pleased with me. There were certain threats made in the field in Vietnam.

It was a more discreet version of fragging. I was threatened by Marines I was in the field with. I took whatever precautions one could take in a fairly hostile situation, but I went to bed saying, "Oh, they'll never do that." I didn't have much more defense than that! I'll tell you, there were three or four days in there when I realized that it was a very close thing. One more beer that somebody shouldn't have had could have made the difference in terms of thinking, "I'm gonna get that S.O.B."

I don't think I am a particularly courageous person—or particularly foolhardy. I may have been a little more foolhardy then to live among those kinds of threats. But reporting is what I do. I've always believed a great deal in not necessarily the value of what I do, but in doing it the best way you possibly can. I would have found it near impossible to have compromised and backed off. I would have found such unseemly behavior so embarrassing to myself.

Hard-bitten reporters aren't much accustomed to identifying their feelings, much less talking about them. It's against the rules. But it's likely that just as America, as a nation, suffered from a collective guilt over the futility and carnage of Vietnam, Safer, as a man, suffered his share of remorse over what the Vietnamese still call "The American War."

Twenty-five years after his first tour of duty in Vietnam, Safer went back there looking for a form of forgiveness. Maybe even absolution. He didn't expect it.

I was petrified about going back, petrified of my own feelings. I love that country a lot. It's just physically a wonderful place. I like the people a lot too. But I was petrified of my own emotions, that I would somehow not hack it if the place conjured up some bad memories. There were bad memories about the waste of life of kids, really, young boys, American boys, young Vietnamese children. I was petrified that there might be such a store of bitterness among the people to any, as we described ourselves, "round eyes."

It was remarkable. It was just the opposite. The resilience of those people is really something to behold because there was no rancor. That absence of rancor, that admiration that they had for Americans, is in itself a rough moment. You remember then the full significance of the waste of lives and the great treasure spent over such a long period for no point—no point whatsoever. To have the enemy crawl out of the rubble you created and say, "Let's get on with our lives." That's something!

I had some bad moments, but for the most part, it was really quite joyful because I had no experience with that country other than at war. The first most extraordinary impression that I had was of silence! It was serene! People travel by bicycle, for the most part anyway. It's a wonderfully serene way to get around!

I remember just driving along outside of Saigon approaching the city on a country road, and there was a young woman carrying two penyas of rice, the yoke. They get into a rhythm when they do it. It's really quite heavy, but they sort of go into a trot which makes the burden bearable. There was something so beautiful about the movement of that young woman, and there was just something so eternal about the sand and the wealth of the earth, sustenance, and the essence of life. What is more essential than a rice paddy? There was heaven in this one little scene, and I cried when I saw it. It was quite wild but I did.

CHAPTER 37

JOHN STOSSEL

I first knew him as Rick. He'll hate me for telling you that. His name was Rick Stossel until he changed it to John. We called him Rick John for a while there until the Rick part became vestigial and died out. The names on our college degrees had barely dried when we arrived in New York, a crew of fresh young blood sentenced to work the weekends on local television. John Stossel and I and two other newbies, John Tesh and Arnold Diaz, were friends. We'd sit in police shacks together and stand on stake-outs together and after the eleven o'clock news, we'd go to the nightclubs and dance together. I couldn't get them to make a move on some unsuspecting outsider to save my sanity. We watched each other grow up and move ahead, but I still cherish that time when we were just becoming what we wanted to be when we grew up.

Stossel had everything required back then for TV. He had fierce intelligence and a nose for snow jobs. He was a good writer, and he was camera-ready. He still is. But he also had something you wouldn't expect of a major broadcaster. He had a stutter. Not just a stammer but a really serious stutter.

He's joins an impressive club. Damosthanies tried to beat it by stuffing marbles in his mouth (it doesn't work). Charles Darwin, George the VI, Thomas Jefferson, and Winston Churchill all coped with it. Carly Simon and Mel Tillis sang their way through it, and now you know that the breathy, sexy vocal thing Marilyn Monroe did was to hide a stutter.

For the first thirty years of his life, ABC News magazine correspondent for 20/20, John Stossel, was so frightened about stuttering that sometimes he could barely speak up. Yet, in addition to network television, he's been one of the top grossing speakers on the lecture circuit. He simply figured out how to get through it, and we haven't been able to shut him up since. But it wasn't simple. In the great panoply of afflictions and barricades to people's success, stuttering makes barely a blip on the radar, but it's very serious.

Stuttering may seem like a silly problem, but let me tell you, it's serious if you have it! It probably deserves to be only a small blip on the radar, and people can overcome it, but it's a very nasty problem when it's your problem.

I was thought to be stupid or snobby or shy at different times. I guess I am shy, and it is a coping mechanism. When you're not sure the words are going to come out and you fear that you'll be horribly embarrassed by blocking or looking funny, you just don't talk.

Stuttering often begins around the ages of four, five, and six, when children, trying to express themselves put pressure behind their stammer and begin to stutter. In my case, instead of saying Mary Alice . . . Mmmm Mmmary Alice Williams (a normal stumble), I would say, "Mmmmm Maaarrryyyy Al . . ." The pressure behind the stammer builds up and then stuttering begins.

I was never a severe stutterer. My stuttering would come and go. It would mostly come when I was afraid of speaking. For instance, I used to work on Channel Two in New York City, and at the end of the broadcast, we had to do fifteen seconds of live talk. I was petrified. I woke up every morning, scared to death. Oh my God, what am I going to have to say live? And I'd be scared all day, anticipating that time, which seldom was as bad as I feared.

One would think that stuttering is a psychological problem, however it's hard to know how much of it truly is psychological. Stutterers stutter more when they want to be fluent and when they are tense about being fluent. Since stutterers who have had a lot of psychotherapy don't stutter any less, the psychological aspect doesn't seem to affect it much. The newest theory behind stuttering is that it has something to do with muscles in the middle of our ears which control the way we hear ourselves. Being born with an ear muscle that contracts at a slightly different rate than the rest of the ear interferes with the way we hear our own voices. If you get delayed auditory feedback [as you sometimes do in your television earpiece when you hear your own voice come back in your ear a half second after the word leaves your throat], it can often make fluent people stutter. It is interesting to note however that such a phenomenon does the converse to stutterers; it makes stutterers fluent. Therefore, that theory is the most sound so far.

I have gone into therapy, seen specialists and even tried hypnosis and acupuncture to get rid of my stuttering problem. However, none of it worked. It wasn't until I went to a good clinic that I got my stuttering under control.

The first thing they did at this clinic was to reteach me how to talk. It took three weeks' time. I was retaught how to make each and every sound. At the time, it was incredibly boring; however in retrospect, I find it fascinating. If you look at stutterers' speech on an oscilloscope, it's very blocky. Normal speech is much smoother. Mine, however, even when I'm not stuttering is blocky. I hit sounds too hard. The clinic had me drill on my vowels and slow down my speech to two seconds per syllable in order to reteach me how to make the correct sounds. I can't stress to you how much my experience there helped me with my problem.

I never intended to be on television. I never thought that it would happen. I took my job which led to my first job on television because it provided me with a free trip. When a Seattle magazine offered me a job, I thought, "I'll take it. Hey, after all it is a free trip to the Northwest!" When the magazine went bankrupt, they said, "We don't want to lose you. Why don't you try working in our Portland, Oregon, newsroom as a researcher. I immediately agreed. One day, it just so happened that nobody was around to cover the day's pressing story, so they asked me to do it. I accepted because I knew that my broadcast was going to be on tape and they could snip out the stutters in the edit room. It was fine.

However, there are times where I have stuttered on live television. I will never forget the first time it happened to me. We were covering the election results in Portland, and I had to report on how much each candidate spent. I got stuck on the word dollars. And what can you say? There are not many good synonyms for dollars. I panicked. No matter how hard I tried, I couldn't say it. I stammered for what seemed like eternity before they cut me off. The show was over, and I was still stuttering in the numbers.

I wish I could say that that experience never happened to me again, but I can't. Even now, when I sit with Hugh Downs and Barbara Walters, I sometimes just have to walk away. I have the most trouble with my speech when I only have a minute to make my point and I don't want to stutter. I'm not cured, I'm just more in control.

Speaking before an audience is different. The reverberation from the microphone helps me speak fluidly. There's not that time pressure. I now feel I have learned things from twenty years of consumer reporting that I want to talk to audiences about, so I don't care about the stuttering. If they want to pay me an outrageous fee to have me talk to people about things I want to share about, I'll do it, even if I am worried about my speech.

As I said, we haven't been able to shut him up since. But there have been a number of people who've tried. Ralph Nader has called Stossel the most dishonest journalist there ever was, and he's also been called the most dangerous.

Much of that vitriol falls into either the category of ox-goring, or ax-grinding. But some may come from the fact that he has a unique style of reporting. All reporters are trained to be neutral and unbiased. At least, that's what they teach you in journalism school. Objectivity is a worthy goal. But as it's practiced on the ground, it means the reporter is often required to pretend that he comes from nowhere, without the human biases associated with his own background or level of education or on which side of the bed he arises. Stossel fills the audience in. He so much as says, "This is where I stand and this is why. What do you think?" Frankly, I think it's refreshing.

The traditional approach in journalism is to pretend we don't bring our own background, education, and biases to the work. I find that to be ridiculous. I think it is pompous to say that even though I have taken three hours of material and edited it down to the twelve minutes I've shown you, I did that with no personal biases influencing it. There is no way that that report is totally neutral. Therefore, when I am reporting I say, " Look, here's where I'm coming from. I think this is wrong! You can listen to me and agree with me, or not." I think that is the best way to report;

whereas other journalists think that I stepped off the curb. I do get grief inside the shop, but not from Barbara and Hugh.

For twenty years I was a consumer reporter, and every day I would report on the evil some business was doing. Then I came to the conclusion that government was doing more harm than business; the rules that were supposed to protect us from bad business hurt the consumer more than the businesses do. When they rip you off, those businesses don't do well—people find out about it, the press publicizes it, and they go out of business. The businesses that deliver you good services thrive! And the market corrects itself without the influence of big lawyers and big government propelled by Ralph Nader. In my opinion, Mr. Nader viewed that as a betrayal.

When you work in network television, embarking on a personal journey of self-discovery and serenity has to get sandwiched in between takeoffs and countdowns, or worked into the research you're doing on a separate issue. Every so often, you hit a story in the middle of which you see yourself in a new way. The story Stossel found himself in the middle of was about the science of happiness.

I always thought, if I only get that job, then I'll be happy. If I only make a little more money I'll be happy. If I get that network job, or if I get *20/20* I'll be happy. Then if I just get my own show, which I'd love, then I'll be happy. I finally had to realize, I was still waking up anxious and upset in the morning. All these traditional measures of success weren't working for me. What does make people happy? We looked into it, and amazingly, there are shrinks who spend their lives studying this. A lot of people look at what makes you unhappy. But here were some people trying to figure out what does make people happy. Half of it turns out to be biological. You are just born that way. In twin studies, experts find disposition in twins, even if they were raised apart, is much more similar than in people raised in the same family—that biology makes a big difference. They now have brain tests to see if a part of the left side of the brain, your happiness center, is active or not. They tested me, and sure enough, mine was pretty low.

If that part of the brain is very active on these CAT scans, then you tend to be one of these people who describes themselves as happy. It's slightly mushy science in that you can't measure happiness like blood pressure. So they just ask thousands of people how they feel—are they happy—and then measure people's brains. They've given a million people another test using a chart that shows six faces with different expressions (very happy, happy, semi-happy, sad, very sad, miserable). Most Americans put themselves somewhere between very happy and happy. I put myself in the semi-happy category. A lot of this is biological.

Also, it can be environmental. My mother had raised me with the philosophy that you have to work hard and study when you don't want to, and get that paper done even if it takes you all night, when you don't want to, because if you don't get good grades and get into a good college, you will starve and die or freeze in the dark. There was no mention of a benign welfare state that was going to take care of me. I was scared to death as a kid. So I had to grit my teeth and push through it, or I would be a failure and terrible things would happen. So that's how I've lived my life.

Now the idea is that you shouldn't push kids too hard. They have to feel good about themselves. Maybe there is benefit to that. What I was taught made me work hard and be more successful, but perhaps, less happy. I'm not happy unless I'm working hard to achieve the next goal. That's not so healthy either. I'm working on that.

But you can improve, they say. It's not hopeless. People who have lots of friends say they're happy. If you have five or six people that you could call when something good or bad happens to you, then you tend to be a happier person. People who have work that makes them feel well used are happier.

Religious people are happier, too. You can't always do something about that. I just sort of ignored it for a long time. I was raised in Wilma, Illinois, a place where it was just cooler to look blond, tall, Scandinavian, and Catholic. To be Jewish was to be shorter and dark, like I was. It was less cool, and I was not happy to hear suddenly at the age of twelve that I was Jewish. My parents said that they were not trying to conceal it, though they had come from Germany. They were just joining the church that their friends had joined. I was confirmed as a Congregationalist; I went to church every Sunday. But I have married a Jew, and my children are being raised Jewish. Did I convert, in that I believe in Judaism? No. I envy the people who have the benefit of deep religious faith and the happiness that brings. I don't have that. I've tried to listen, and I've tried to get it, and I don't get it. There may be a God who made all this happen. I just don't know. I think I worked hard. I was lucky. I had breaks. And maybe it was all piloted by God, but I can't say I really believe that.

Stossel's dream is to spend his days playing beach volleyball and seeing his children smile. I suspect it will come true. And maybe he'll investigate whether there is a pilot.

CHAPTER 38

ROBERT MERRILL

No strides are ever really made nor goals achieved without a dream behind it. Robert Merrill is a born dreamer. He has been called the greatest dramatic baritone of the twentieth century. But at heart he's still a poor Jewish kid from Brooklyn who played stickball in the streets and stuttered so badly he could barely speak. At night he would crouch by the stove, the family's only source of heat, and dream. He didn't dream that his preternatural voice would touch a billion people, though it really has. He didn't envision performing for every United States president from Roosevelt through Reagan, and going on to win a National Medal of the Arts from President Clinton. All he ever dreamed of was baseball—Yankee baseball.

My dream was to pitch for the New York Yankees. I played semiprofessionally in Brooklyn. I used to get ten, fifteen, twenty dollars on a Sunday to pitch, and I loved it. When I was out on that mound, that was the life. That was it!

My mother, of course, had other ideas. She was a singer but couldn't make it big. Her ambition was for me to sing. I'll never forget the day she pulled me off the baseball field because I had a lesson waiting for me in my house. I was so embarrassed. I said, "Oh my gosh. This is awful." But thank God for my mom; she did the right thing.

My mother found a voice teacher for me at the Metropolitan Opera House. His name was Samuel Margolis. My mother told Samuel that she would pay him one dollar a lesson, which was a lot of money at the time. However, when he heard me sing, he immediately waived his fee. I studied with him for several years. It was probably the greatest thing that ever happened to me as a young singer. I used to take the subway from Bensonhurst to the Metropolitan Opera, get off at Thirty-ninth Street, take the elevator up to his studio, and I thought I heard Caruso and Jenny Lind. It really inspired me.

He taught me how to enjoy singing and how to be proud of my gift, realizing I could never make the Yankees..

It was the Depression era. My poor father used to catch the subway at six o'clock in the morning. He was a tailor and worked in a sweatshop. He got me a job in his sweatshop as a delivery boy. I used to roll huge carts down the street filled with dresses. I realized that that sort of life was not for me. I wanted to do something bigger and better. My uncle, for whom I worked, couldn't understand why I needed voice lessons. He said, "Can't you talk?" One day I pushed the cart filled with dresses past the Metropolitan on Fortieth Street. At that time, the Metropolitan used to deliver their scenery and costumes to a warehouse by wheeling them down this ramp at Fortieth Street and Broadway. I immediately seized the opportunity. I rolled my cart of dresses up the ramp; nobody stopped me because they thought my dresses were costumes. I got all the way backstage. I'll never forget it. I stood there and listened to my first matinee performance. They told me it was Lawrence Tibbet and Helen Jefferson. I was completely enthralled. I forgot where I was. Finally, one guy said, "Hey, what are you doing here? What's up, buddy? Get out." I rolled the dresses back. It was a great experience. When I got back to my uncle's dress place, I was in another world. I made up my mind then that I would one day become a great singer.

Robert Merrill was already eighteen years old before anyone, with the possible exception of his mother, knew he had a trainable voice. As success stories go, eighteen qualifies as a late start. When he reminisces about his life, he skips the tough parts. Memory has a kind way of illuminating only the high points. So he didn't volunteer that even after training a voice that was growing in size and power every day, he still needed training in the kind of game decisions that can only be made before a live audience. He got it in the most unlikely venues. He hit the old borscht belt of the Catskills, serving as straight man for Red Skelton and Danny Kaye. That's what made a performer out of him.

In 1944, he debuted in the Newark Opera production of Aida. *The very next year, after only eight years of training, he won the Metropolitan Opera Auditions of the Air. That gave him a shot at the Met, The Metropolitan Opera. Not as a spear-carrier, but as Germont, the father in* La Traviata, *a part reserved for the primo baritono. It would be the first of a record-breaking 788 performances at the Met, his home field.*

The 1945 to 1946 season was a very important time for me. During that time, I had a Sunday show with RCA. When Toscanini heard me sing the aria from *La Traviata* on the radio, he engaged me to sing it with him in the NBC Orchestra's performance of *La Traviata.* Until I met him and until I began rehearsals, I still didn't believe that I was going to do it. My first rehearsal with the old man, took place on the sixth floor of NBC. I expected the cast, but it was only the two of us. He sat behind the piano and stared at me for five minutes. It was terrifying. If I had had a pill, I would've taken it. Finally he said, "Roberto, are you a father?" I started to stutter. I said, "No, M-M-Maestro, I'm-I'm-I'm not even married." He stared at me for another minute or two and then began to play the role for me. I immediately started to sing. After I finished, he spoke. He said, "I will make you a father."

I couldn't believe my good fortune. There I was, I had a debut at the Met and I was singing *La Traviata* with Arturo Toscanini. It was something that I couldn't believe. My parents were in the audience that Monday night. My father, who did not want me to be a singer, sat next to my mother, who of course was in another world. She just sat there, beaming, "I'm the mother of Robert." After the performance was over and I had finished signing my autographs, my father looked at me and said, "When is your next performance?" I replied, "Thursday, Papa." He said, "It's not a profession. No, it's not a profession, not a steady job." We got into the subway and went home. When we got home, I kissed them both goodnight and went to bed as a member of the Metropolitan Opera. It was very exciting.

On that debut night, when the audience, the critics, and even his father learned that he could sing with the pipes of the angels, no one knew he couldn't speak clearly. Stuttering is far more common, not to mention more psychologically crippling, than I had ever assumed. The affliction may not have killed Merrill's career, but it was getting in his way. And he is not a man to defer dreams.

When I first got into the radio business, I had to introduce my music by reading from a script. Whenever I would start the script on a consonant, I would panic. It scared the heck out of me. As a result, I decided then that I must get rid of my stuttering problem. The Stuttering Foundation helped me a great deal. They told me to sing the words to my scripts because stutterers don't stutter when they sing. It was wonderful advice that really worked.

Growing up as a stutterer is definitely the most frightening and brutal thing I have ever had to go through. I used to hate going to school because kids would make fun of me. My teachers didn't understand. My teachers would ask me to get up and say something in front of the class. I would have to turn my back. When I turned my back I could sort of speak. Everyone would laugh. It was awful, terrifying, and cruel. People don't realize that stuttering is an affliction; it's a nervous physical affliction. When I finally realized that, I felt empowered. I became the spokesman for the Stuttering Foundation.

As the spokesman for the Stuttering Foundation, I teach fellow stutterers to slow down their speech, sing before they say anything, and put vowels before their consonants. If I say, "My name is R . . ." it is difficult. However, when I add an "uh," a vowel, "Uh-Robert Merrill . . ." I can get it out. When I was at the White House, I noticed Eisenhower, when he was interviewed, did the same thing. I heard it. When I finally met him, I mentioned it. He took me to a corner and said, "Yes, you too?" I said, "Yes. I noticed, Mr. President, that you put a vowel before your consonants." He said, "That's right, that's right. It's helped a great deal."

I'm a very lucky and fortunate guy to be able to be invited to the White House in the greatest country in the world and meet these presidents and chat with them and become part of history. I'm thrilled every time I walk into that White House. I don't take it for granted; I know that I'm privileged. I'm at the White House.

Even the White House is no match, in his mind, for Yankee Stadium. Even at the White House, Mr. Merrill wears his trademark meticulously tailored white-flannel shirts made of real Yankee pin-stripes. He has twenty-five of them. He even wears a World Series ring.

Maybe that's his greatest contribution to opera. He has brought to Yankee fans who might not know Rigoletto *from rigatoni his beautiful voice delivered high and fast right from the pitcher's mound.*

I have two World Series rings. I received them when I sang the national anthem at the World Series games and playoffs in 1977 and '78. It may sound strange, but I consider myself to be a New York Yankee. One afternoon at an Old Timer's Day game, Mr. George Steinbrenner said, "Get yourself a uniform, get down there, and manage the team." So I went down and found Bobby Mercer's pants and somebody else's shoes. But I didn't have a top. Then Billy Martin called to me, "Bob, come on in. Put this on." It was his number, one and a half. He never got it back. It's now my official number. So now I'm called Mr. One-and-a-Half Yankee. I get such a thrill out of that.

I'm part of the Yankees family. Every time I walk out onto that mound to sing the anthem, I feel like a kid from Brooklyn who has made it. I don't think of myself as a singer when I go out; rather, I am a part of the New York Yankees. I'm pitching a World Series game.

I think everyone at one point in their lives has a dream that they want to fulfill. And most of them never make it happen. I've been fortunate that I made both of my dreams come true. I'm a Yankee and a Metropolitan Opera star. I am lucky and my story is unique. I meet people all the time who are frustrated in life because they wanted to be an important lawyer, somebody on television, a famous ballplayer, or somebody involved in show business; and never had the opportunity or the talent.

People talk to me and mention the fact that they didn't have the opportunity to study. They had to go to work, they had to make a living, they had families. I say that's very important also. I tell them that their dream may not have brought them the success that they experience in their fields. I tell them to be happy with their lives and happy with what they have.

Sounds easy for him to say. He made it to the top. But he has confided that opera is the toughest of the arts. The pressure is enormous. He watched it eat other men alive. His two greatest friends and mentors, Leonard Warren and the great tenor Richard Tucker, both died onstage. For years you are lionized, he says, and then you are forgotten.

In the half-century that Robert Merrill gave to opera, he used classical music to build a classic American success story. Baritones usually portray the villains in opera, but Merrill has been a hero. Ever since his meteoric rise from local Brooklyn kid to international superstar, he's served great music and great baseball with great artistry and great humanity. Because he never got jaded, never lost that part of him that's just an awestruck kid who knows he got a really good deal just by chasing his dreams.

CHAPTER 39

EDWARD JAMES OLMOS

I expected Martin Castillo, Miami Vice*'s laser-eyed lieutenant who always looked cool, if slightly laconic, to saunter into the room, but that's not Edward James Olmos. He doesn't like that role much, though he recognizes it's what made him famous. He is an energetic, unpretentious, ordinary man who tries hard to do the right thing. And who loves to play hero.*

Olmos has a face any air-brain in central casting would pick for the glowering bad guy. Thick-skinned and so deeply pitted that you wonder whether he walked into a round of buckshot. But it's the good guys whose portrayals are important to him. He won't do gratuitous violence or play unredeemably evil villains. Yes, he is typecast as Latino. No getting around it. But he uses that to make Anglos confront their own prejudices and to bring Latinos face-to-face with their cultural icons. In film roles carefully chosen, he's given us a new perspective on the legendary Mexican folk hero Gregorio Cortez, who the Texas Rangers considered a desperado. He's celebrated the innovative leadership of the remarkable barrio math teacher Jaime Escalante in Stand and Deliver. *In* Zoot Suit, *the story of Latino youths wrongly convicted of murder in 1942, he played the narrator, El Pachuco, the flamboyant Chicano who raised the ire and consciousness of angelinos back in the Forties. And in a chilling piece of agit-prop, he played the Mexican-American druglord Santana in* American Me, *a warning about the birth and growth and infestation of gang violence in America. As an actor, producer, and director, he's given us a unique perspective on the American experience.*

Edward James Olmos sees himself more as educator than performer. He spends a lot more time in classrooms preaching the values of self-respect and perseverance than he does onscreen. He has combated gang violence at home and tried to ease the suffering in his ancestral home. During the Zapatista guerrilla war in Mexico, he smuggled food and medicine behind guerrilla lines in the mountains to feed children who were dying in the Mayan village of Chappas, his grandmother's home. In the grim aftermath of the South Central riots in Los Angeles, he picked up a broom and dustpan in the smoldering ruins and began to sweep clean the carnage. It wasn't just for the TV cameras, though they were there. He met with the mayor and became a member of the Rebuild L.A. Committee.

Maybe it's because he's been there. His way up was sports. He was a helluva baseball player. While still in grammar school, he was Golden State batting champion. And at fourteen he caught major league pitchers in the California winter league. But at fifteen he dropped the ball and began performing in a band. He says he couldn't sing, but he could dance. So he'd dance for five minutes, then scream a song and dance some more. Eventually he developed a style of screaming that worked. But once he discovered drama at East Los Angeles City College, Olmos dissolved the band and bought its van, a three-quarter-ton truck, and delivered furniture to support his dream.

But Olmos came up in poverty in Los Angeles, growing up Latino in the Fifties before Americans had begun to realize that color doesn't count, character does. His first home had dirt floors. His dad left when he was little. His mom raised the kids alone. But his memories of those years, the ones he likes to share, are happy and positive without a sliver of resentment.

He once said, "I came from a dysfunctional family. I'm a minority. I have no natural talent. But I did it, and if I can do it, anybody can do it. I take away all the excuses."

When I was seven years old, my mother and father got a divorce. While my father left the household, he didn't abandon me. He never missed a day or an opportunity to be with his children. So we were always together. At first it was tough, because the courts made it clear that we were only to see him eight hours every other week. But we soon learned that if I was playing baseball, my dad could come and see me at the ballpark. Since it was a public place, he was allowed to visit me. So I started to play baseball every day, seven days a week. I became a great ballplayer. I remember having my mother and father in the stands; it was great. At the end of the ballgame, my dad would come up to me and say, "Good game." I would thank him, give him a kiss, and then go home with my mom. And that was it. But we saw each other every single day. He would come to practices and sit on the bleachers, watch the games, and watch the practices. So I was always around him. It was extraordinary.

In the final months of his life, I was with him every day. Every day, for about four months, I would take care of him. He had diabetes, which kicked off a heart problem, which then kicked off other problems. He was only seventy-four years old. He didn't want to be put on a life-support system; so his health just slowly deteriorated day by day. It would have been very easy for me to become angry with him for his decision, but I did not. Since it was what he wanted, I was okay with his decision.

In retrospect, I realize that our continuing relationship through all those years really led me to understand a life different from the standard single-parent household experience.

Being Latino in Boyle Heights, East L.A. in the Forties and Fifties was fantastic. I call it the Ellis Island of the West Coast. I remember there was a sign on the wall at my grammar school which said, "If it isn't worth saying in English, it isn't worth saying at all." Thank God that I didn't listen to that statement and I became bilingual. I think it's much better to speak more than one language. People who only speak English have a long way to go in understanding the future of this planet.

I remember the day after the Rodney King verdict, we were driving down Sunset Boulevard. It was about twelve-thirty at night on Thursday. The riots had been going on since three o'clock Wednesday afternoon. I remember jamming on my breaks when I saw someone get shot two lanes across from me. From the force of the shot, his body was propelled two lanes backwards. It was awful. We immediately jumped out of our car and tried to resuscitate him, but it was no use. When I put my hand underneath him to move his head, I couldn't help but think that his head felt exactly like an eggshell. It was all granulated and there was nothing left. I realized that there wasn't a reason to try any further; he was gone. I broke down.

That was the spring of 1992. South Central Los Angeles had exploded from pent-up rage over what its citizens believed was institutional police brutality and the failure of the "system" to do anything about it. The world had witnessed the ruthless beating of Rodney King, looped over and over on every TV set on the planet, and then the perpetrators had gotten off scot-free.

As Olmos stood over the dead boy, another kid ran up and began pounding on the dead kid's chest, saying, "Don't die!" And then the kid looked to Eddie Olmos and said, "What are you gonna do, Actor Boy? This is real life, Actor Boy!" How do you take that kind of pessimism in the heart of that child and turn it into positive action? How's that for a challenge?

You have to allow children to experience something that will allow them to come to terms with what they've gone through; they need to have the opportunity of changing their own cynicism into constructive activism. Therefore, the only thing that you can do to help is to continue your attempts at understanding your own life. You must continue to move forward. And that's exactly what I did. There was no way that I was going to talk to that boy at that moment about what he was going through and how he couldn't feel what he was feeling.

Children who live in violence often lack the experience of unconditional love. In my opinion, unconditional love is the most necessary aspect of survival on the planet. Most of the young people who have experienced unconditional love will be able to move forward in a positive way. Those that don't have unconditional love are trapped and end up being destroyed inside. Oftentimes, they become a statistic.

Over the span of the last twenty-three years, we've begun to get an understanding of violence. We've begun to understand that one of the basic factors in violent outbursts derives from the male/female issue. In today's society, we started to notice that, especially in the last twenty years, the confrontation between male and female has grown an extraordinary amount. With that confrontation came violence. In my opinion, as women became equal in voice and equal in understanding to men, it became more of a threat to the males. And as a result of this threat, the violence escalated.

My wife, Lorraine Bracco, believes that it is extremely important to educate people of all ages about the dangers of domestic violence. She understands that people think it won't happen to them. It is hard for people of all ages to fathom marrying someone who could turn out to be a batterer. Therefore, we decided to make a film aimed at educating both the elderly and the young about the prevalence of domestic violence.

Our film, *It Ain't Love,* was a most extraordinary commitment at looking at the problem of domestic violence. Even from the beginning, no one wanted to be involved in making it. It was really difficult to find sponsors for the film. I think it is because the subject matter is both hard to deal with and hits so close to home. The story stars a real-life twenty-five-year-old mother, who has two kids, lives in a safe house, and whose husband batters her.

Our hope in making the film was that the elderly would look at the story and say, "I remember that happened to me. I wish I would have understood it better." Or, "I have friends that went through that. I wonder if they're now suffering from domestic violence now that they've gotten older." And that youngsters would say, "I won't allow that to happen to me."

I believe that violence is a health problem. It's not a judicial problem, even though we continue to try to get at the core of it through the judicial system; rather, it is a problem that we have to treat like polio. We have to vaccinate against it at a very young age and continue our vaccinations against it throughout our lifetimes. I believe that one way of vaccinating against such violence is to learn how to do easy, confrontational type work. We need to make sure that when people become impatient, they don't resort to physical or emotional violence. I believe this is a learned behavior; it is learned from the society, learned from parents, learned from the environment. It is a behavior that is passed on.

So we're trying to make sure that there's no way for people to get confused about what it means to be violent. Through our work, I hope that we have taught an invaluable lesson; the problem of violence is out there and it is up to us to stop it.

I never lose perspective as to where I come from. My heart,

my roots, are in East L.A. With roots, I understand my present. And by understanding my present, there's hope for the future. Without roots, you have no present. And without present, you have no hope. There are children today who have no sense of roots whatsoever. But among the majority of our young people, there is no poverty of spirit.

The only thing we can ask of ourselves is to be the best that we can be—period. Accept what has been given to us, not as an excuse for failing but as an opportunity for succeeding.

There's something inspiring about ordinary men and women doing extraordinary things, like standing up for what they believe in. Living right gets you a triple-A rating. Acknowledge what is true in your life, accept it with gratitude, and then take action. Edward James Olmos is an impressive case in point.

CHAPTER 40

RITA MORENO

Rita Moreno is roughly the size of a dinner mint, but her personality can be monitored from geo-synchronous orbit. She is huge, with a loud belly laugh, and dancing eyes, and a "neener neener" kind of schoolyard taunt when she's making jokes at her own expense, which she does all the time. She has spent a lifetime railing against her typecasting as the "Latin Spitfire." But she is that, and a lot more.

She's earned a place in the Guinness Book of World Records *as the only performer, man or woman, ever to win the grand slam of entertainment awards: the Oscar, the Grammy, the Tony, and two Emmys. For a person who's spent a lifetime trying to make the entertainment industry take her seriously, that's a triumph.*

She came from very little. Her father left before she was born. Her mother left for America to earn enough money to give her only child a life. When she was five, Rosa Delores Alverio sailed for twelve hours on a boat to come to New York from her native Puerto Rico. She was planted on the West Side of New York, in a nation embedded in depression that spoke a language she'd never heard. In more ways than one, it must have felt like an alien abduction.

We moved here to find a life. My mother became a seamstress in a factory where many Puerto Rican women worked. While I don't know if they were treated miserably, it was a sweatshop. They were treated as cogs.

My first two experiences in this country were very difficult. After coming over here by boat since we couldn't afford the airfare, we moved into a tiny tenement apartment. Almost immediately, I was struck with the chicken pox, and for reasons that to this day that I still don't understand, I was taken away in an ambulance to a hospital. It was awful. These two men wrapped me up in a sheet like a little piece of candy and carried me down the stairs.

Imagine being five years old, not able to speak a word of English, and being carted away by two strange men to a hospital. I remember screaming and yelling because I didn't know what was happening to me. They put me in an ambulance, and I guess for fun, because it certainly wasn't an emergency, they turned on the siren. It was like a nightmare. I didn't know where I was being taken. All I knew was that these men were taking me away from my mother. Imagine that being your first experience in New York City.

My second experience in this country was when my mother took me to kindergarten. At that point, I still couldn't speak a word of English. There were no bilingual programs in those days. I remember my mother taking me to the roof garden of the school where the children were playing, and she didn't know what to do. (I think she was only eighteen or nineteen years old at the time.) She told me that she would be back soon because she was going to get me some chiclette gum. While I waited for my mother to return, I sat on the steps of the roof and watched the other kids play. At some point, the teacher came up to me and said, I assume, "It's time to go in, Rosita." And I said to her, "No, no, no, porque mi mommy me va a traer chicle." And the teacher said, "No, no dear, you have to come in, we're going," and I started to cry. Again, I had no idea what was happening to me. I was very scared because I thought I was being taken away from my mother again. It was a very difficult childhood. And it was very scary.

Rita Moreno's childhood may have made her feel second-rate, but it soon became clear that she had first-rate talent. And that talent saved her. She was put to work early, starting in the toy department at Macy's department store to supplement the family's meager income. By the time she was thirteen, Rita Moreno was on Broadway. In the white world, one big hit leads to more. Not so in hers. Latino, back then, meant closed doors and closed minds. So Rosita passed through her teen years singing at weddings and bar mitzvahs, then graduated to tacky nightclubs doing Carmen Miranda with bananas on her head—second-rate stuff. When she finally worked her way to Hollywood, she discovered that the studios considered dark-complected foreigners all the same: interchangeable, second class. She played a Latin, an Arab, a Native American, whatever. She's referred to it as the "Yonkee Peeg School of Acting." Oh, and of course, Rita the Cheetah, the Latino spitfire!

When I was little, back in Puerto Rico, I used to dance for my grandfather. As I danced, he would clap in time to the music. I loved those times; I loved performing for him. When I came to the United States, a friend of my mother's saw me dancing to a record, and she said to my mom, "Gee, Rosita seems to have a lot of natural talent. Why don't you take her to my dancing teacher?" Which is exactly what happened. I went to my mom's friend's dancing teacher, Paco Cansino, who happened to be Rita Hayworth's uncle!

Carlos Montelban, Ricardo Montelban's brother, directed all of the MGM movies that were being looped into Spanish. I got to be the Spanish voice of Margaret O'Brien and Elizabeth Taylor in the MGM movies. For a child who wanted to sing and dance, MGM was the studio of my dreams! That was the studio of Gene Kelly and Judy Garland and Esther Williams and all these great musical stars. That's where I was going to make my mark. When I got to Hollywood, I fully expected to be the next Lana Turner. You can imagine, then, that the falls were great and vast and deep because that didn't happen.

It didn't happen because of my name. My true name is Rosa Delores Alverio. It was a beautiful name, and I'm so sorry now that I changed it, but Rosa was not a pretty name then. That was a June Allyson world. I didn't look or think like June Allyson. But I sure danced a hell of a lot better than she did! However, no matter how hard I tried to assimilate to Hollywood's standards, it didn't work. I was typecast as an ethnic girl.

I had to play the role of Oola in a Twentieth-Century Fox potboiler. Dressed in very dark makeup and a black wig, I was the epitome of an ethnic stereotype.

I actually said, "Why joo no luv Oola no more?" And when he

told me why he no luv me no more, I threw myself over the cliff! That was the story of my life at the movies. I aspired to so much more. I was thinking Chekov, and Shakespeare.

But it was not meant to be, and it simply verified my worst fears about myself. I believed I didn't really have a great deal of value. I was, after all, just a little Puerto Rican. It solidified in my mind all of the insecurities that I felt about being who I was and what I was, because if that's all I got, then maybe I wasn't worth more than that.

It's hard not to let other people make decisions about the value of your own life. You have very few alternatives in terms of how to pull yourself up when things go bad. You either fall by the wayside and feel sorry for yourself, or you pick yourself up and say, "I know, somewhere inside of me, that I'm better than this. There's something good here, something valuable and worthy in here, with talent and skill." That's the one that's very tender. The tender side of you can easily get lost.

The "Rita the Cheetah" stereotype was reinforced by Rita Moreno's tempestuous personal life. She was young and fiery and her eight-year-long, on-again off-again fling with Marlon Brando was religiously documented by every Hollywood gossip columnist. Another famous boyfriend, Geordie Hormel of meat-packing fame, was falsely arrested for possession of marijuana. Rita, at five-foot-two and ninety-nine pounds max, got caught up in the imbroglio, doing battle with the cops.

And then it all came crashing down. Depression can strike anybody. But women get hit the hardest. Genetic researchers believe some depression has its origins, not in female hormones, but in the genes. Researchers at the National Institutes of Mental Health, using positron emission tomography (PET) scanning are just beginning to trace the physiology of chronic sadness. Accelerated circulation occurs in a deeply recessed primitive part of the brain called the limbic system. This area is eight times larger in size in women than in men. Twenty percent of women between the ages of twenty and fifty will suffer at least one episode of clinical depression. It is very serious, usually unrecognized, and more often than not underdiagnosed. Only one in five get help.

Rita Moreno got help by trying to end it all. It was a rotten beginning, with the aid of an overdose of sleeping pills. But when she woke up in a hospital, she was oddly reborn. She'd exorcised all her demons, and she decided to build a happy life.

I tried to do away with myself. I was twenty-six years old, and I tried to kill myself. I now understand why I attempted to do what I did. People who feel they are without value, or feel unworthy, inevitably believe that there is nothing that can be done to remedy their situation. You really feel that you're going to live in this hell for the rest of your life and you can't bear it. I want to say to people who might be contemplating something like this that, as painful as the situation may be right now, it does change. I'm a living example of understanding that it really does change. However, in order to make a change, the first thing one must do is seek help. Whether it's a clergyman, a psychotherapist, or a friend who you trust implicitly, go to them and tell them you need help. It is a very difficult thing to do at first; however, if you do it, you will save yourself and your loved ones from inevitable pain and suffering. I'm thrilled that I had the sense of desperation to go into psychotherapy. It was the best decision I could have made.

I've talked about this publicly only twice in my life, and I have found that on the two occasions in which I talked about it, it helped a lot of people. The first time I spoke about my attempt at suicide, I was on a television show. I guess I must have struck a lot of chords because about a month after that show was on the air, I was walking in the lobby of the Hilton hotel and was stopped by a woman. I knew she wasn't a fan from the look on her face. The moment she hugged me, she began to cry. She said, "Thank you for talking about your suicide attempt. After listening to you, I was able to throw away the notion of doing something like that." It was an astonishing and scary moment at the same time. I suddenly realized what an enormous responsibility I had as a well-known person; I was a role model. All that business about role models, which I despise sometimes, had come back and slapped me in the face.

It happened to me again in another place where a man told

me that he was going to commit suicide the night of the show. However, by chance, he had turned on the television and watched my interview. The man told me that I saved his life that night. He said that my story prevented him from committing suicide. I can't claim to have saved this man's life because I wasn't there to stop him. All I did was share my story. I guess that is the point. Since he didn't try it that night like he had been planning to, it is a testimony to two things: the power of the famous individual and the power of television.

I have worked hard to come to a point in my life where I can honestly say that I am a good person, I am a person who has value. I attribute this ability to my many years of therapy. My doctor used to ask me why I hated myself so much because I had so many wonderful qualities that he wished I would recognize. Finally one day, I was able to admit to what kind of person I was. On the day I told him that I was a good person, I burst into tears. I knew that I was going to be okay; it was one of the most difficult things I've ever had to do, but I did it. It was wonderful.

Rita Moreno's blueprint for relationships was etched at home, as they all are, living with a mother who married and remarried a number of times. She was likely to follow that path; adults often duplicate the environment of their childhood. But she didn't. She met and married a man who was a cardiologist, didn't go to the movies much, and didn't figure out she was that *Rita Moreno until their sixth date. By then she was healthy enough to stop searching for someone to make her happy. She knew how to make herself happy and was ready to share that little miracle. She was thirty-four on her wedding day. She and Dr. Leonard Gordon are still married, and their daughter, Fernanda Lu, is all grown up.*

My husband is not a dreamboat. He's just as impossible as I am. But what we've learned, if nothing else, is that, when the time comes when you're sick to death of one another (and it comes all the time on a regular basis), when you are so irritated and annoyed by one another's foibles and quirks, you must recognize that there is no other person in this world who is a better person, or who is better for you, and who is better for this marriage. By understanding that, I believe that you have the key to a successful marriage.

When I look at him, it's like looking in a mirror; I see the best of me. He thinks I'm the bee's knees, the cat's meow, the cat's whiskers, and the Latin spitfire, Rita the Cheetah! In fact, just two days ago I was doing my actress thing by getting all crazy about something that was unimportant, and he said, "You're getting Puerto Rican on me! Please don't get Puerto Rican on me, we need to be logical about this." I openly acknowledge the fact that I'm not a logical person; I am all about my emotions. Therefore, I am lucky to have been able to find a partner in life who is able to quell some of those storms.

As I look back on my life, I am proud to say that I have no regrets. I am proud of the person I have become. The only thing I wish I could do is tell Rosa Delores Alverio that she has great value, that she is a good person, and that she should always believe in herself. But saying something like that is abstract. Since I am a person of the moment, what I would tell her does not mean that much in my life now. I have learned what I've learned, and I'm grateful that I have learned so much in a short amount of time. I'm sixty-six, and to me, that's a short time in which to learn such difficult lessons. Whenever I say the saying, "Life is hard, and then you die," I have to smile. I know that that saying is true.

It is nice to hear someone with genuine acceptance say life is hard. It is nice to hear someone say with genuine humility that they have a good heart. But then you have to affirm your value over and over again, every day. Try it. Look in the mirror and say something really nice to yourself every day. If you're not gentle with yourself, the world won't be very gentle with you.

CHAPTER 41

MICHAEL LEARNED

The day I met Michael Learned was the kind of day that proves Murphy's Law. Anything that could have gone wrong did. The puppy chewed a precious toy. Someone spilled orange juice on her school clothes. Someone misplaced her backpack. We missed the school bus. Traffic was backed up to Indiana. And it rained. I blew in, late and sodden, with all the charm of a tsunami and uttered something that would have made God Himself drink vodka from the dog bowl, and Michael whooped and said, "Thank God, she's just like me."

Michael Learned has created characters on film and on stage that have lingered in our hearts for their humanity. Particularly memorable are her roles as caretaker: the nurse supervisor on Nurse, *and most resonant, the matriarch who presided over television's most traditional family, the Walton clan. The Waltons came to represent an island of serenity and security for Americans amidst the chaos of the Seventies, but it was a time of tremendous personal upheaval for Michael Learned.*

Today Michael is a practical, thoughtful, part gracious, part bawdy blonde who's gone through more character-building crises than Olivia Walton ever dreamed of.

Marriage is a complex business. Ask her. She's had four of them. People who move through many marriages sure know what they don't want in the next one. Often what they don't want is hidden from their view and the next marriage is what they don't want in triplicate. Maybe that's because they've been so focused on the ex-from-hell that they neglected to figure out their own participation in the demise of the marriage. We can't change the predicament or its other perpetrator. The only thing we can change is ourselves, that part of us that is either drawn to destructive relationships or is bent on destroying rela-

tionships. Michael Learned has changed herself. She's identified her role models, reconsidered her more troublesome perceptions, thrown out her unrealistic expectations, and delivered to her three sons a good mother. It exacted a toll but increased her odds of making a happy life. They are lessons Olivia Walton would be proud of.

At the time that I was married to my first husband, people married for life. It was a Fifties mentality. We seemed like the perfect couple; however, what seems isn't always a reality. I was dying inside. Our marriage was falling apart. I broke my vows and left my husband; it was a very hard thing for me to do. It was shattering to the kids. That time brings up a lot of sadness for me.

I went immediately into therapy. I needed to deal with the fact that I couldn't make my marriage work. I really was heroically trying to keep it all together. I remember falling to my knees in front of my husband and weeping, "This isn't real, and I can't go on like this. I'm suicidal and I just can't go on like this." And he looked at me and said, "I'm happy with things just the way they are." I felt like a door closed in my heart.

It's not that he didn't love me; it's just that his needs were being met and mine were not. He's a lovely man. And we are good friends. And I still love him. He's the father of my children. But at that time, he didn't want to work on the marriage and I did. I knew our marriage needed work. I just didn't know how much work I needed. That's always the joke; you think if only the other person would change, then everything would be all right. Then you find out it's you that has to change.

After our marriage was over, I asked my husband if he thought I could have made our marriage work. I asked him if I had been a little more of this way or a little more of that way, or if I'd pushed a little harder, if he thought I could have saved it. And he said, "No way. If you had done all of that our marriage would have ended sooner." It was a very kind thing for him to say because it let me off the hook.

I am happy to say that I am now in a healthy relationship with a man. He is my husband and I love him very much. I chalk it up to the messages I was taught by the women's movement. I learned that I no longer had to buy into the Fifties mentality for women. In retrospect, I can't believe that I bought into that Fifties wife thing, but I did. I believed that a wife's job was to bring her husband's slippers, rub his back, and refrain from burdening him with her troubles. I now understand that these beliefs caused me to lose the most important thing in my life; they taught me to lose my own identity.

My husband brought home a page from a home economics book published in the Fifties. It read like a blueprint for slavery. It truly said in order to be a good wife, when your husband comes home tired from his busy day, the house should be quiet, the lights dimmed, dinner should be waiting. You should be fresh and smelling good, and the children should be bathed and out of the way because he's tired, he's been out fighting battles. Don't ask him to take you out to dinner. Don't bother him with your problems of the day. Compared to his problems, your problems are nothing. It really made me sad to realize I'd bought it, hook, line, and sinker. I had catered so. At a buffet, I would stand at the end of the line, get him a plate, serve him and then go back to the end of the line again and wait to get myself a plate. I'm not saying he forced me to do that, but he certainly didn't tell me not to. I wouldn't dream of doing it now. My sense now is both of you stand in line and have a good talk while you're waiting.

When I got divorced for the first time, I panicked. I didn't know who the heck I was; I had always defined myself as a wife. Now that I wasn't a wife, who was I? I had to find a new identity.

I think, because I had no center within myself, I felt I needed to be in a relationship to define me.

I was only seventeen when I married my first husband. My second marriage was a mistake. We'd both come out of divorces and we were scared to death to be alone.

My third marriage lasted thirteen years. It was wonderful and difficult and painful and very turbulent and I so deeply wanted it to work that I think I lost myself in him. It was typical codependent stuff. I was very much the caretaker. He was very charismatic, and I got lost in there somewhere.

Unfortunately, I think it's easy to get lost in relationships. I did and many others do as well. I see young women today—gorgeous, dear, beautiful, talented, sweet, funny, wise girls—struggling with no self-esteem. But losing yourself can be extremely detrimental. I learned that giving yourself up for someone is not always doing that person a favor.

I learned that I was patronizing and condescending to my husband. I learned that my way of survival was to take care of others, and in doing so I lost myself. It has taken me a long time to realize this, but my behavior cost me a lot of important things in my life.

I think you do try to fix in your relationships what didn't get fixed when you were a kid. Then eventually, with luck, you finally realize that that can't happen. You can't fix it. You can support someone that you love. But you can't save somebody. Then you're free.

I think some people are just plain selfish and mean. But I think you can be selfish in taking care of yourself. If I'm well rested, I'm a much nicer person than I am if I stay up all night cleaning the house. Then in the morning everybody gets up and says, "Boy, the house is so clean. Why is she being such a bitch?" I used to be that woman. However, now I allow myself to go to bed and worry about the house in the morning.

I wish that all marriages would mimic the type of relationship portrayed on *The Waltons,* but sadly, they don't. Olivia Walton had a husband who respected her, who worked side-by-side with her, and who never cheated on her. She had a husband who treated her as an equal partner; she was just as important to maintaining the family as her husband. They were a family unit. She had the help of Grandma and he had the help of Grandpa. We don't have that sort of family unit today. To me, that is very sad.

In this day and age, most women try to do it all. Sometimes, it is enough to drive us crazy. However, it is important to remember that the women of earlier generations didn't have the opportunities that we do today. My poor mother was an intelligent, witty, and well-read woman who was trying to be a Fifties housewife. In my opinion, she had it much worse than I did; she was trapped. My mother went mad from trying to be something that she wasn't. But even though there seemed to be no way out for her, she taught me that I deserved a better life than she had had. She instilled in me values that made me a person rather than a maid.

When I had sons, it became extremely important for me to teach my sons how to cook. I didn't want them to get married because they wanted someone to cook for them. To my credit, my sons have turned into wonderful husbands. In fact, I have one son who I worry about a little because I feel like he's wearing himself out. He does the laundry. He works a full day. He's always got a kid in one arm. But he's alright. My kids are wonderful people. They have troubles like everybody else, but rather than run, they deal with such problems right then and there. I'm very proud of them.

My career took me away from home a lot. It was difficult for my children. I remember coming home one day to the kids saying, "You know, Mom, sometimes we have things we want to tell you and you're not here." And I said, "You know what? If you really have something important you want to tell me, good or bad, whatever it is, write it on a piece of paper and stick it in my jewelry box. And when I get home at night, I'll look in my jewelry box and if there's a note from you I'll read it. And in the morning we'll talk about it at breakfast." Sometimes I'd come home to find a note saying, "I hate you, you weren't here today. I got an A on my paper and I wanted to show it to you." And sometimes I'd get a note saying, "Mom, I had the best day today, I'm so happy, I love you so much." It worked for them. It was like a release for them. If something was really bugging them they could write it out, and they knew I would look. I always did. If it was something important, we would talk about it over breakfast. I always tried to get up and have breakfast with the kids.

Being an actress and mother was a really hard balancing act for me. I was always so torn when I'd get a call from one of my sons on the set. I remember my youngest son saying, "Mom, if I ever get sick, would you walk off the set and come home and take care of me?" I said I would. And it happened. Luke was sent home from school. I immediately went to the director and said, "I have a son who's sick, can I leave the set?" And he said, "Yeah, we'll work around you." It never occurred to me that I had the right to ask something like that, but it was wonderful because I was able to go home and be with Luke and mother him.

God has helped me get through the hard times in my life. There have been many times in my life, especially with my kids, when I didn't know what to do. I'd cry for help and somehow I would be helped. I'm not a religious person, but I think the more you learn to connect with yourself, the more spiritual you become. I am grateful for the person that I have become and for the values I have instilled in my children. I'm old now. But for me, in a way that's a good thing. I look at these young women today who are still struggling with the same self-esteem issues and "Who am I?" issues that I was struggling with as a young woman. I've read Gail Sheehy who said she feels invisible. Maybe it is my age, or maybe it is my experience, but I've never felt more visible in my life. Frankly, I want people to see me. I feel like there is a person inside myself for the first time. It took me fifty years to get here and I feel great. I finally feel free.

CHAPTER 42

ROBERT KLEIN

America's most famous clown ever was Emmett Kelly. His face, as all clown faces are, was trademarked. He had the dark cheeks of a complexion that hadn't seen soap, much less a razor, for too long a time, and a big, red, painted-on smile. But beneath the mask, his human mouth was turned way down in a permanent depiction of sadness.

Comedian and actor Robert Klein is one of America's best clowns. Back in the Sixties, his hilarious social criticism gave voice to the cynicism that was percolating just below the surface everywhere. It's not, I think, an exaggeration in calling it a revolutionary time. He unabashedly points out that he liked the sexual revolution best. It was a lot more fun than the Bolshevik revolution, says he.

We worked together in the early Seventies at a roast for football great Fran Tarkenton, and we became fast friends. He's a news freak, and he loved to pick my brain. I'm an intelligence freak, and I was fascinated by the intellectual turns of his mind. We'd talk for hours. His face was always animated by a light just out of view, and a giddiness would break the surface in waves that would make his eyes dance. He was a happy guy.

We were friends when he was perfecting his craft, calling at two in the morning demanding that I meet him at the famous Improv comedy club where he was trying a new routine he wanted me to check out. He was working on the edges of what became a new era in comedy: blunt, hip social commentary with attitude. When he was introduced to the nation on The Ed Sullivan Show, *Klein was already straddling the fence between decorous and raunchy, gentleman and brat. And his brilliance was electrifying. He went on to marry his great love Brenda Boozer and star on Broadway, in musical theater, film, and television. For over three decades, he's continued to make America laugh.*

Today, he still makes me laugh, but his eyes have changed, colored by an Emmett Kelly melancholy. In the long trek from single, and singularly funny man, to single father, he's hit seriously fractured roadbed. Calling it a rotten, painful divorce is redundant; I don't know of any other kind. But his was also very public, and very expensive—half a million dollars by the time the dust settled. And that was just legal fees.

The personal stakes were high. I think divorce maims everyone. Robert and Brenda had a little boy, Allie, who they had to protect in the heat of a battle not entirely of their own making. Fighting hurt or fighting in pain is not a position of strength. And learning how to be a single father to Allie took the heart of a lion. He is still fighting to find humor in any of it.

We went through a very nasty divorce. It was not as public and messy as some have been. Thank God I wasn't Madonna. I always kept a pretty neat profile.

I have little to blame directly for problems in the marriage because people do change and they drift. I already had a going career for a while and my ex-wife became a bit of an opera star. She was very impassioned about her career, but she was talented, and she had a right to be. I think that we really had different philosophies to begin with—different ways of living our lives—which was not so apparent when we met. I was thirty-one, she was twenty-six. We shared great music together, like Bach and Mozart, which was the major bond. But after a number of years, I felt like there was a stranger there, and apparently she felt the same.

The divorce should have been handshakes, minimum trauma, minimal expense, so that we could have the maximum money to go on with our lives. But it wasn't. Even though we shook hands on divorcing very civilly and promised to think of Allie, our son, who was three years old at the time, it was clear that the proceedings were not going to go forth as planned. When I was hit with divorce papers a few weeks later, I was prepared to settle amicably all financial aspects. However, before I would do that, I needed to make sure that I would have access to my son. For some reason, my ex-wife made an issue of that. She said that she would allow me access, but it was going to be strictly controlled. That was a nightmare to me. I was afraid that for some reason I would be extremely restricted in my access to my own child, who I was with from the day he was born. I'm not a nine-to-five father. I was a big diaper changer. I was the only man on the playground his whole childhood. That's all I care about. I'm home during the day usually. I was going to make sure that she didn't have her way.

That's when we gave in to the lawyers who, I think, contributed to our pain. They both fueled our anger at one another. We were no longer in love. To have loved her as deeply as I loved her when we were first married, and to feel that way at the end, was burden enough. Our lives were falling apart, and the lawyers made it worse. She was right about getting a divorce. Maybe when I agreed, my acquiescence was painful for me. I was naïve. I was resistant to change in my marriage. There's no blame in the marriage itself; it wasn't working. As it was, we were just trying to get this over with, but instead we were besieged for two years, and it was very destructive. I found it hard to be funny, and she found it hard to go on singing. It's all a waste, a waste. I must say I find it difficult to forgive.

Preparing Allie for what was going to happen to our family in the midst of the ill will was probably the hardest thing I ever had to do. I wanted to make sure that my son felt that he was loved in the process. I wanted to make sure that he felt he could come to me, that I would be there. I wanted my son to know how much I cared about him. I wanted him to know that he would not have a relationship with me like I had had with my father.

I loved my father very much, but I could never please him. My father was a gifted comedian, and I think I got my sense of humor from him. However, he had a short temper, which made it difficult to talk to him about sex or peer-pressure problems, cigarettes being thrown my way, or anything. I think my father may have been slightly depressive. He was a brooder. He was strong as an ox and took care of business, but he would go into moody declines. He was extremely sad, easily embarrassed, and could bear and hold a grudge. He didn't know how to let something pass. He was unapproachable. I couldn't approach him about my deepest sadnesses. Therefore, I have made sure that my son Allie can approach me about anything. I think the divorce that we had probably has made me even more sensitive to my son, because I wanted so much for him not to have to face it.

It is easy to blame the other guy, wallow in disappointment, and take no responsibility for your own part in the death of a marriage. It's not so easy to point your finger at yourself and figure out what must change in you. Robert did it the hard way. He got healthy, he cut out alcohol, he incorporated trusted friends to love him, and instead of making lists of what he'd lost, he quantified all that remained. And it's a lot.

Rule one: Locate the rough spot! You've got to know where and what the rough spot is!

Rule two: Humor, humor, humor. A life without humor is not life to me, not life because you can find humor in anything, even the direst situation. There is something to smile about in almost anything. It is not human to think of a life without laughter. Humor is a saving grace in the best and worst of times.

It's dime-store psychology, but to count your blessings is always a good strategy as well. I'm very blessed in that my sister and my core of male friends were there for me at this time.

My cousin, Lou Stanger, died a couple of years ago from multiple sclerosis. Whenever I feel badly about something, I think of him. Far worse things could have happened to me, but they didn't. That knowledge gives me the courage to go on. I know it sounds like real dime-store stuff, but I try again and again to realize what I've got going for me. I see inspiration in others. And time always helps.

When I've seen or read interviews with wealthy men like George Steinbrenner or Bob Hope, they always seem to have a universe of regret with respect to their children, which I shall never have because I have one child. I've been with him from the start. I participated in his life completely. I think it's enriched me too, and I wouldn't trade it for anything.

The thing about him is that unlike the romantic love I've had for different women, my love for Allie is truly unconditional.

I'm a coward, but I'd stop a bullet in two seconds for him. I love the sacrifice. I love the whole fatherhood thing. I also don't like to smother him. My parents would yell, "Watch out for that lamp cord! Don't cut that bagel towards your neck!" I just watch him grow. He's got to learn intrepidness too. But he's brave and he's agile, and I want him to expand. He is a really special boy.

I like to feel a kind of pride in that I was not destroyed by my divorce. I survived all the bad times and the adversity. I weathered it. I survived it.

Mary Kay Blakely has written, "Divorce is the psychological equivalent of a triple coronary bypass. After such a monumental assault on the heart, it takes years to amend all the habits and attitudes that led up to it."

Robert Klein is using those years to learn about himself, which takes monumental courage. The payoff, I think, is that he's learned to be a father in the process.

CHAPTER 43

JENNIFER O'NEILL

Jennifer O'Neill walked into my life on one of those gray days in Nashville when full fall had just given way to the bleakness of November. Hers was the face that had launched a thousand magazine covers and, in its fiftieth year, could launch a thousand more. She was a top model at the age of sixteen; she's had her own TV series, her own line of fashions, and hers was the idealized face behind Cover Girl cosmetics for an incredible thirty years. She's even in the Smithsonian. But she may be best known for what she did in the Summer of '42. *She was only on-screen for twelve minutes, but that twenty-two-year-old face on-screen has still had a staying power that even Cover Girl couldn't manufacture.*

Wearing her most formal black riding togs, a long skirt, boots, and a Victorian-lace collar, she lacked only the crop to make the time warp official. I expected her to radiate everything I thought she stood for: beauty, talent, fame, wealth, real power. Except for the beauty part, she seemed none of those things. I thought of her as a woman in control. She had broken the traditional rules of marriage—she's had eight of them—and broken out of the traditional roles expected of wives, earning several fortunes on the strength of her own business acumen and will.

She also lost a lot, several times over. Jennifer O'Neill's troubles transcended the tabloids, and the big-league newspapers had chronicled most of them. She fell off her horse and broke her back. Her teenage daughter dragged one of Jennifer's husbands through a year long court battle after accusing him of sexually abusing her. Then there was the gun incident. Official reports still question the proximate cause: attempted murder? Suicide? Jennifer told me it was just a dumb accident that caused a bullet to pierce her body. She did not share with me what on earth a gun was doing in her house. While she was hospital-

ized from that injury, she learned that her entire fortune, which she'd relied on her husband to manage, had disappeared.

You never know what's going on in someone else's soul. What kind of dependence or codependence underpins serial choices that punish instead of nourish. But guessing that the quality of love one has grown up with has something to do with it is a chip shot. People given unconditional love do pretty well despite what life throws at them. If the love has been conditional, it sends its recipient on an endless search for love in all the wrong places.

Jennifer O'Neill has found her unconditional love. When I asked her, after all her torment who she trusted, she fell silent. Her eyes filled with tears. Then, finally, she answered. It seemed to me that it frightened her, yet at the same time relieved her, that she could only come up with one name. God. Hey, if God's all you've got to go on some days, that's pretty darn good.

Most people look for love all their lives. But I think some look for love more than others. In God's words, love is patient, love is kind, and love keeps no record of wrong. It's quite an amazing thought. Love puts someone else before you. Love is unconditional. Love makes the world go round. And if you connect to the real love, there's nothing better.

My parents are madly in love. They've been married fifty-two years, and they are extremely dedicated to one another. I love my parents a great deal. However, when I was growing up, I wish that they had shown me love by being more sensitive to my needs. My parents weren't the stereotypical PTA parents; rather, they were people who were extremely involved with themselves. When my parents wouldn't come to my horse shows, I would get upset. They would console me by saying that even though they hadn't shown up, they loved me a great deal. In fact, they would say my brother and I were a product of their love. In retrospect, I believe they were good parents, but they just weren't good at being sensitive to our needs.

The way it translated in my life is that I became an overachiever, constantly seeking approval and love. I think a child should grow up feeling unconditionally loved. When a child grows up unsure if they're loved or accepted, a void is created inside them. This void can't be filled by money, activity, fame, or marriages. It is a void that can only be filled by God. Unfortunately, I didn't know God at that point in my life. However, I am glad to report that now I do.

I'll tell you a quick, funny story. *People* magazine was doing a piece on me and called my mother to ask her if she too was a born-again Christian. My mom responded, "Well, heaven's no! I never had to hit bottom!" They used that quote in the article. When I read the article, I immediately called my mother. When I asked her why she said that she wasn't a born-again Christian, she said, "Well, I've always associated born-again Christians with some sort of California cult or odd group. I am not a part of that. But I will say that I've always believed in Jesus Christ, and I pray every day." And I said, "Mom you are wrong about born-again Christians. There's a point in your life in which you become an adult and you make decisions based on being an individual rather than a child. As a baby you can't make the decision, but whenever that time comes for you to receive the Lord in your life, you become spiritually born again. That's all it means. It is just a decision you have to make."

I believe that the Bible is the word of God. I go to a nondenominational church, and I believe very much in the study of the Word. I believe in applying the word of God to my everyday life.

Women's libbers are not going to be very happy with this one, but I believe that God has made a natural order for men and women. In marriages, men are accountable to the Lord, while the women are accountable to their husbands. That's the part that gets people angry. However, I believe that the people who get angry just don't understand what God is saying. In my opinion, God would never advocate for a husband to abuse his wife. Rather, God advocates for a man to love his wife more than himself, to lift her up before himself, to respect her and hold her blameless in front of the Lord. Therefore, a man who is in right relationship with God, and right relationship with his family, actually lifts up his wife.

To those people who say that the Bible advocates a secondary role for women, I disagree. God never spoke against women making their own living. Rather, God encourages us to make our lives richer; and if that is done by getting a job, then so be it. However, it is important to realize that it takes a guy who is very secure with himself to understand that even if I am out there making money, he is still the man of the house. If he's right with the relationship, he will know that no matter how successful I am, no one will be able to take his manliness away.

When my daughter accused one of my husbands of sexual abuse, I thought that I was married to a guy that shared my beliefs; I could not have been more wrong. It all started when my daughter went to a counselor, and confessed that my husband had been sexually abusing her. At the time, I'd never heard of anything like that. Frankly, I didn't believe my daughter. There was no way that my husband could do that to her. In retrospect, I wish that I had believed her, because my husband turned out to be a very bad guy.

I finally realized that my husband was a man to be reckoned with when I came out of the hospital for a self-inflicted gunshot wound. I know it sounds bad, but let me assure you it is not as it sounds. I should probably explain. One day I came home from the doctor with my son, who had had an ear infection. When I came home, I saw that the door to the safe, where my husband kept his gun, was open. I was furious. My son could have easily reached the gun; I couldn't believe my husband. Without thinking, I picked up the gun, went over to my bed, and jumped on it. When I landed, the gun went off in my lap. The gun's 38-caliber bullet went right through me. I was going unconscious. I knew that if I didn't get someone on the phone, I would die. So I called the office and the caretaker; yet no one answered. I called the operator and she told me to call 911. But I couldn't. In the end, it was she who made the call and got the police there. When the paramedics arrived at the scene, they couldn't figure out why I wasn't bleeding. They immediately operated to make sure that I wasn't hemorrhaging internally. It was a miracle that I wasn't. The bullet missed my spinal cord by fractions; it was truly a miracle.

However, right when I left the hospital, the miracles ended. My bank account was wiped out. I was in debt for several million dollars. I divorced my husband.

I lost my home. I lost everything. I was told to go into personal bankruptcy, which I just found offensive, so I went back to work, took a series, and built everything back up again.

One would think that during this time I would have lost all faith in God; however, I did not. I believe that God never makes anything bad happen. However, he allows things to happen in your life which make you grow into a believer. Difficult times are used to mold and shape you, and bring you to a stronger faith. They are important times which are definitely not comfortable.

I know that God will survive my press and my craziness because we're all on a road to being good stewards in life. I am trying to do that. As I have grown up, I have realized that God is there for me. God says, "Give me your worries, give me everything you have that is troubling you, and let me handle it. Come to me." And I didn't want to. I think a lot of people have trouble doing that. Especially if they like control. I would negotiate with God. I'd say, "Okay. I'll give you this part, but this other part's really important to me so I'll take care of it." I think in the last two years, he was really allowing certain things in my life to strip me down and get to the core of really understanding what love is.

I am very curious to see what's in store for me; and I know it's about to reveal itself, because I feel very aligned. Therefore, I know that I can be a good steward to whatever comes my way. I know that I have a lot to offer, and I will offer it. I just don't know which way I am going to do it.

Then she blasted me with her dazzling smile. But behind it was a mix of melancholy, trepidation, and relief.

CHAPTER 44

RICHARD THOMAS

For five years in the mid-Seventies, Americans faithfully stayed up to hear him say, "Good night." Richard Thomas' life and work have gone way beyond Walton's Mountain. He's been at the top professionally. He's hit the bottom personally. And he's looking at both sides now. John Boy, at mid-life, is a real man.

As the sensitive John Boy, the eldest son of the reassuringly traditional Walton clan, Richard Thomas came to embody what might be called the quest of youth, searching for answers, fulfillment, and purpose. As he's made his own real-world journey, he has gained his own insights into all those questions John Boy asked his journal so many years ago.

Richard Thomas is one of the single most prolific people in his field. He became a professional actor at the age of seven and made his silver-screen debut at the age of sixteen. He's acted in or directed an entire catalog of movies for television. He's done a raft of feature films and is considered one of the most important classical Shakespearean actors of our time. He never stops working. But for all the mad kings and murderous lovers he's brought to life, none of it registers like John Boy.

The Waltons *was not just a TV show, it was a franchise. It only ran for eight years (not counting reunions for Thanksgiving and Easter specials, and one wedding in the Nineties), but for most Americans, Richard is frozen in time as the fawn-faced John Boy.*

My obituary's gonna say, "John Boy, Dead at Ninety." Let's say ninety-five. Why skimp? There's nothing I can do about it. I just have to let it be. I know a lot of folks who've done shows from which they just wanted to run screaming while they were doing them, let alone afterwards. So I feel pretty good about *The Waltons* because that was a show we all liked. I'm proud of the show. It gave me huge leverage and enormous material to work with. It's a memory show. So it is idealized to a certain point. Someone in *TV Guide* wrote, "It's the show we all watch to feel bad about our own childhoods." I think that's what was wonderful about that show for people was that at the time we created it, the nation was torn apart. It was torn apart over Vietnam. There were huge changes taking place, huge revolutions. Feminism was moving forward and gay rights was just making the right early noises. Everybody had an opinion. Everybody was pulled apart. And *The Waltons* was a show where everybody at least came together at dinnertime to hold hands and love each other. So it had a healing and a tonic quality at that time. I can only be grateful for that. It's a pain every now and then to hear it over and over, but so what? It's a small price to pay.

My dad had an existence very similar to the Waltons. He was an only child but he was raised with his aunts and uncles, who were very young, in a small town in eastern Kentucky during the Depression. I was born and raised in New York, but I spent all my summers as a child at my grandparents' farm in eastern Kentucky. So mine was a schitzy childhood. The subway's fine, but every summer I'd be barefoot, running down the lane, and riding the mule.

If you ride mules long enough, you're bound to get bounced off. John Boy at mid-life has been bounced. His sixteen-year-long marriage to Alma Gonzales dissolved in a divorce he neither expected nor desired. He said at the time that it just brought him to his knees. Not only did he have to cope with his personal loss, but he also had to incorporate the feelings of his son and identical triplet daughters. Even in his own mind, he had become so associated with the picture-perfect Waltons, a family who struggled and had challenges but worked hard and were faithful to each other and made it together as a team, that recognizing anything different knocked him flat. I had, I confess, idealized his life.

So had I. I had done the same thing.

It's just one of those sad things where we looked pretty perfect but it wasn't developing the way it should for a lot of reasons—many of which I wouldn't talk about, but a lot of which are understandable. I was twenty-four when I got married, which was probably way too young. But I wanted a family, and I'm a committer—the committer from Hell. I have the commitment capabilities of a nun or a priest and I get into a relationship very, very quickly and very, very deeply and stay with it. So I was doing everything to make it work and she was doing everything to make it work. We just really weren't doing it together.

It was the last place that I looked for trouble. You fear death, you fear your kids and loved ones going through bad stuff. Some people live in fear of being broke and losing their career. But I just had no idea the divorce was coming. It just caught me looking away, like a really good pitch. It went over the plate and I was out. I never saw it coming, and I should have. But I have to forgive myself for some of that. I just never thought that that part of my life would come unglued. And there are a lot of reasons for it. My youth. Unawareness of what the deeper aspects of intimacy are in terms of relationships and how they're developing. But there are two people involved. It takes two people to keep it together. My ex-wife just reached a point where she just did not want to be married anymore and it was over for her. So it was just left for me to catch up with that and for the kids to catch up to that and finally accept it and let it go and move on, which was not easy.

It's hard sometimes, especially if you're in the position that a lot of people find themselves in after the breakup of a marriage or any life-threatening event. So many people around you seem to have known so much more than you did or intuited so much more or been aware of so much more. It makes you feel so foolish. Why couldn't I see? Why was I so blind? But when you're in there working to make the marriage work, you don't want to look left, you don't want to look right. You just want to go forward and make sure it all stays together. Clearly, I'm a person with some control issues.

The thing that I learned that was really amazing for me was that I really knew how to get help for myself. I went into therapy, which is something I never thought in a million years I would do. I wasn't raised to do it. I have nothing in my upbringing to recommend it. And it was the smartest thing I ever did. It was enormously helpful. But I also have a resilience, which I'm very happy about, that helped me a lot. I'm extraordinarily resilient. That's what I learned.

Our marriage had this "together" quality. I was always very "together" around friends. I was willing to help them, and it was perfectly okay for them to fall apart but not for me. Ultimately I did, and it was great for me to fall apart so that I could actually be a real friend. Not just someone who looked good and could go to dinner and make good conversation, but somebody who was really in need. I think they liked it. I think they loved seeing me come to my knees. Actually, they just loved seeing me being human. You can't be a friend unless you're willing to be vulnerable with the people that you care about. It was great to just totally fall apart and have people come in and be loving and supportive.

The kids were a wreck, too, because it was a big surprise for them as well. You just have to really be careful. You have to just be who you are and where you're at. It's okay to let them see what you're feeling, but you have to, at some level, let them know that you're going to handle how you're feeling. They want to take care of you because they think if you're okay, they're going to be okay. So all their wonderful little taking-care-of-the-parents instincts go into full gear.

It's great, and they're wonderful at it. They're just the best. They've cheered me up so many, many times when it was really dark. However, a pattern can begin to develop where the kids start looking out for the parent, and it creates an inappropriate relationship at some point. So you have to really make sure that that doesn't get out of balance. Of course, when you're in a divorce I think it's very natural for you to want your kids to have sympathy for you, to see that you're suffering. It's manipulative as well as honestly emotional. You just have to be a cop whenever you can and make sure that you're not using them the wrong way.

My oldest boy is twenty-two and on his own. One of my daughters is with me full time and two of them live with their mom full time. This is their choice. There was a tendency at the beginning to try to create a false sense of connection between the two of us once it became two separate households. The kids liked it because they could continue to try to pull their parents together. But sometimes to try to give them an illusion of a connection and a closeness when in fact it isn't really there anymore doesn't give them the real story. It's okay for them to see the conflict. I think it's important, provided the parents aren't beating each other up or beating the children up. If there is conflict, it's better for the ex-spouses to be out in the open about it.

Badmouthing your ex in front of the children qualifies as beating them up. And you avoid it as much as you can. You just try to keep from doing it. But nobody's a saint. Nobody's perfect.

One of the reasons that it's all right for the exes to have conflict, for the kids to be aware of it, is that then the kids can see that the problem is with the parents and not their fault.

When everyone's trying to be so nice to everybody, the kids are thinking, "Well, then, what's the problem? If everyone wants to be so nice why aren't we still together? Why isn't this picture working for me?" But the parents must own the conflict that they have and to some degree act it out, as long as it doesn't become too destructive. It's painful for the kids, and it's hard. But it's real. It's the real world for them. I think it also depends on the age of the children. My kids are teenagers, so they understand that they are not the problem and that they're caught in the middle and that they have a lot of pain and a lot of anger about it and they have their feelings. But the problem didn't start with them. They've got to sometimes see Mom and Dad really go to it, get angry, have conflict, so that you know that they can handle that.

My ex-wife and I are not at all close. We communicate around the kids. We have to because they go back and forth and spend a lot of time with each of us separately. Our relationship is polite, but I wouldn't call it friendly. The divorce just was not a happy thing. No one's making trouble for anybody right now so that's good. That's really the best way to have it.

But life every so often delivers second chances. When he was most bereft, Richard wandered into a new possibility. It was a family-owned curio shop. The manager, a single mother named Georgianna Bischoff, said to a friend, "It's John Boy. No, he's too good looking to be John Boy." She helped him select a leather belt and gave him directions to a museum. Then he came back, every day. He finally screwed up the courage to invite her to his play, Love Letters, *and dinner and lunch the next day, and dinner after that. Six months later, on his grandparents' Kentucky farm, he married her. His son was best man, all five girls—his three and her two—were bridesmaids.*

I was down in Scottsdale, Arizona, alone for the first time, flying solo for the first time in sixteen years. I was a wreck, a disaster. I was doing a play there and had just set up camp at my little rented house. I went in to a Western goods store to buy souvenirs for my kids and met a wonderful woman whom I married. We have a two-year-old little boy now.

So we have seven children altogether. Georgianna has two teenage daughters, Brooke who's eighteen and Kendra who's thirteen. And my triplet daughters, Pilar, Barbara, and Gwyneth, are seventeen. Richard, my oldest, is twenty-two. Georgianna had always wanted to have a home birth. She had natural birth experiences with the first two children. She'd wanted to have a home birth the second time but couldn't because of her complications. So she decided when she got pregnant that she wanted to have this baby at home. There were no complications. She had a very healthy pregnancy. Fortunately it worked out. Montana, our two-year-old son, was born at home. And all our kids were there.

Oh, yeah, they were all there. They didn't have to be. Attendance was not compulsory. But the home birth was great. We had a magnificent midwife and it was hassle-free. It was wonderful. If the circumstances are right and you have a good midwife who you really trust and you have good prenatal care, I recommend it highly. Georgianna, my wife, is really a crusader for it. She believes it should happen as often as possible.

Before the birth, we had every conceivable teenage reaction

to the prospect of witnessing an actual delivery, ranging from, "Oh, I can't wait" to "Mommy, the last thing in the world I want to do is stand in the room and look at your genitals."

When it came time for the moment to happen, they were all there and in various states of euphoria and tears. Richard was there. She said to him, "Now look, it's not going to be modest. I'm not going to worry about anything except having this baby, but you're welcome to be there if you want to be." And he was. I think it was a great experience for him. She said the next morning he looked at her and said, "Can I get you anything? Can I get you some breakfast? Is there anything you need?" He had a very, very, very new kind of experience. It was an extraordinary blending of a family. This is an ancillary benefit.

Blending a family is a really hard thing to do. I call it graduate work, post-graduate work. The only people who get to do the post-graduate work are people who've already failed the course. So it's really hard to do. So having this baby with all of us being together was the most extraordinary event for us to come together as a family.

Brooke, our oldest girl, said, "This baby made us a family." And it's true. He's the family kid. Everybody's got an investment in Montana, and that's a lot of pressure. But he'll survive it. He gets a lot of love. He's got five sisters who adore him.

People suggest the universe is making these good things happen for me. I don't really think the universe cares. I think the universe has its own business to deal with. It's just a euphemism for God. I talk to God all the time. I can't honestly say I know if anyone's listening, but it doesn't stop me from doing it. I have a faith, which is there and present. No matter how I bang it up and throw it around and question it and tear it apart and put it back together again, it always seems to land on its feet and remain intact, so I don't question that. I have a huge respect for the science of psychology, about which I know very little but for which I have, through my own work, developed an enormous respect. But I have a stubborn old faith, which just seems to kick in and stay put. As long as it's there, it's a gift, and I'm happy to be a home for it. I think it's an inalienable part of each of us. If it's in you, you can't pull it away. It's a blessing for me. It's like a dialogue. It's an ongoing discussion with some part of myself, through some part of myself, to something else. And it takes up a good part of my day, I'd say.

CHAPTER 45

KEITH CARRADINE

Keith Carradine looks like he's been lassoed right out of the Cowboy Hall of Fame. He's got an incorrigible shock of blond hair that falls over his brow, an Oklahoma twang that he picked up somewhere between Ojai and Okalala, and a demeanor that gives him an "Aw, shucks" country-boy quality. Taken together, all this makes him darn near irresistible.

Whether singing in the movie Nashville *or telling tall tales with all the folksy populism of Will Rogers in* Will Rogers Follies *on Broadway, Carradine has glittered. His very name evokes the dazzling culture of Hollywood's golden days, when his father, the legendary John Carradine, romanced his way through chorines and stars alike.*

Keith relishes his father's glorious, notorious past while he underplays his own harrowing history. It was a mess marked by too many brothers by too many mothers and long months in a joint with bars on the windows while his father lived in a Hollywood mansion. Keith became a ward of the state, a pawn in a bitter custody battle. At the age of six, his mother was taken from him, barred by the courts from raising her son. Keith seems to have accepted his childhood for what it was, forgiven everyone for all of it, and moved on.

He also says that in consciously trying not to recapitulate his own background, he's learned that denial doesn't work and he's off-loaded the survival techniques that held him back. He's says he's learned that coping isn't good enough. And it's taken a leap of faith worthy of a balladeer. But how do you get beyond your own history?

My family was a real mess, a typical Hollywood mess. My father left his first wife when he met my mother. He was actually out auditioning actors for his Shakespearean repertory company. Instead, he found my mother. She was a nineteen-year-old student at the Pasadena Playhouse. She came in and read a scene from Hamlet. She blew him away with her reading. Instantly, he fell in love with her, which changed his life immediately and completely. But by the time she was thirty-five, she left him for an eighteen-year-old beatnik painter from San Francisco. So what goes around, comes around.

When my father met his third wife, it became a wildly extended blended family. His first wife already had a son, Bruce, when they married. Then they had a son together, Jack David. With his second wife came Christopher and me and Bobby. Then he married his third wife, who already had two sons, Michael and Dale. My father split up with this third wife (she left him actually). Then he met his fourth wife, whom he married and spent seven years with. If that was not enough, when he was eighty he decided he had enough of her, and walked out. For an eighty-year-old man, I thought it was an amazing thing to do.

When my mother left my father and married Michael Bowen, the beatnik painter from San Francisco, they had a child who was also named Michael. So I have seven brothers, two of them named Mike. One is a stepbrother, one is a half brother. No girls. My father actually had a funny line about that. People would ask him about the fact that he never had any daughters, and he'd say, "No, I could always make women, but I could never produce them."

So I grew up clueless about women.

When my mom left him for the painter, they battled over custody of the three of us. It was ugly. There were a couple of kidnappings. On one of those occasions, my mom and her new husband came and picked us up at the house. I was six and Chris was eight, and Bobby was just a baby. He doesn't remember any of this because he was an infant at the time. My mom had Bobby with her and they came and took Christopher and me, and we went up to some big old house in Argura. We were there for a few days, and then they decided we had to go to school, so they took Chris and me down to the Argura elementary school. I guess my father had called the police and said we'd gone missing, and he figured we'd been taken by our mother. We'd only been at school a couple of hours when these two plainclothes guys showed up and took us downtown. We wound up in juvenile hall. Christopher and I spent three months in juvenile hall while they tried to sort it out.

For eight years after that, I didn't see my mother because that was the custody arrangement. When the custody battle was over, my father was given absolute, complete custody because my mother was so far out there. She was extremely Bohemian—really kind of gone—and judged not responsible enough to have custody of her children.

I think that might have left me mistrustful of women on a certain level. Yet on the other hand, I've had several really extraordinary relationships. I think that unless one goes to sleep, one is growing for his entire life; and the growth never seems to have stopped for me.

For whatever reason, I became very self-sufficient very early on. That was the effect it had on me. I realized at a very tender age that I really had nowhere to look but to myself for my own well-being. There can be a downside to that. But I managed to go through that phase of my life and come out the other end. I don't think I'm unscathed at all. I think I'm deeply scarred by that stuff, but everyone responds to those kinds of scars in different ways. I think it made me stronger. I think for some people it can become an excuse for how they live the rest of their lives. For other people it can become a kind of foundation on which you build. I think that's what happened to me. I don't take any particular credit for that. I think I'm lucky in that whatever my nature is, whatever that part of my nature is that enabled me to get through that and grow into adulthood, I seem to be doing okay.

I've certainly forgiven and accepted what happened. But it's a funny thing, it's not like I had some other experience as a child to compare. All I had was that experience, so for a six-year-old child, what's normal?

You talk about forgiveness and acceptance, but I feel like I'm really a lucky person. I've had an amazing life. I've been given the gifts. I feel sorry for the rest of the folks who haven't had the kind of life I'm having. I'm a lucky man.

Keith Carradine followed in his father's footsteps, hitting the stage in the Sixties musical Hair. *He had a child with an actress he met in the cast. He married another woman with whom he had two more children and from whom he's now separated.*

For seven years we've been separated. But having got through the worst part of the collapse of the marriage, we are now in a parenting partnership that works really well. It took about a year to get to that point—maybe even less. You start to realize what's important and when you have children, they are what is important. So you tend to put your own needs, wants, desires, aside to a certain extent.

Obviously there are very deep-seated reasons why a marriage fails, but once you've looked at that and accepted it, okay, that's what happened, now what? Well, there are these two children and they need us both. So we're there for them.

If you are able to see certain things about yourself—patterns you fall into, the way you choose to be, or the kind of person you choose to be with—you start to realize why you make certain choices. For me it was a matter of waking up at one point and seeing the choices I had made and why I had made them. I saw then how out of control I was in my own life, how reactive I was.

I was doing things automatically out of a set of patterns that I had developed in order to survive growing up. I dealt with adverse conditions: divorce, abandonment, a custody battle, time in juvenile hall. And as a child, I figured out certain ways to get through it.

As a grownup, those patterns started to be a hindrance. I was lucky in that some people don't figure this stuff out until they're sixty. I started to get a hold of it when I was in my late-thirties and early-forties. I started to understand a little bit about myself and how I operate and why I was doing things in the ways I was doing them.

My father's third wife, who was my stepmother from the time I was eight years old until I was on my own, had a strong personality. I didn't necessarily feel good or right about her behavior at the time, but it felt normal. So as an adult, I went out and I managed to create that same atmosphere around myself because it felt normal.

It was a real revelation when I understood what I'd done. My choices had nothing to do with happiness. They just recreated a feeling of familiarity and normalcy. When I realized that I had chosen normalcy over happiness, I had to consciously learn to choose happiness as a normal state. It's like having to jump out of the airplane.

There's certainly no guarantee I won't recreate that same situation again, but it certainly does improve your odds I think. Any self-knowledge is going to improve your odds of actually making a conscious choice to live consciously as opposed to unconsciously, actively rather than reactively.

I never felt as though anyone was to blame for anything, because I never felt as though I've had it particularly bad. Or that there was any reason to blame, anything to blame anyone for. I've never felt ashamed. I do believe that it's up to me to make my own life work. I'm active in terms of the choices that I make.

CHAPTER 46

KENNY LOGGINS

You know how you feel when you say something really dumb? The moment the words leave your mouth, you flush red and hope the floor swallows you whole? Can you tell I've done that a lot? The first time I met Kenny Loggins happened to be one of those times. It was just before a concert; I was standing at the top of a winding staircase in the entrails of a Broadway theater. It was so awful. The moment I saw him, I gushed something about his song, "House at Pooh Corner," and realized (in a nanosecond) how insulting I'd been; leave it to me to dredge up one of Kenny's most ancient tunes when I knew that he had done better work since. I felt dreadful. That night, Kenny Loggins blew open his show with "Celebrate Me Home," unleashed a couple new tunes, and then said, "Okay. I'll sing the song about the bear." And the audience exploded. My embarrassment immediately vanished; I was not the only one who still loved that song.

Kenny Loggins broke into the music scene as part of the rock 'n' roll duo Loggins and Messina. Now Kenny Loggins is part of a very different duo whose message is embedded in the music of love. Throughout his career, Kenny Loggins has sung a lot of songs about love. But his words have perhaps never been so eloquent or so universal as they are now. Kenny Loggins and his wife Julia have written a guide book to life and relationships that a lot of critics and psychologists have called essential. The book and its companion album are a breathtakingly candid account of where they were, the psychological twists and turns that brought them to themselves and then to each other. It is called Unimaginable Life.

While Kenny and Julia are an extraordinary couple (Kenny is a remarkably gifted musician and Julia is no slouch as a poet), they also share the same ordinary problems many of us struggle with. They never really believed that love could last or that we're meant to be genuinely happy. They were as swamped as the next guy, with houses to run and laundry to clean and meals to slam on the table and, oh yes, work. And no time to think.

But they took the time to do something practical. They wrote down what they were thinking and how they were feeling and saw right there in black and white what was real in their lives. It wasn't all pretty but it was real.

The route they took was fraught with danger. Painful realities were dredged up. They risked losing people they loved. They found that the only way to happiness was searching for it alone. But through it, they found love for themselves and for each other. They found they had a right to happiness. They found that a third party (who they call Spirit) was there all the time, coaxing them through it. And through this process, they found that they had never really been alone.

When I hit a place in my life I like to refer to as midlife clarity (rather than midlife crisis), my life completely changed. It started at first with some business things. I was doing and accepting things that I didn't really believe in, mostly out of fear. This manifested itself as working with people who didn't really believe in me or my talents. It was a difficult time, which forced me to reassess my life and see what was honestly going on. And as I let myself get in touch with what I really felt, I was able to change; I was able to carry forth new goals, a heart-based vision.

First I reassessed my business partnerships. At the time, I had a very lucrative record deal; however, lucrative deals mean nothing when you are surrounded by people who don't believe in you. Whenever I would submit an idea, these people would tell me that they wanted somebody else to write, produce, and practically sing the songs. They didn't know what to do with my work at all. It was a bad situation. One day I suddenly experienced an important epiphany, which showed how clearly I needed to make a change. I realized I needed to be where people believed in me. I needed to believe in myself. So I began by calling up all the negative people surrounding me and letting them go. It was a tough but important learning experience for me; I learned I had to make the commitment to myself first, to surround myself with people who believed in me; and now, I am proud to say, I use that belief as a metaphor in every aspect of my life.

I attribute my ability to change my surroundings and my attitude to the pain that I was in at the time. When one gets to a place where they realize that they're not happy, the pain that they feel can motivate them to learn what they need to know. By facing this pain, instead of taking pills or alcohol to avoid it, one is able to find his direction in life. Therefore, I believe pain is an essential motivating tool in the quest to better one's life. Julia and I say no one moves who's not in enough pain.

The pain one feels also allows that person to ask relevant and important questions about their life. I found myself asking "Whose life am I living here? Am I living this life for the money? Am I living this life for my spouse? Am I living this life as if I were my parents? Am I really living my own life?" These questions brought me to a great conclusion; they forced me to stand up for myself and make my life happen.

As I inspected my life, I sadly realized that my marriage was not working either. I knew something had to change. My wife (at the time) and I really examined our relationship and decided that it was best for us both if we parted ways. It was a very difficult and very painful thing to come to; but we ultimately decided that the pain of living somebody else's life would be more painful to us both.

We were forced to face the truth about our marriage. While it was extremely painful, it helped us both find the truth in ourselves. By being in touch with the truth of my life, I became a totally different person than I was previously. I was a person who held to my convictions, a person who had beliefs, and a person who I could be proud of.

When I fell in love with Julia, I experienced a love so huge it was undeniable. Yet, of course, I would try to deny it a few times in the months to come. This is natural with love, when the heart starts landing and the mind loses all control. Lucky for me, Julia had been mentor and my teacher for six years. Because of that relationship, I had nothing left to hide. She taught me not to be afraid of my feelings. She taught me to be true to myself and my needs. She taught me how to get in touch with my inner self by writing down everything I thought in a journal. She told me that by writing and reading these thoughts, I would get in touch with my own inner truths. Boy, was she right. Through this process, I was able to more fully explore my two loves of life, my music and my relationships.

Creating music has always been a major passion of mine. However, prior to my CD *Leap of Faith* I had reached a point in my life where my love for music had begun to fade. I was drowning in my own low self-esteem. When I let myself feel my life and write from my heart, using my journaling to put my truth onto paper, out jumped the most transformational music of my career, *Leap of Faith.*

When I was young, I kind of wrote my songs without thinking. I would sit down to write; I guess you could call it a stream of consciousness thing. As a result, my songs came from an innocent heart. It didn't matter so much if the words made sense, since they contained a simplicity and a naïveté that made them work. In that way, my old songs were fine songs. But because of what Julia had taught me, I discovered that by being honest with myself, I could write great songs again, but with a level of depth and honesty that could actually change people's lives.

Julia taught me perhaps my most important lesson; she taught me that honoring the truth is the essential element of an alive relationship. However, what she didn't tell me, but what I soon learned, is that telling the truth to your partner is not always the easiest thing to do. Telling the truth to your partner can be a very scary thing. By telling the truth you may feel that you're risking your relationship, but you are not. Whenever I withhold the truth from Julia, a wall grows between us. You see, the truth helps to blow up the walls between your hearts. When I talk about it, the issue, the wall, immediately dissipates, and we fall in love again. So to me, our awareness of the truth is the quickest route to keeping our hearts open and keeping our love alive and juicy.

I believe one's ability to love another is directly proportionate to loving oneself. That's what people mean when they talk about self-love. The way you get to self-love is, first you have to be willing to feel your life, and admit to yourself what is and what isn't real. That gets you in touch with your heart. By listening to your heart, you connect to your intuition. Your intuition will tell you to do things no matter what your head tells you to do. But the key here is to act on your intuitions, not only when they're convenient but also when they're against the grain. That's what creates self-love, doing the courageous thing. You create a relationship with yourself that says, I love you enough to do what you tell me. This is key.

There is a big difference between hearing what your mind is telling you and hearing what your heart is telling you. Each of us has got to come to a place where we can recognize the difference. The core issue of the philosophy that we're talking about is that I trust what my heart tells me, therefore I am inner-directed, and I know that my heart is taking me to love because it did that. I know that my heart is taking me to happiness, to joy, because that's the whole point. My heart is the hotline to the Spirit. Therefore, can you trust your heart? Can you trust what your heart tells you? Absolutely! This is what it's all about! Trusting God.

Love itself, or Spirit—God, if you will—is the third entity. As I fell in love with Julia, I became aware of our connection to Spirit. The very first thing I came to understand was there is a Spirit that loves us, and wants us to have love in our lives. No matter what. Everything we do is taking us to love. That is Spirit's only agenda, and the key importance of that is I believe when I follow my heart and when I act on my intuition, whatever I do is one more step to love. Spirit's are loving arms that catch me each time I take a leap of faith.

Most of us spend the majority of our lives thinking that we're the ones in charge. Part of the illusion of being in a body is that we think we have something to do with the things that happen around us. Playing that game and moving those chess pieces around is what keeps us busy. But it is important to realize that God's in charge. Learning to trust that, and not fear that, is what we're here to do.

Perhaps this generation is finally beginning to get the idea that we should not placate one another's fears anymore, but we should really trust what we feel as true for us and true in our lives. We believe that what works for our hearts is going to work for everyone around us. When I listen to the inner voice, and I act on that voice, that takes me into a place of peace, where my children, my relationship, and everyone around me are positively affected.

By following my heart, by letting my passion lead, I'm teaching my children that they have the power to follow their hearts, and to make their lives work for them. That it's okay to have passion in their lives. They can have love and work at the same time. They can be free.

EPILOGUE

MARY ALICE WILLIAMS

Okay. It's my turn. I have always been reluctant to share anything deeply personal about my life in public. Why should anyone care about my experience? How dare I set myself up as someone whose life is more compelling than events or ideas of others, as though the episodes that have informed me were more valid than yours—so valuable that you should well take my advice. What has failed for me, or worked for me, has no bearing on what helps or hinders you. But recently I have learned through fire that mine is the only experience I have any right to share.

On March 20, 1997, I found myself face down. My eyelashes were pinned by the oak boards of the kitchen floor. My ears had plugged out all sound except the pulse of blood to my brain. My only focus was breathing. In hurt; out was harder. Breathing was all I could think of doing. And trying to breathe took all the strength I had left. It was the bottom. Lying there on the kitchen floor. It wasn't a body blow that got me there on the ground next to the dog's kennel in a ratty bathrobe.

It was a picture, in stark relief, of all the pain I had witnessed, all of the submerged conflicts I'd fallen prey to, all of the real feelings I'd stuffed into a strongbox, the key to which I'd lost along the way to losing myself. Feelings so long buried that when, in that galvanic moment, they erupted. They made Mount St. Helen's look like a snowdrift.

All my dreams had come true. I'd reached the top of my game, the top of my industry, collecting national Emmy Awards, and great-get interviews, and honorary doctorates—the hood ornaments of which piled up like soft-sculpture on a closet shelf of treasures next to the baby clothes too beautiful to give away. I had things. Houses and cars and clothes and hairdressers and a wedding ring the size of a wall sconce. I was omnipotent. I could handle my own problems and yours too. I could be dictator or servant, depending on what was required. I could solve problems and smooth things over, run companies and tell the world how to think. I could make you laugh and make you cry. I could think and write and perform like a champ. The only thing I couldn't do was feel.

I had faced challenges before. Some of them heartbreakers. My heart's desire was to have children. After a decade of infertility, I conceived a child, twice, and lost him, twice. When finally, through the breath of God and a steady diet of tuna fish and broccoli, I was able to carry a baby to term, she was born with a hole in her heart. But I was in charge, remember? I had a strategy for getting through it. I studied. I researched. I talked to experts and used the craft and craftiness of a killer journalist to find a solution. I became a trustee of the March of Dimes Birth Defects Foundation to get up-close access to the scientists working on the edge. I got the nation's top pediatric cardiologist to take the case. And by the time she was five, the baby's heart had healed. Yet, despite my zealous intervention, her heart had healed all by itself.

My marriage had been going south big time. We were diving ahead in our careers, getting businesses and a family off the ground. Yet, while we were acquiring what we needed and what we wanted, we were far too busy to look at each other and far too unversed to talk. So even though we slept in the same bed, a wall of pillows and rage emerged between us; we lived separate lives. We stopped sharing friends. I found my safety in fear. So I isolated myself from anyone who dared to love me, because the way I controlled my world was to take all the blame for what went wrong. No matter who the perpetrator was. How's that for omnipotent?

How do you research soul-sickness? They don't have remedies for that on the Internet. And none of my old tricks worked anymore. I couldn't clean my way out of it. The house was already spotless. I couldn't clarify my way through it. I had never learned to distinguish what was real in my life. I couldn't think of a single place to turn, a single person who would hear me. If there was someone trying to get through to me, and there was, I didn't know how to open the door. When you encrust yourself with the blame and shame and guilt of the ages, even a decent cookie recipe has a tough time breaking through it. Never mind a kind word or the pat of your baby's hand on your face. I had invited a pervasive sadness into my life and had lost my self-esteem in the process. I was a monument of self-destruction. I had spent so much time paralyzed or focused on what had happened to me that I forgot I had choices about what happens in me.

And I am grateful for it all. I don't judge anybody anymore, including myself. It is such a relief.

We all tend to think we've invented ourselves, making our lives up as we go along. But I have come to suspect that there is that essential, authentic person we were created to be that is always pulling us toward our true north. It's not so much that we are predestined to live as we do. It's just that each of us has an inherent, unique yearning that helps us spot the guideposts so that we don't lose our way completely. This book has been an exercise in finding that authentic self.

Some of what you've read may resonate with you. Some of it may have made you feel you have no right to be distressed over your own niggling issues. Forget it. This is not a contest. Just because someone's experience seems a lot worse than yours does, it doesn't invalidate what you're going through. It doesn't matter what others have experienced. When you're in trouble and in pain, it feels like no one has ever felt like you do and nothing could be worse.

Recovery from anything difficult is a process. We are built as triumvirate beings: physical, emotional, and spiritual. When life gets unbearably tough, the first thing that goes is spirituality. We get cut off from God and start living in isolation and fear. The next thing to go is our mental abilities to perceive the truth accurately, make decisions, and act on them. The last thing to go is our physical being. Your body starts to betray you. Eating and sleeping patterns run amok, and you start getting sick. On the climb out we recover in inverse order. First your body gets healthier, then your mind begins to function more effectively and your emotions realign. You begin to react rationally and act sensibly. That last thing that returns is your spirituality. But feelings do follow behavior. Sometimes, I've found, you have to "act as if" for a while. Fake it 'til you make it, and you may come to realize that what you viewed as your pretense is, in fact, reality.

I am not one for advice. Take it from me, I am an expert in nothing with the possible exception of getting really bad stains out of children's ready-to-wear. I'm not giving advice now. But I have developed my own personal To-Do list based on what's worked for those who've shared their experiences:

- *Write it down.* The more ham-strung you are by your crisis, the more you get to write. Write down the names of everyone you've ever known, everything you've ever done, every incident you've ever witnessed, and all the feelings they kick up. Trust that the important ones will get on paper. They will. Then read it. What emerges is a very clear pattern that helps you see what is true in your life, helps you come out of denial if you've been in it, and helps you make decisions about setting a course of action. There is much in these stories that smacks of the compulsion identified by Sigmund Freud (who wasn't wrong about *everything*) to endlessly repeat the troublesome environment that framed you. That notion is the underpinning of the phrase, "Hell is repetition." His view was that we are doomed to repeat the damaging part of our past over and over. Maybe he's right. But I don't think it's a life sentence. Once you recognize your own pattern, you just have an opportunity to react differently.

- *Focus on yourself.* Admit where the boundaries of your personal power lie. No matter how hard you try, you can't control anything or anyone around you. Give yourself the best gift of all: Stop trying. Control yourself. It will fill up your time nicely. Cataloging other people's faults and misdeeds, like counting other people's beers, is a sorry occupation. Counting my own blind spots and self-imposed barriers and addressing them is a full day's work for me. Stop trying to control everybody else by pleasing them and taking care of them. Caretaking is condescending and they won't like you for it anyway.

- *Try to identify your participation in the bigger picture.* When you focus small, you tend to get tripped up and miss the fact that sometimes we blunder into doing something terribly hurtful, to ourselves and to other people, and in the process of flagellating ourselves over it, we may never realize that we have been the instrument for others to heal.

- *You be the judge.* As tough as it is, try not to base your own value on other people's view of you. If you are rigorously honest with yourself and can identify your stresses and resentments, you'll know who you are. Be gentle. You're human.

- *Accept it.* Whatever happened, however ghastly is it, accept it. It's the only way you can find the good behind it. And the good is there.

- *Forgive.* Forgiveness has nothing to do with having power over someone else. The person you may self-righteously feel is in dire need of your magnanimously bestowed forgiveness is probably living a fine life and getting a good sleep. You're the one who's not. As long as you're tightening the noose around someone else's neck, you're the one who's choking. Don't forgive for anyone else. Do it for you. Without it you can't get on with your life. Forgiveness is not forgetting. It's just letting go of the hurt.

- *Be grateful.* Find something to be grateful for. Good. Now find another thing. Make a list. Make it long. Early on, the best I could come up with to be grateful for was indoor plumbing. It takes practice, but eventually I got as many as three really legitimate things to be thankful for. Now I stop at twenty-five or I'd be at it all night and unavailable to do the exhausted-working-mother and overachiever thing. Gratitude is all in your attitude.

- *Remember that we all have choices.* One of them is to decide to be happy. If you're in a burning room and the only way out is through the fire, you have a choice. You can die in there or go through the fire to freedom. So what if you get scorched?

- *Change.* Change the only thing in this wide world that you can change—you. True insanity is doing the same things over and over expecting different results. Change your procedures. Do something different.

- *Make time for stillness.* Busy is good, but if you're wildly busy all the time, you may not get the message you've been waiting to hear. To twist an old saw, don't just do something, sit there.

- *Give time, time.* It doesn't matter if you're twenty or bearing down on fifty. It's not too late for patience if you're ninety. The lowly caterpillar crawls around for a powerful amount of time and then wraps himself in a cocoon and hangs-ten for a while. While he's in there, buffeted by the winds, he looks the same on the outside, but something's happening on the inside. When he comes forth, he's got the same DNA, but he's a completely different animal. Making a magnificent butterfly just takes time.

- A*cknowledge your mistakes, and make amends for them,* even if you fear they'll be used against you. I'm Irish Catholic and a working mother of three. Guilt is my middle name. Get rid of it. You can't face life head-on when your head's down.

- *Say what you mean and mean what you say* when you're dealing with other people. But don't say it meanly.

- *Live for now.* Right at this moment. Wallowing in the past keeps you from stepping forward. Projecting into the future keeps you in fear because so very often your expectations are simply predestined disappointments. The next thing really will take care of itself, and you'll have a lot more fun doing it.

- *Crank up the network.* Call a friend. Reach out. You can't accomplish any great thing alone.

- *Try to distinguish the difference between an emergency and a crisis.*

- *Dig back for your original dream and then cling to it.* As long as it wasn't totally unrealistic in the first place, that's your pole star.

- *Never stop asking what you want to be when you grow up.*

- *Pray.* It doesn't matter to whom you pray as long as it's something or someone or a collective entity that is larger than you. (I call mine God.) It's not just the default position of atheists in foxholes. I am learning from everyone I've talked to that it is immeasurably helpful. There's no right way to do it. Give that greater power the letters of the alphabet and He'll figure out the words. I don't pray for things anymore, just that I hear what God's will is for me and that I have the strength to carry it out. I'm learning to pray for people I resent. It's weird at first. (Alright, I'll pray damn it.) But with practice, you can pray that the person who hurt you receives all you yourself want. And the resentment goes away.

And keep in mind this one:

- *It doesn't matter what the question is. The answer is love.*

Luke, the gospel writer, tells the story of two guys on their way to the village of Emmaus desolate over the execution of a friend on whom they'd relied for their very salvation. A stranger fell in step with them along the road, listened to them, and suggested another way of viewing their loss—a hopeful way, demonstrating that even in their worst despair there is always opportunity for hope. It was only after the stranger had dined with them that they realized he was The Man and he had given them a glimpse of their salvation.

This has been my road to Emmaus. I don't have the protection of my sanctuary anymore. Don't look for the cool, dispassionate television anchor who couldn't let anyone touch her anymore. She's gone. And I've emerged in her place. I am here acknowledging who I am and what I feel and what I believe in.

I am grateful to the maniacs who've allowed me to play in television, allowed me to witness history and the bravery of the men and women who've made it. But all of them together have been no match for the up-close-and-personal bravery I have seen on a daily basis in my husband and my three indomitable little girls.

I am grateful to all the men and women who walked with me, fellow pilgrims who turned my journey into an adventure. I am grateful to the countless others whose names I will never know and who will never know themselves how much they've meant to me along my road to Emmaus.

God, grant me the serenity to accept the things I cannot change,
the courage to change the things I can,
And the wisdom to know the difference—
Living one day at a time
Enjoying one moment at a time
Accepting hardships as the pathway to peace;
Taking, as He did, this sinful world as it is,
Not as I would have it,
Trusting that he will make all things right
If I surrender to His will;
That I may be reasonably happy in this life
And supremely happy with Him forever.

—Rev. Dr. Reinhold Niebuhr